BLACKTHORN AND BEYOND

THE SORCERER'S REDEMPTION

ELLIE TILLEY

The Book Guild Ltd

First published in Great Britain in 2024 by
The Book Guild Ltd
Unit E2 Airfield Business Park,
Harrison Road, Market Harborough,
Leicestershire. LE16 7UL
Tel: 0116 2792299
www.bookguild.co.uk
Email: info@bookguild.co.uk
X: @bookguild

Typeset in 11pt Minion Pro

Printed on FSC accredited paper
Printed and bound in Great Britain by 4edge Limited

ISBN 978 1835740 613

British Library Cataloguing in Publication Data.
A catalogue record for this book is available from the British Library.

For my mum, my biggest fan.
And for the dreamers of worlds.
Keep dreaming–
It is your greatest power.

PROLOGUE

THE CREATION OF THE FOREST

A golden frame that still shone through the layers of dust accumulated over many years encased the forest scene. The artist had expertly depicted both the tranquillity and the mystery of the trees. Their black branches snaked around each other in strange harmony as their thick trunks stood rooted firmly into the earth. A challenging maze of spiky arms reached out – arms that threatened to force the lone traveller off the path. The only greenery in the painting belonged to the long trails of ivy that wound themselves up around and suffocated the towering trees.

The small boy stood and stared at the intricate frame, drinking in the richness of the painting. As he lingered in the draughty corridor, he became entranced by the painting, feeling its strange attraction. He stepped closer. He made dreamlike contact with the earth underneath his bare feet, and goose bumps emerged on his skin as he felt the breeze that swayed those awful branches. The faint rustlings of small animals hiding in the undergrowth entered his ears. He reached out a shaking finger, feeling that he was doing something forbidden, and touched the painting.

The scene changed before his very eyes. It was as though someone had thrown a bucket of boiling water over wet paint. The trees melted into the ground, and discoloured lines streaked the canvas from top to bottom. The boy was in shock. He gazed in horror as the canvas ripped and branches forced themselves out of the frame. The musty carpet became soil, the candlesticks on the wall morphed into leaves, and the corridor was a corridor no more. The trees grew up to the ceiling and encroached into every available space. They travelled along the passage and into adjacent rooms until the entire house was taken over by the knotted boughs. They broke forth from the four walls of the house and stretched their roots deep into the earth for miles around. Shoots of ivy sprouted forth from the frame, and their long trails crept over the old house until, like the boy, it became lost to the trees.

PART ONE

JOANNA

ONE

I moved the old rag wearily up and down the golden frame for what seemed the millionth time, being careful to avoid direct contact with the fragile canvas. I sighed and cursed my parents for leaving me here. 'Leaving' may be the wrong word. Perhaps 'temporarily housing' me may be more appropriate. I knew this wasn't entirely their fault, however I couldn't help but wonder how long it had taken for them to realise that their financial security had been compromised.

Their eager investment into a new business had fallen apart, and their money became tangled up in a web of failed enterprises. They could not keep a household intact for much longer and were threatened by the loss of the family home. To disentangle the mess they had created, they had, in fact, handed me the short straw. Until further notice I had been sent to live under my Aunt Agatha and Uncle Frederic's protection in Blackthorn House.

My parents delivered the news with grave faces. I was soon uprooted from my old life and planted into a cold, dusty house in the middle of a forest. The stories about Blackthorn House were abundant: that it was haunted, that children from the village had disappeared, that it was hiding something from the rest of the world. On the other hand, the stories about Agatha and Frederic Woodgate were non-existent. I knew better than to fall for bedtime horrors and fanciful tales, however it would have been a little reassuring to know at least one thing about these mysterious relatives who lived in the woods.

Mum and Dad assured me that Agatha and Frederic were perfectly nice people who simply kept themselves to themselves. I asked myself, if Aunt Agatha and Uncle Frederic really were perfectly nice people, why had our family had nothing to do with them until now? There could only be a handful of reasons why relatives become estranged: a family disagreement, a family dishonour or perhaps a wrong that could not be put right. I racked my brain for days on end to dig up any childhood memories. I kept on drawing a blank. I had to accept that I knew absolutely nothing about my aunt and uncle except for their names.

My arrival in the rain at Blackthorn House two days ago had involved a bitterly cold trek, as the house stood hidden from the rest of the village deep in the forest. The welcome I had received from my aunt and uncle had been even colder. Their frosty exterior blew a draught all the way through the house, and my thick jumpers and cardigans had become my new best friends. A sharp, awkward hug, a brief tour of the house (it would have taken a week to give me a proper tour) and a short-lived disappointing dinner had been my first introduction.

I can't say it has improved much since. In return for my occupancy, my parents had promised that I would be more than willing to help with chores. I soon understood that this included cleaning, gardening, shopping, washing and anything else that needed doing. I had worked laboriously at the frames of the paintings for many hours.

Despite the dust, cold and mustiness, there was no doubt that Blackthorn House was extraordinary. The wings of the house were set out on the four points of the compass. My room had been prepared in the east, and I was under instruction to go anywhere I liked but not to try and enter any room that was locked or looked like it was in disrepair. In all honesty, that did not leave many at my disposal.

Monstrous candelabras lined the corridors that when lit cast eerie dancing shadows along the cobwebbed walls. The house was a maze, and the rooms were endless. I could not fathom how just two people could live here. Uncle Frederic frequented the house very rarely; from what I gathered he preferred the outdoors.

Blackthorn House stood in a clearing surrounded by trees in all directions. Frederic spent most of his time chopping wood for the fire or sweeping leaves off the twisted steps at the front of the house. I would often look down on the perilous staircase from one of the windows at the top. The cracked steps were overladen with wet leaves, and I would regularly grimace at the thought of my uncle slipping on the leafy mulch and plunging to his death below. If I could not spot him, that meant he had taken the main forest path to the village to pick up supplies. I had been warned that if I ever did go into the village not to stray from the main path. I would need to go soon, as Aunt Agatha had hinted she needed new knitting needles and wool.

I would have no desire to go exploring off the path. Blackthorn Forest looked like it could swallow you up in a heartbeat.

Grand staircases and elaborate high ceilings aside, there was one thing about the house that really drew my attention. I say one thing, but there must have been hundreds. They lined the corridors and took over the walls. They judged you, invited you and followed you wherever you went. I could not escape from the paintings. If I didn't know any better, I'd have thought I was staying inside an art gallery. Blackthorn House was full to the brim with canvases, miniature to colossal, all complete with intricate handmade frames. I didn't know a great deal about artwork, but it didn't take a genius to understand that they must have been worth a small fortune.

I had spent the morning cleaning these interminable frames and had only made a small dent in the workload. Aunt Agatha had instructed me to polish the frames and dust the cobwebs off the walls, however I must not, under any circumstance, touch the canvases. They were all too fragile to touch with bare hands, which would explain the pair of special gloves I had been given that made me feel like a strange surgeon.

A great number of scenes had been depicted at the hands of these skilled artists. I shall attempt to do justice as I recount them: vast misty mountains that stretched for miles up to the sky, babbling brooks and winding rivers that guided you through enchanting forests and down into green valleys, the perilous waves of a choppy sea at night, twinkling moons and stars in a magnificent galaxy of light and colour, portraits of individuals and families with their piercing eyes that followed you when you weren't looking, a grand library with stacks upon stacks of priceless classics, animals of all shapes and sizes sleeping, fighting, eating and gazing like a human into the distance.

"Joanna!" I jumped out of my reverie and dropped my filthy rag at the shrill voice of my aunt. Agatha was framed at the end of the corridor and had been watching me polish the architecture that encompassed these scenes. "Aunt Agatha!" I exclaimed, feigning happiness at seeing her. "How long have you been there?"

"Never you mind, child," she replied, furrowing her grey eyebrows at me as she shuffled down the corridor. "I have another job for you, you've been polishing those frames all morning. I do hope you've been careful not to touch any of them directly, I don't need them being ruined by dirt or grease."

"Of course I've been careful, Aunt." I sighed, wondering what she had in store for me next. "I've finished all the ones in this corridor anyway."

"Very well. Come with me. I need you to help me in the kitchen and stoke the fires before dinner. It's a bitter wind out there." Agatha's wizened frame hobbled back up the corridor towards the main part of the house as the windowpanes shook from the force of the gale outside. "I thought you'd finished polishing these ones…" She raised her voice over the elements, ignoring their plea for attention.

"I have," I said defensively.

Agatha's tasselled cardigan draped along the floor and followed in her wake as she disappeared around the corner. "You've missed one."

I scanned the walls quickly. She was right; I had missed one. It was the largest painting in the corridor and hung proudly on the wall opposite. I stared at the canvas wondering why I had subconsciously avoided it all morning.

The longer I looked, the stranger it made me feel. A forest scene with trees so black you could barely see through them. A well-trodden path that led to nowhere. A gate half open on its hinges symbolised the beginning of a journey… or perhaps the end of one? Cold air rushed down the corridor and I shivered, pulling my cardigan tighter about me. I put one foot in front of the other and approached the painting.

There was something about this painting. Something out of the ordinary.

Perhaps it was the dead trees that looked so unnatural, or perhaps the gate which I longed to reach out and close, or perhaps it was because the forest reminded me of the very one Blackthorn House stood in. The painting appeared three-dimensional, and if I took another step further, I felt I might pass through the brushstrokes and feel the leaves underneath my feet.

The tip of my nose was millimetres away from the canvas. Had it been a mirror it would have misted up by now. I narrowed my eyes, eager to see the finer details.

Those awful branches seemed to sway ever so slightly in the wind.

"Joanna!" I jumped once more and cursed my aunt. I stepped back and picked up my cleaning rags quickly. My back prickled as I turned around and the trees watched me disappear.

TWO

Aunt Agatha had me peeling carrots and potatoes as she stood by my side and stirred a foul-smelling broth that I hoped I would never have to eat. The kitchen was located down the main staircase in a side room off to the right of the house. This meant that we could both stand in front of a big window and watch my Uncle Frederic go about his work in the clearing.

I was surprised by the agile nature of my uncle compared to my aunt: he moved swiftly whereas Agatha's movement was more of a hobble. Frederic's energised demeanour outside of Blackthorn House made it clear that he wished to spend as little time as possible inside its dark, oppressive walls. I didn't blame him.

I sighed and thought suddenly of Mum and Dad. I would have given anything to be back in our house instead of feeling like a visitor to a museum or a maid trapped under house arrest. As we sat down to dinner and I moved the broth to and fro in my bowl, I watched Agatha and Frederic eat, waiting for them to slip up and reveal something behind their secretive barriers. Whenever Agatha spoke to me it was always in short, sharp sentences that made me prickle and bite my tongue to prevent a few choice words leaving my mouth.

Whenever Frederic spoke, it was just short. He was a man of very few words but, I suspected, very many thoughts. He had fine brown hair and a mostly plain face, but if you caught him with the right expression, he had a touch of adventurous youth about him. Agatha, on the other hand, gave the impression of everything but youthful. In the two days I had stayed in the house I had the delights of listening to her moans about her bad hip, sore ankle, stiff back and displeasure with the youth of today. It was Agatha who replied when I enquired about the paintings.

"What do you mean, where do they come from?" Her beady eyes narrowed.

I sighed. "I mean… who painted them? Why the hell do you have so many? I've noticed that most of them have no names or signatures whatsoever and the few that do just say 'anonymous.'"

Agatha glanced at her husband who was busy pretending to be engrossed in his broth so as not to meet her eye. "Joanna. You would do well to remember that the paintings are fragile and extremely old. I have already told you that they have been here for as long as I can remember. I have also already told you that, even if you are cleaning them, you must not and will not touch the canvases under any circumstance. I noticed today that you were getting dangerously close to them. I will not have them destroyed at the hands of an ignorant sixteen-year-old girl."

I jumped to my own defence. "But I only—"

"Curiosity killed the cat, Joanna. Now eat your dinner and I'll hear no more of this." I gritted my teeth and didn't bother telling her what a stupid phrase that was. The meal was finished in silence. The judgemental face of a distant Woodgate ancestor frowned down at us from above the fireplace.

*

I awoke the next morning to a rare ray of sunlight filtering through my curtains. I begrudgingly emerged from beneath my warm sheets and into the cold air. My room smelled musty, and I knew it hadn't been aired out properly for many years. I wrinkled my nose and undid the latch on my window. I had to work at it for a while, and I forced it open eventually as it gave a great noise, complaining at me.

My bedroom presided over the front of the house and Uncle Frederic glanced upwards with a very old broom in hand. He reached for his cup of tea on the window ledge, took a sip, and resumed his methodical sweeping, ignoring my disturbance. It was going to be an eventful day.

Despite the sunlight, it was still a bitter December morning, and I opened the creaky wardrobe to search for some suitable attire. The clothes I had brought from home did not shield me from the elements, and even my woolliest jumpers did nothing to alleviate the cold.

The temperature in Blackthorn was unlike any I was used to. The best garment that I could see for now was a gigantic dressing gown tucked away in the corner. I brushed a few cobwebs off it, tried not to think about who it belonged to before, and wrapped it around my small frame. It engulfed me, but at least I was warm. It would do for breakfast. I padded down the corridor in my slippers, trying to remember the way to the main staircase.

Even though I had been here for three days now, Blackthorn House seemed to sprout corridors at will, making it impossible for me to find my way around. I passed magnificent mountain scenes and marvelled at the mist that floated over the peaks. No wonder Agatha was always shouting my name; I was too engrossed in a painting to get anywhere in a hurry.

I didn't recognise any of the paintings in this corridor and was about to turn around and retrace my steps when a flash of gold caught my eye. It was a shiny doorknob half concealed by a black drape at the end of the corridor which I assumed was hiding a window. I pulled my dressing gown tighter around me. I had to squint in the darkness; this part of the house hadn't seen sunlight in years.

I lifted the black drape to pull it across and struggled with the heavy, tasselled material. With a great cloud of dust that set

10

me off coughing for a few minutes, the sunlight streamed in and lit up the corridor. As the light caught the doorknob to my right, it shone even brighter. All thoughts of going downstairs for breakfast abandoned me. I looked closer. I could see my own curious reflection staring back at me. I turned back to the empty corridor. The house was still. The temptation was too much. I twisted the knob and crept inside.

It was lucky that I had pulled the drape across in the corridor and exposed my eyes to the bright sunlight. If I hadn't, I think I would have been blinded. A vast window stretched from one side of the opposite wall to the other. I blinked several times, feeling like I was finally waking up since arriving in Blackthorn House, and gazed out of the frosted glass. The surrounding forest framed the window, and I suddenly felt like I was trapped in a fairy tale: the big old house in the woods with the paintings that were always watching.

The room was old, yet grand, and I wouldn't have been surprised if it had witnessed many great triumphs and tragedies. It was weathered by time and there was a slow hum as though it were in a deep slumber. I gazed up at the shelves that stretched to the ceiling. They groaned quietly under the weight of all the heavy books. I stood, marvelling at the grandeur of this room and all that it contained, and do not know how much time passed before I came to my senses. I had stepped foot into a magnificent library.

THREE

I peered up at the shelves. Impressed by the sheer quantity of the exquisite collection, I ran my fingertip along the edge of one, leaving behind a mahogany trail of exposed wood underneath. The spines were so dusty that I could not read the titles or authors of these great volumes. The library looked like it could have been there for hundreds of years, sleeping, undisturbed, guarding the secrets of the past.

As I wound my way through the remarkable shelves, I pictured many generations of Woodgates whiling away the hours in there, and the life of my ancestors entered my ears. I heard small children running around and giggling behind the books, the pages being turned impatiently as the reader became engrossed, and the wise voices of a mother and father saying it was time for bed. I pictured the sparkling windows thrown open onto a green lawn in the heat of the day, the sound of laughter as others played outside and the library all aglow, renewed by the rush of life.

I shook my head. The picture faded and the dust set in. This beautiful yet somehow sad library had not been alive in years.

I sat for a while in a quaint window seat and watched the still clearing outside. The terrible trees of the forest looked less intimidating through the frosted glass. I could have spent all week in there, poring over the great classics, discovering the ancient lost worlds and shivering at candle-lit thrillers. I felt a strange familiarity in the room, as though I had been in it before, but that would have been impossible.

Had I seen it before in a photograph or a... My thoughts trailed off and it came to me in a heartbeat. Hanging up in the same corridor that my bedroom was in, inviting me in every morning and encased in a delicate silver frame, was this library. Whoever had lived in Blackthorn House previously, or perhaps a visitor to its formidable walls, had decided to paint a picture of this grand show of wealth.

I closed my eyes and the painting swam before them. It was etched onto my mind; I had seen it every morning when leaving my bedroom. The towering shelves, mahogany surfaces, and glittering spines that invited the reader to lift them right off the shelf. Yes, it was this library alright, only somehow different... I opened my eyes and looked around. There was something that didn't quite match up between the painting and the real thing.

Perhaps the shade of the wood was slightly darker, or the shelves slightly taller, or... Aunt Agatha wasn't standing framed in the doorway with an expression of pure horror unfolding on her face. I jumped a foot in the air and almost fell off the window seat.

"How dare you come in here, Joanna Woodgate."

Therein followed a fifteen-minute lecture over the breakfast table about honesty, respect and bad behaviour from children who lacked discipline. Agatha took a sharp breath in between her ranting to stop from going purple and buttered her toast with such aggressiveness that the knife almost skidded across the table. I refrained from telling her that in my defence, the library had been unlocked and the door ajar, however this probably would have added to my prosecution instead.

I was given the opportunity for redemption by accompanying my uncle into the village to purchase some knitting needles and wool for Agatha. I must admit, thinking about trekking through the forest was no enticing thought, but if it saved me from another of my aunt's lectures, I couldn't get out of the house quick enough. I hurried away from the breakfast table as soon as I had swallowed my last bite of toast. The wizened eyes that presided over our every meal watched me leave from the canvas above.

I turned my back on the well-dressed old man with a tingle down my spine, hurried up the main staircase and took a right towards the east wing so I could go and get dressed. As I approached the door to my bedroom, I couldn't help but glance left to the wall opposite. I recognised the polished mahogany wood, the glittering letters on the spines of the books and the sparkling window beyond onto the forest. I felt a sudden respect for whoever had painted this; the quality of the artwork was outstanding, to the point where I felt I was back in the library gazing at the tall shelves above.

I tore my eyes away and entered my room. It had been a mistake leaving the window open. The room was ice cold, and I could see my own breath as I moved quickly trying to find the thickest jumper I owned. I dressed hurriedly, not wanting to expose any part of my body for too long, and closed the creaky window with difficulty. I turned around and caught sight of myself in the mirror on the wall opposite.

I hardly recognised myself. My features had become thinner, and my small frame looked ridiculous in the woolly clothes. My skin looked paler and my eyes narrower and sore. My lips were red raw from the cold. I hadn't been sleeping very well but only realised now how much of an effect it had on my appearance. My lack of vitality was partially down to Blackthorn House and how it made me feel: it was dark, oppressive, and inside its walls I felt trapped.

There was no denying that the other contribution to my declining health was because I had not heard a peep from my parents since arriving here. This saddening fact was something that I had been trying to ignore. They had not visited the house, written to me, nor shown any sign of communication. I sighed and shook my head. Perhaps they were biding their time until they had sorted everything out and I could return home as though nothing had changed.

Although, I did feel changed. Blackthorn House was changing me, and if my parents didn't hurry up, they might find a very different girl awaiting their arrival.

I shook my head, wrapped my scarf tightly around my neck, and closed the door on these dangerous thoughts. I took a few steps down the corridor towards the main staircase and then stopped dead in my tracks. Something was different. Something had changed in those five minutes between my entering and leaving the icy bedroom. I reluctantly looked back on what I thought I had seen, retracing my steps back to the bedroom door. I stared at the library.

Were my eyes deceiving me? I blinked several times, took a deep breath, and stared closer until the tip of my nose was close to touching the canvas. Suddenly fearful that I was being watched, I took a step back and looked either way up and down the corridor. How could this be?

On my entering the bedroom and glancing upon the library, the shelves had been polished, the spines glittering and the window sparkling. Now when I looked, the dark brown of the wood had become grey with a thick layer of dust, the letters on the spines were obscured, and the windows were cobwebbed and dirty. In those five minutes the library had aged fifty years.

I stood in disbelief trying to find an explanation for this sudden time lapse. It had fallen into the state of decline that the library was currently in. I searched the corridor for another painting of the library, thinking perhaps I had been looking at the wrong one, but to no avail. I was tempted to reach out a fingertip and try to wipe the dust away to return the library back to normal. But there was no mistaking it; it was in the brushstrokes and detail of the canvas. The dust and the cobwebs had been painted in, as though they had always been there.

I began to worry that being cooped up in the frosty house with only my aunt and uncle to talk to had driven me to insanity.

What I needed was fresh air to clear my head. Venturing into the village would be an excellent distraction from the peculiar paintings of Blackthorn House.

Perhaps it was simply a trick of the light, I thought, as I wandered towards the sound of Agatha's summoning voice.

Perhaps this unfamiliar house and these unwelcoming corridors had made me feel a little out of place.

Who could blame me?

FOUR

Two pairs of footsteps crunched their way through the forest as I followed my Uncle Frederic through the trees towards the village. It had taken us ten minutes to descend the twisted staircase, during which I repeatedly cursed whoever had designed them as I slipped on the wet leaves. Uncle Frederic grabbed the sleeve of my fur coat to steady me and gave me a silent look of reproach.

I had been strangely touched by his kind gesture when he handed me a magnificent fur coat before we left on our journey. He had obviously made it himself, and I debated whether the warmth and protection it provided were enough to outweigh the unfortunate souls of the animals he had destroyed to make it. I wrapped it tighter around me as the trees grew closer together and the path seemed to shrink and slither away.

Frederic expertly manoeuvred his way through the forest; he had clearly done this countless times before. If it wasn't for my experienced guide, I would have easily strayed from the path and been lost to the trees. Thankfully we soon neared the edge of the forest and the border of the village. We passed a little cottage with the wind whistling in its chimney and rattling at the weak windowpanes. I peered over the dilapidated fence. Whatever had been growing in that vegetable patch had long been ravaged by the elements. The cottage looked abandoned.

We walked in silence towards the centre of Blackthorn. As I continued to put one foot in front of the other, I grew a little uneasy. I felt we were being watched. Every villager we passed by would stare, or stop mid-conversation to peer at us strangely; some even turned their heads to get a second look. I looked at Uncle Frederic. He was unfazed by the attention and stared straight ahead to avoid eye contact with anyone.

Perhaps he was used to people looking on strangely; he was the owner of the big old house in the woods after all. I, on the other hand, looked sheepishly about me, afraid that we were doing something wrong. As we walked down the cobbled streets (I was hoping that Frederic knew where he was going) the sun disappeared behind the imposing clouds and the village was cast into grey shadow. Once again, I caught sight of my reflection in the apothecary window. My complete lack of direction and gifted gigantic furs made me look like a fish out of water; no wonder the villagers seemed disturbed. Uncle Frederic looked back at me and furrowed his brow.

He had stopped in front of a bookshop and peered mistrustfully through the window as though he were expecting to see something other than books inside. "There's a haberdashery just round the corner there. Why don't you go and get your aunt's supplies?" he said, without looking at me. "I'll meet you back here in ten minutes." The bell on the door tinkled as he stepped inside.

It began to rain. I looked around me furtively. I felt more and more uncomfortable as the seconds passed by and thought I'd better get inside somewhere quickly, not just because of the rain but to avoid everyone's accusing stares. Frederic's sudden disappearance had not left me much choice but to go in search of Agatha's needles and wool on my own. I felt vulnerable without his presence; he had been my guide.

I squinted through the heavy droplets that now fell unreservedly from the sky. By all accounts the appearance of the sun that morning had been a strange and uncommon event in Blackthorn. Frederic had said the haberdashery was just around the corner. I made a decisive right turn down a darkened alleyway; I couldn't stand outside the bookshop forever.

I immediately collided with a hurried villager who was trying to get out of the rain. Her rain-washed features scowled at me. "Watch where you're going, girl!" Taken aback, I apologised quickly and swept aside my hair plastered across my face. "I'm sorry, I didn't see you through the rain." The woman looked at me again as she passed by, and her features rearranged themselves as she saw Frederic through the glass front of the shop behind me.

"Oh…" she stuttered, eager to make a quick getaway. "That's okay. Have a nice day." I glanced back at my uncle through the raindrops on the glass. He was too engrossed in the spine of a book to have noticed the commotion on the street. The encounter had ended as the villager left abruptly, an expression of pure fear upon her face.

Questioning why all the villagers seemed to fear the Woodgate family and how I had known nothing of their peculiarities until now, I opened the door to the haberdashery and the tinkling bell announced me, in my confusion.

The shop was empty apart from what looked like a friendlier and younger version of Aunt Agatha sitting on a stool at the front till and an elderly man to the left of me who was peering intently at a shelf. The shop was lined with shelves on either side that contained brightly coloured bundles of wool and sewing materials that would have made sense to someone who knew what they were looking for.

I dug out the list that my aunt had scrawled on a tiny piece of paper for me. The list had become wet, and the ink was starting to run as the paper began to disintegrate in my hand. Thankfully Agatha had repeatedly given me a verbal list and I could remember the items she wanted.

I walked over to a stand that had needles of various lengths and sizes hanging precariously on its wobbly shelf, and the lady at the till glanced up from her book, readjusted her reading glasses and smiled encouragingly at me. I picked up what Agatha had requested, and she went back to her novel, uninterested in me. I turned to my right and began to examine the vast range of colours on offer to me.

I gathered everything that I needed apart from a bundle of baby-blue wool. Spotting it just within an arm's reach on the shelf below, I reached out and went to grab the soft material. What I had not noticed in those last few minutes was that the elderly man had joined me and was also in need of a bundle of blue wool. Our hands made contact and I withdrew mine in surprise.

He chuckled and turned to face me. "My apologies, young lady, I'm under instructions from my wife today, and it seems she wants the same colour as you." I smiled and looked up from the shelf, about to tell him about my aunt and how I too was following instructions. My smile vanished.

It took me only a few seconds to recognise those ancient, wrinkled eyes. My mind flashed back, and my stomach fell out from underneath me. I felt physically sick. Those eyes had watched my every meal so far at Blackthorn House. The nose, the eyes, the lips... Every feature was indistinguishable from the ones in my memory. Even his posture and his fine fabrics matched the canvas – the canvas that hung above the dining table in Blackthorn House. The canvas that, I had been told, was a real-life portrait of a distant Woodgate ancestor. The canvas, as my aunt had informed me after my many questions and upon closer inspection I had confirmed, that had been painted over 150 years ago.

FIVE

"I say, you look rather pale. Are you alright?" I recoiled from the old man and nodded my head. I tried to regain a form of consciousness in which I could reply to him, but he had already gone up to the front desk, paid for his items and left the shop, looking strangely at me one last time before the bell tinkled on his way out. He must have thought I was a mute.

Young Agatha looked at me and frowned. "Are you going to pay for those or are you going to stand there all day like a lemon?" she said, not unkindly. I gulped and hurried my purchases to the till, fearful that the old man would come back. "Good lord, child, you look like you've seen a ghost! Are you sure you're alright? Joseph, bless his heart, I know he can be a bit scary, but he was only trying to help. Normally he just keeps himself to himself." She entered my items individually onto the till and could have charged me £100 and I wouldn't have taken any notice.

"W-Who?" I stammered.

"Joseph," she repeated slowly, "the elderly man who left just now." I began to place Agatha's items absent-mindedly in my bag and looked at her as she continued, "Joseph – he's lived in the village his whole life, bless his heart." That infernal bell tinkled once more and put the fear of God into me. It was not Joseph as I had anticipated but Uncle Frederic, looking like a drowned rat.

He grunted, asking me why I had taken so long, and I gave him a despairing look in return that he ignored. He handed over some money to the haberdashery owner (who had fallen silent) and ushered us out of the shop as she returned to her book and immediately forgot about the whole ordeal.

Frederic looked up at the dark sky and checked his watch. "It's getting late. We'd better go back." I followed him without a word as we retraced our steps on the cobbles, out of the village, past the dishevelled cottage with its weather-beaten vegetable patch and through the muddy forest.

I felt as though somebody had taken my head in their hands and rattled it around. My thoughts were all jumbled up, and I couldn't make head nor tail of what was going on. If there was one thing I was sure of, it was that I hadn't been mistaken. I understood that people could look alike and that family members could bear certain resemblances, but this was uncanny.

The old man may as well have stepped straight off the canvas and into that haberdashery. It was the same person, there was no denying it. This meant that I had to try and comprehend how it was possible that somebody who had their portrait painted 150 years ago could be walking about the streets of Blackthorn today buying knitting materials for their wife.

The more I thought about it the more I could not comprehend it, not because it was incomprehensible but because it was impossible. Things like this simply did not happen; magic was not real, and people do not exist centuries after they are supposed to.

And yet, I had seen it. Hadn't I? Seen him. The one they call Joseph.

*

I tipped the contents of my bag out onto my aunt's sewing table, and she frowned. "There's one colour missing." My heart sank. In the chaos of the morning's occurrences, I had forgotten to pick up the last bundle of wool.

"They didn't have it," I lied.

"That seems odd, Joanna, as they always have the baby blue. It's quite popular, you know."

She picked up the bundles of wool and examined them as I scowled. She looked up and I looked back at her blankly. She sighed and put down the wool. "Now go and have a hot bath or something, you're dripping all over my floor and I can't be doing with having an invalid to look after if you catch cold. You can help prepare dinner later." No thanks, no gratitude, no nothing. Just a blunt dismissal. I turned on my heel and walked out of her perfumed, bright pink-coloured sewing room with all the dignity I could muster in my heavy furs.

I trudged up the main staircase and turned right towards the east wing. As much as I didn't like my aunt, she was right, I was desperately in need of some warmth, and I certainly wasn't going to get any from her. Slightly further along the corridor from my room was a separate bathroom in which I proceeded to lock myself in for the next few hours. I didn't pause to look at any paintings or to marvel at impressive scenes on my way. I ignored the library. I was tired. Tired of being treated like I had always done something wrong and tired of this big, oppressive house.

I wanted to go home. I wanted to go back and forget about the past four miserable days of my life. As I lay there amid the hot steam and closed my eyes, I thought vaguely of my parents and wondered when any of this would begin to make sense.

I felt a little more relaxed and a whole lot warmer after I had got dressed a few hours later. I had spent half the time sitting by the window in my room, huddling in a blanket and looking out over the clearing around me. It reminded me of how beautiful Blackthorn House really was, and even though the people who lived there were not beautiful in any way, I was lucky to have been able to see it. Perhaps it would have been better to have seen it from the outside rather than the inside, but right now I had to be grateful for my situation: warmth, a roof over my head and a hot dinner waiting for me (albeit one that I had to go and prepare).

Again, I didn't even glance at the library as I walked past the door to my bedroom and ignored all the canvases on the way down to the kitchen. They had done enough harm for now. As the three of us went in for dinner it felt as though four of us had sat down: me, Uncle Frederic, Aunt Agatha and the withered old man above us. I glanced at him once or twice and then tried to focus instead on my meal and the conversation taking place. That did not last long as the conversation soon stopped, and we lapsed into a stagnant silence.

I couldn't help myself. "Who is the old man in the frame?" Agatha jumped into defensive mode as her knife and fork made a clatter against the china.

"We've had this conversation before. He is an old ancestor of our family."

"Who painted him?" I fired back, making it clear I would not let this go.

"How should I know?" Agatha snapped. "Freddie, do you know where the painting came from? Put an end to Joanna's infernal questions, will you."

It was the first time I had heard her call my uncle Freddie and wondered if this was what she called him in private. Frederic's expression had changed. He looked at me and he knew. It hadn't occurred to me until this moment that as Joseph had been walking out of the haberdashery, my uncle was walking in.

"I don't know," he replied and calmly took a sip of water.

"There you go, Joanna, it's just an old portrait of a very old man..." She paused and gazed away absentmindedly. "I do seem to remember that his name was Jimmy or something... perhaps John..." I didn't bother to correct her and looked again at the canvas. I knew full well that his name was Joseph Woodgate.

24

"I saw somebody in the village that looked like him," I blurted out. "It looked so much like him it could have been him."

"Don't be silly." Agatha shut me down. "A lot of people probably look like him. The Woodgates have been around these parts for hundreds of years." Frederic remained silent and continued to eat his meal, displaying an apathetic lack of appetite.

A sudden chill rushed about the dining room. One of the curtains fluttered and a candle was extinguished in the draught. Agatha stood up with her back to us, relit the candle that had gone out and Joseph Woodgate winked at me from the canvas above. I dropped my knife and fork with a deafening clang and stared. It was only a slight movement, but it happened alright.

The portrait was alive.

SIX

"What's the matter with you now?" Agatha looked me up and down as the candlelight flickered and cast shadows on the table. I swallowed. In fact, I felt strangely calm. Yes – today I had seen an old man who shouldn't be alive anymore walk around Blackthorn as though he had just stepped straight off the canvas. I knew that I wasn't crazy. I knew that I wasn't making things up. Frederic also knew that I was telling the truth. He was looking everywhere about the room but the canvas.

Aunt Agatha was simply ignoring the whole thing. It made perfect sense that the portrait would move because, with everything else that had gone on in Blackthorn House, how could I be surprised anymore? The immediate shock was over and now I just wanted the truth.

As I took the final bite of my dinner, there was a loud noise that didn't originate from the three of us. I looked up and Joseph Woodgate was blowing his nose on a handkerchief taken from his jacket pocket. I gazed above and watched him replace the handkerchief as though it were the most commonplace occurrence. He resumed his position back to the one in which he had been painted in.

Agatha and Frederic's eyes met and then looked quickly away. They arranged their features as if nothing had happened. I stood up and knocked over my chair. "Are you telling me that you neither heard nor saw what just happened? You're both just going to sit there and ignore what is clearly happening with that canvas above you? Because if you are you must think I'm one hell of a fool."

Silence fell around the table. A different silence to the usual silence I expected at the end of dinner. This was not an awkward silence or one that had arisen from me being told off yet again. This was a silence in which Frederic remained as still as a statue and Agatha was thinking very carefully about what she was going to say.

She cleared her throat calmly and looked me in the eye. "It appears you're not feeling well, Joanna. You've had a long day today. I understand that you might be a little upset about your parents, and I've made certain allowances for that over the past few days. However, I think it's best that you go up to bed and get a good night's sleep." She placed both hands firmly upon the table and stood up, indicating that dinner was over.

I laughed at her derisively. "You've got to be joking. You're trying to convince me that I'm imagining all of this? How can you deny what's plainly in front of you?" I was half laughing half shouting now, and anybody who didn't know me or the situation may have indeed thought I was crazy.

"Frederic. Please can you escort Joanna to her room and ensure she is comfortable. I will get your uncle to bring you up some nice soothing tea."

"I don't want your sodding tea. Or your lies. I will not be escorted like a child. I'm packing my bags tomorrow and I'm going home." I left the dining room, blinking back tears of frustration and shaking my head. I walked swiftly to my room and slammed the door behind me.

*

I lay on my bed, shivering in the cold, for what must have been hours. I had to get out of Blackthorn House. There was something supernatural occurring inside its walls and I too had become trapped, like Joseph in the canvas. If I stayed here any longer, I didn't know what I'd do. The simple fact that I had been ignoring was this: the portrait of my ancient ancestor was not the first painting that I had seen move.

I had seen others but had simply put them down to tiredness or tricks of the light. Those imposing black branches of the forest had swayed in the wind when I had stepped closer to the frame in the corridor. The dust had gathered and settled on every surface of the library as I stepped outside my bedroom door. I had seen animals move out of the corner of my eye as I went about my daily chores. I had pushed these odd occurrences to the back of my mind for the past four days. I now saw them as clear as day.

The paintings of Blackthorn House were not only uncannily lifelike, they were, in fact, alive.

I jumped as a sudden knock at my bedroom door disturbed me from these frightful thoughts. I sighed a little in relief as Uncle Frederic peered through a crack in the door, bringing me the promised tea from earlier. "You can come in," I said wearily, and watched him set down a flower-patterned cup and saucer on my bedside table.

"You should drink this. It will help you sleep." He backed out of the room and left the door slightly ajar after our brief exchange.

I huddled underneath my bedcovers. I felt more lost and alone than I had ever before. Why had my parents not let me know what was going on or when I could go home? Why hadn't they come for me? Did they not want me anymore? I angrily blinked back stinging tears. The heavily perfumed scent of Agatha's sweet tea wafted into my nostrils. I took the cup in my hands and blew on the steam. What was the worst that could happen? At least it would warm me up.

It was not until I had eagerly drained the last few drops that Agatha's tea began to take effect. Not an innocent, comforting cup of tea as I had assumed but instead, one that had been laced with something bittersweet that made my eyelids droop and my limbs become heavy. The pale light from my bedside lamp was obscured by my eyelids as I gave in to the darkness. As I began to drift off into an uncomfortable slumber, my ears picked up the faint murmur of voices that gathered pace and clarity as Agatha and Frederic made their way up the main staircase.

Their words bounced around in the great chamber of the ceiling and floated down the corridor. I caught snippets of their conversation as their words echoed in my ears.

"...should have seen their faces..."

"...people have started talking... keep this a secret... figure it out soon..."

"...she'll soon... family gift..."

"...not gift – curse..."

"...we'll have to call them ... she'll have to go..."

"...she's better off ... Blackthorn..."

I fell out of consciousness as their last few words faded and slunk away into the night.

SEVEN

I awoke abruptly drenched in a cold sweat. I checked my watch and briefly registered that it was three o'clock in the morning. The effects of Agatha's sleeping elixir had worn off. It was the early hours of the morning, and I was wide awake.

I sat bolt upright in bed as though I had just been shocked. I tried to recall the snippets of conversation I had overheard between my aunt and uncle before I was unwillingly forced into sleep. I racked my brain and came up with something about people talking, being better off away from Blackthorn and a family gift... no, a curse. For all I knew I could have made this conversation up during my night-time fevers.

I threw the bedcovers violently off me and reached for my dressing gown. I wasn't going to find the answers hiding beneath my covers. It was time to go searching for the truth, and I knew exactly where to find it. I had to go back. Back to where it all began.

Aided by the moonlight, I padded barefoot down the corridors and up the staircases of Blackthorn House, so close to the answers I desperately sought. I found the painting of the forest quickly. It was as though I had subconsciously mapped out the house and now had a better sense of direction than ever before. I stood before the painting in a patch of silver on the musty carpet and looked – properly looked – for the first time.

The gate, which before had been half open, was now shut and padlocked. I could feel the wind whistling in my ears now.

I watched as the leaves of the forest playfully danced, teasing me with their boldness. I listened as the owls called out to each other, speaking their curious nocturnal language to which I was a stranger. I shuddered as I felt the damp earth beneath my toes. A crack of a twig startled me, and I looked down the corridor behind me, suddenly aware that I might not be alone. All was still. I looked back at the painting of Blackthorn Forest. It had become motionless, trapped in time, a mirror image of the trees that surrounded me.

The moon passed over to the other side of the corridor. "Joannaaaa…" The faint whisper disturbed me a lot less than it should have done, and I responded instinctively by following the noise. Something was calling my name. Calling out to me, enticing me to follow it into the darkness.

"Joanna Woodgaaaate…" I followed it all the way back to the other side of the house towards the east wing. My footsteps were muffled by the old carpet, and the rest of the house remained silent. I put one foot in front of the other, forgetting about my aunt and uncle, forgetting about my parents. All that existed in this moment was me and the disembodied voice.

"Joanna…" It sounded like a woman's voice. One I had not heard before but one I did not fear. I should have known better. I should have feared it. It led me to a corridor I had not seen before. The voice was growing faint, and I felt as though I was nearing its origin.

Goose bumps emerged on my skin from the bitter cold. The corridor was draughty. I looked up. The voice had led me to a painting. I think it was the most beautiful painting I had ever seen. A breathtaking night sky stretched across a deep navy-blue canvas that was lit up eerily by the shining white light of the moon.

Black figures floated across the night sky. Black figures with hooded cloaks that began to trail behind them in the wind. "Joannaaaa…" I moved closer. The stars twinkled, and the moonlight shone upon the cloaked women. The painting had me in a spell. Had I the sense to look at my watch I would see the hour approaching four… then five…

I had lost all sense of time and place. The painting entranced me. The strange women called out to me from beneath the canvas. I blinked only when my eyes became sore from the cold. My entire body became frozen to the spot. The moonlight lit up my eyes, and I had the sudden desire to touch that shining object in the night sky.

As soon as my finger contacted the canvas the surface was destroyed instantaneously. The moon melted away onto my fingertip, and the corridor shone with milky white light. There was a great tear as the canvas ripped from top to bottom. A gnarled finger appeared from beneath the rip and was followed by a cunning, twisted face and a long black cloak that put the fear of death into my heart.

I watched with horror as the hideous figures emerged triumphantly from the frame. As they twisted their way out of the canvas and looked gleefully at their new surroundings, I stood paralysed and looked at the tragedy I had created.

This was my curse. I had been warned never to touch the paintings, and now I knew why. I felt that instead of bringing something to life I had in fact brought death to Blackthorn House.

The witches began to chant in another language as I looked about the corridor desperately trying to find an escape. If it were not for the loud shrieks coming from the foul mouths, I might have heard my parents' footsteps crunching on the leaves outside. I might have heard their hopeful voices as they began the steep ascent to Blackthorn House as the sun came up.

When the sun comes up, most fairytale creatures shrink and disappear never to be seen again.

Unfortunately, these were not fairytale creatures.

PART TWO

SOPHIE

EIGHT

Our house was rid of possessions, our bags were packed, and the hire van groaned on the drive under the weight of our belongings. This was it: moving day. I sat glumly watching the chaos as Mum and Dad rushed about like headless chickens, checking and rechecking the contents of the vehicle, terrified of leaving something behind. I plonked myself atop a pile of suitcases that were due to arrive at our destination later and sat with my head propped up on my arm.

I shifted on the uncomfortable baggage while Mum shot me a glare. "Are you going to sit there all morning, Sophie, or are you going to lift a finger to help?" I sighed, slowly heaving myself out of my makeshift chair, and grabbed a cardboard box that sat waiting on the front porch of our apartment block.

The luxury penthouse on the top floor had been our home for ten years. I thought sorrowfully of how I would never again be able to gaze out over the Thames that stretched below us and watch the hustle and bustle of everyday life in the streets of London. I was a city girl through and through, but that was going to have to change.

My mother, Anne Lockwood, a renowned doctor in Windsor, was able to take her work with her. Mum had applied for a new position in the sleepy village of Blackthorn and had succeeded. It would be a significant step down in our annual income; however, I was informed this did not matter, as it allowed Dad to pursue his dream, the real reason for our move.

A well-established banker in the heart of London, with his six-figure paycheque and perfect client record, Harvey Lockwood had it made. Or so we had thought.

During his mid-life crisis, Dad revealed to us that his new dream was to become an author. He said the drab cover of grey buildings and drizzle that we lived under in the city had finally taken its toll. It had repressed his imagination and stopped him from living up to his full potential. Thankfully, he had already made his fortune, and we were assured that moving to the country would not affect his ability to look after his two favourite girls, who both stood in front of the glass window that presided over the river with arms crossed and sceptical faces upon receipt of this news.

My inability to comprehend why on earth Dad would want to give up the extravagance of his high life was silenced by Mum's love for her husband and willingness to make him happy. A frank chat between me and Mum had ensued. She was very quick to remind me that Dad had put in many laborious hours for us to have everything we wanted. It was time for his girls to return the favour.

So, I had swallowed this dry pill with extreme difficulty, and resigned myself to the fact that I was leaving old Sophie Lockwood behind. I must become a country bumpkin. I grimaced at the thought and pulled my phone out of my back pocket. Rearranging my auburn bob around my face so no sleek strand could go awry, I snapped a quick picture of a puppy dog face and forwarded it to Jessica and Amelia. Upon facing the realisation that I would have to leave my two best friends behind, I was surprised that little emotion bubbled to the surface, and I began to re-evaluate our friendship over the years.

I couldn't help but think they had used me as an excuse to participate in the long pamper evenings and exotic holiday breaks that had come as a bonus of the Lockwood family's money. They hadn't replied to my messages in two days.

After rearranging some of the boxes like a giant game of Tetris, Dad managed to slam the doors on the van shut and looked up resolutely at our old home. His dark brown stubble did not waver as he said a silent goodbye to London. "Come on, Harvey," Mum took his hand gently and smiled at me, "there's nothing left for us to do now but leave." He played with a strand of Mum's red locks and kissed her gently on the cheek.

"What would I do without you, eh?"

Even though my parents' affections were slightly embarrassing, I had to count myself lucky that they were both so in love, and their marriage had survived the continuous stresses of life as a doctor and a banker. Their unsociable hours and mountains of paperwork had only reinforced the old saying that absence makes the heart grow fonder. I shook my head and stored away these tender thoughts. Tossing my hair, I clambered into the van. "Let's get going then." We'd dragged out our goodbyes for long enough.

The crowded streets and high-rise buildings of London were left behind and replaced with green fields and open spaces. I turned my head to look out of the window as the trees and hedgerows passed by in a blur. I settled myself down and plugged in my earphones, only to remove them ten minutes later when Mum accused me of being ignorant. Begrudgingly partaking in a family game, the time passed surprisingly quickly, and three hours later we pulled up in front of our destination with bated breath.

I released mine with a gentle sigh of relief; the house was indeed beautiful. Not quite a luxury penthouse suite; it stood semi-detached at the end of a little row of houses in the village. Eyeing the colourful wildflowers that grew in the front garden, I toyed with the idea that maybe yes, it might be possible for us to make a home here.

NINE

Three hours later we finished unpacking the boxes and collapsed onto cellophane-covered chairs in exhaustion. Two high-pitched syllables of music sounded, and I set down my espresso. "Do we have a doorbell?" Mum jumped up and stubbed her toe on a mirror that hadn't quite made it up onto the wall yet. "Ow!"

I hovered by the staircase, peering over their shoulders as Mum and Dad opened the door to greet our visitors. A couple stood side by side, dressed in black from head to toe, as though they had just departed a funeral. The woman handed over a woven basket of fruit with a red-lipped smile. "Welcome to Blackthorn!" she exclaimed through a toothy grin. "Wilhelmina and Christopher Nightingale. We thought we'd come and see who our new doctor is and to welcome you to the village. Forgive the intrusion."

Mum tentatively returned her smile. "That's very kind of you. We've just finished unpacking." She gestured behind her. "This is my husband, Harvey, and our daughter, Sophie. It's lovely to see a friendly face!" Wilhelmina's pale face lit up as she moved her arms around, and her sleek black hair moved slightly in the breeze.

"Well, you've come to the right village then! I'm sure everybody here will help you feel right at home."

"That's great," Dad replied. "I'm sure we'll settle in quickly." I looked up at the sky. There was a storm brewing.

"And…" Wilhelmina continued, ignoring the worsening weather, "our girls will be such good friends. They look about the same age…?" Mum affirmed that I was seventeen whilst passing me the colourful basket, and Wilhelmina smiled. It was an unnerving movement that stretched her mouth far too wide for it to be genuine.

"It's lovely to meet you, Sophie. Say hello, Cassandra." Wilhelmina gave her daughter a gentle push into sight. The girl looked me up and down as though scrutinising every part of me. She eventually gave a shy smile. My first impression of Cassandra was that she was, well, a little odd. With her wide eyes and tangled mane of black hair, Cassandra Nightingale looked like she was in a world of her own.

"You can call me Cassie," she mumbled quietly. "I think we'll be in the same class at school tomorrow." I opened my mouth to reply, but my words were interrupted with a rumble from the overcast sky. The Nightingales cut short our exchange, whipped out their black umbrellas, and set off home as the heavens opened. They disappeared down the cobbles, and we shut the door with relieved expressions.

"Is it just me or are the Nightingales a little… strange?" I asked, walking to the kitchen and setting down the basket on the table.

Dad chuckled. "They were nice enough, although that husband wasn't very talkative." I caught Mum's eye, and we exchanged dubious expressions as she silently confirmed what I was thinking. It wasn't Christopher that I thought odd but rather Wilhelmina. Her fake niceties and crimson lipstick gave me goose bumps.

My new room was smaller than my old one but complete with a large windowsill that jutted out above the street below. I retreated upstairs after dinner and grabbed a blanket from my bed. I sat huddled, contemplating my day at a new school tomorrow, watching the rain lash the windows. New classes, new people, being the 'new girl'... The thought of everything made me want to hop into the van and joyride all the way back to London. I sighed and thought of Cassandra; at least I would know one person.

I whiled away the remaining hours of the evening gathering pens, papers, books and timetables, which I stuffed clumsily into my bag. I laid out my uniform in the hope that it would have changed appearance come morning. Knee-high socks, a pleated skirt and a green-striped blouse were not exactly what I had in mind for creating a good first impression. With the thought of postponing the next morning for as long as possible, I avoided going to sleep, until Mum poked her head through my door.

"Are you still awake, Sophie?" she whispered. "You know it's eleven o'clock?"

"I'm just going. Trying to get myself ready for tomorrow," I said with a sigh. She smiled and patted my arm reassuringly.

"You shouldn't worry, Cassie will look after you." She backed out of the door, and I heard her bedroom door open and close further along the landing. For some reason her final words were anything but reassuring.

I clambered into bed and tried to forget until morning. The rain kept me awake. Gigantic droplets beat against the windows, and the wind rushed violently past the house. It felt like the very foundations of the house were shaking as the storm persisted. I checked my clock. It was just turning midnight when I noticed a streetlamp shining eerily through a gap in my curtains. I stumbled over to the windowsill, rubbing my eyes, when something on the pavement below caught my attention.

A woman walked hurriedly, braced against the rain with no umbrella and a long black coat that billowed out in the wind. She kept her head down, like she didn't want to be seen. I looked closer as she passed the house. I recognised that hair – long, black and wavy. Like Cassandra's, but not quite. More styled and tamed. More like her mother's. I hesitated at my window in confusion.

Why would Wilhelmina Nightingale be prowling the streets of Blackthorn at midnight in the middle of a howling storm? I tried to catch sight of her again to check that my suspicions were correct, but too late; she had passed on.

I closed the curtains slowly and sat down on the end of my bed. I was sure that the woman I had seen was Cassandra's mother; her hair and her height were the same as I had been introduced to earlier. No shops were open in Blackthorn past eight, so she couldn't have been picking anything up. Could she have been visiting someone? A relative? I shook my head. Surely no one would have a reason to go visiting people at midnight in a little village where your neighbours are always watching. I yawned and realised that I desperately needed some sleep if I was to survive tomorrow. I got back into bed, huddled beneath the covers and tried to get comfortable. As I fluffed up my pillow in annoyance, a strange thought occurred to me; a tiny detail that for some reason had stuck in my mind.

Wilhelmina's hair wasn't wet. As she battled against the elements her hair had remained dry. How was that possible? She had repelled the heavy raindrops that ran like a river in the middle of the street. As I was drifting off, I wondered faintly if Wilhelmina Nightingale made a habit of patrolling the cobbles in the dark.

TEN

I rushed through breakfast and grabbed my bag off the kitchen surface. I was late. "Good luck!" Mum called after me as I skidded down the hallway and out the front door. Thankfully I only had a ten-minute walk around the corner, and I arrived at the school gates. The building stood tall and intimidating. Its grey brickwork reminded me uncomfortably of a prison.

I repositioned my bag over my shoulder, swallowed, and walked through the gates with my head held high. I didn't get very far before a mane of black hair engulfed me. Taken aback by Cassandra's hug, I smiled and tried to pretend I was happy to see her. Jessica, Amelia and I had rarely exchanged hugs back in London, and I wasn't used to this level of physical embrace.

"Hi, Sophie! First day – how're you feeling?" I paused. She was a completely different girl to the shy one I had met yesterday. Without the domineering presence of her mother, Cassandra seemed more at ease with herself.

"I, um, yeah, okay, I guess." My poor conversation skills were saved by the shrill ring of the bell. I smiled a little more warmly and gestured to the entrance doors. "Shall we? You can show me the ropes." Cassandra nodded, and we proceeded through the busy doors.

After everyone had disappeared down the corridor, and I resurfaced from the sea of school bags, I finally got a chance to survey my new surroundings. I gasped; for a second, I thought I'd walked into the wrong building.

Black drapes hung majestically from the high ceiling and bats swooped down from every corner. Shining cobwebs hung suspended along the walls, and their giant owners stared out menacingly from their eight eyes. A mechanical cauldron emitted bubbling sounds to my left, and black witches' hats had been placed strategically on science lab stools around it. My eyes widened as they scanned over vials of scarlet fake blood that had been splashed across the reception desk. A giant figurine of an ugly witch perched on a shabby-looking broomstick robbed from the cleaning cupboard took centre stage. She looked so life-like I expected a black cat companion to be rubbing around her ankles.

"Um. Cassand... Cassie, is this what your school normally looks like?" I asked in apprehension.

Cassandra cackled, and I turned to her in alarm. "Sophie... you do know it's two days before Halloween, don't you?" I looked at her as the realisation dawned. With the disruption of the move, I'd lost track of time.

"Of course I do." The cauldron fizzed and belched out a particularly violent gurgle. "These decorations are really something..."

Cassandra tugged me by the arm and mumbled something about not being late on my first day. She was right; I didn't want to be the 'new girl' and the 'latecomer' all in one.

We hurried along the eerily decorated corridor and reached a door sign posted 'Classroom 13' at the end. How apt. I opened the door and exhaled slowly. "What the..." Even the classrooms were littered with spiders, bats and rattling skeleton bones. We located two seats at the back of the room, and I sat down gingerly in front of a grotesquely carved pumpkin that I feared may come alive and pounce on me at any moment. I was briefly introduced to everyone by a young-looking Miss Wood, and all thirty members of the class swivelled slowly on their seats to have a peek. They simultaneously returned to face the front and ignored the new girl to take note of their timetable changes.

I spent the rest of form time contemplating what kind of school celebrates Halloween to this extent. Did everyone else think it was normal to study algebra among pumpkins and inflatable gravestones? My family was never particularly religious, but All Hallows' Eve was not a celebration that we usually acknowledged. I shifted uncomfortably on my seat. It made me feel somewhat uneasy to think that a celebration so often associated with the Devil and his counterparts was encouraged in a school.

My first day at Blackthorn High passed in a blur of trying to remember people's names and the layout of the sixth form block. My preoccupation with my new vicinity meant that I didn't get a chance to ask Cassandra about her mother's night-time wanderings. Perhaps that was a good thing; I didn't want her to think I was poking my nose in where it didn't belong. Perhaps she was used to her mother disappearing into the night like a shadow. We only shared a couple of classes together, and I ambled home alone. My skill for making new friends had not established itself yet, and most of my peers avoided the odd-looking city girl with the ring in her nose.

After extracting Dad from his makeshift office at the back of the house, and waiting for Mum to finally return home, the three of us wearily sat down to a large pizza from the only takeaway shop in the village. We dived for the warm slices gratefully. "Most of them don't even have medical problems," Mum complained through a mouthful of hot pepperoni. "They just want to come in and be nosy... Word travels quickly around here."

"You'll get used to them, love." Dad reached for another slice and inclined his head towards the takeout boxes. "I'm sorry I didn't have a chance to get anything else. I've been so engrossed in medieval folklore I didn't realise what the time was..."

"I'm glad you're finding some inspiration here," I replied smiling.

"What about you, Soph?" Mum leant back in her chair and wiped her hands on a napkin. "How was your first day?"

I groaned. "Weird. You know they've decorated the school for Halloween? It looks like the set of a horror film." I met their quizzical looks. "You'd have to see it to believe it."

Mum retreated upstairs to run a much-needed bubble bath and Dad stretched his feet up on the sofa with a great yawn. I joined him for a while, being in no hurry to be alone with my thoughts; they were brimming with overflowing cauldrons and ghostly faces. I was beginning to doubt if I would ever feel at home in Blackthorn. Everything just seemed so... strange.

First, Wilhelmina Nightingale swoops by the house at midnight with no feasible explanation, and second, the entire school is decked out to welcome ghosts and ghouls alike. There was something odd about this village. And not just because of the time of year. The infamous rain that so often washed the cobbles of Blackthorn reappeared, and I resolved to focus my mind on my books instead.

I don't know how long I had been lying on my bed, eyes blurring at the wiggly lines on the page, when the doorbell chimed. I opened my bedroom door wondering if I would have to be the one who answered it. I was knocked to the side by Mum who had emerged from the bathroom hastily tying up her dressing gown. "It's nine o'clock for God's sake!" She made her way down the stairs in a fluster, rearranging the towel around her head as she went, damp strands of hair escaping loosely.

I tiptoed to the landing and peered down as she passed Dad snoozing on the sofa and rolled her eyes up at me. Who would be calling this late? I had a partial view of the front door from my vantage point and leant further over the banister in curiosity.

Speak of the Devil and she shall appear.

Wilhelmina Nightingale stood framed in the doorway with a big fake smile plastered all over her face. "Wilhelmina! What a... lovely surprise!" Mum proceeded to invite her in for a drink, clearly embarrassed by her current lack of clothing, and tied her robe tighter to protect from the sudden cold that wafted through the hallway.

"That's very kind of you, Anne, but I'm not staying. I have something I need to do. I just popped by to check how Sophie's first day went? Cassandra said she seemed a little on edge."

"Well..." Mum quickly came to my defence, "I can imagine why – first day at a new school and all that... It can be quite unsettling." Wilhelmina smiled a brilliant white grin and wrapped her black shawl around her shoulders.

"Why of course. Poor child. She should know that she's welcome round our house any time she wishes. And the same to you as well! Sorry to disturb your evening. I'll leave you to get on."

Wilhelmina turned away from the house, and Mum arched her back. Something was amiss. "At least the rain's stopped!" she called after her.

Wilhelmina stepped out from beneath the porch and into the continuing downpour. "Oh, it doesn't disappear that easily in Blackthorn, my dear!"

"Oh... right," Mum replied, her voice trailing off. "Get home safe." The door was closed with a snap. Mum turned around with her head on one side, and an odd expression crept over her features. She raised her eyebrows, shook her head and continued into the living room to wake Dad up and complain about late-night visitors.

I refrained from informing her that Wilhelmina Nightingale was no stranger to night-time wanderings. I watched the encounter like a spy from above and tiptoed back to my bedroom. Mum knew that something was wrong but had simply shrugged it off. "At least the rain's stopped," she had said. And for good reason. Wilhelmina's hair was dry again – silky smooth yet she carried no umbrella with her. She displayed no sign of having just been caught in a deluge. That's why Mum had paused when she turned away. Like me, the first time, she must have thought nothing of it. But now I knew better. Something was wrong. A person could not be walking in torrential rain two nights in a row and not have a secret to keep.

I resolved to ask Cassandra about it the next day. I would subtly bring up that her mother had been visiting and enquire into her whereabouts after that.

But something happened the next day that shook the village of Blackthorn to its core.

ELEVEN

It really is an indescribable occurrence when a small child goes missing. The tragedy hit Blackthorn like a tidal wave, uncomfortably washing over the villagers, causing a ripple in the normality of everyday life.

Anxious faces met my gaze from the moment I stepped through the school gates. The classroom was somewhat subdued as I took my seat next to Cassandra. "What's happened?" I whispered as Miss Wood walked slowly up the rows of desks, fiddling with the golden locket that hung around her neck. She turned her wide eyes to face her pupils, who stared back at her with blank faces. The impossible task of informing a classroom of teenagers that something unthinkable had happened right under their very noses had befallen her.

The words uttered from her trembling lips instilled a sense of incredible fear into everyone sitting in that room. "There's no need to be afraid." A deafening silence followed. "I have been instructed to inform you that last night, a child went missing from Blackthorn – Michael Burrows. Now some of you may know him, as he was..." she paused, "he is a part of this school. His parents reported him missing at 11.30pm yesterday evening." She paused again, and her next sentence made me feel a little sick. "Michael went missing from his own home."

Everyone sat stiffly like statues frozen in time. "Rest assured there is an ongoing police search taking place, and I am confident that Michael will be found and returned very soon. In the meantime, classes will take place as normal." And that was that. Quick and painful. We were dismissed for our first class and left in complete silence.

It was only when we were outside the doors that people began whispering and discussing the missing child. I learnt that Michael was eleven years old, and his family was much liked in the village. Cassandra told me that from the few times she had ever seen him he had mousy brown hair and a very timid demeanour. We caught fragmented snippets of people's conversations as the corridors erupted and we battled our way through.

"I can't believe it—"

"I know. From his own home?"

"Where were his parents?"

"I wonder if they'll ever find him."

"Missing?"

"Where could he be…?"

"…the woods?"

"You know how the story goes…"

"Certainly the right time of year for it."

"The witches."

I turned my head to see who had made such a ridiculous comment, and Cassandra pulled on my arm. "Ow… what are you—"

"Come on. There's something I need to tell you." I watched in confusion as she fought past gaggles of students chatting nervously, led me to the girls' toilets next to Classroom 13, and barricaded the door shut. Her cheeks were flushed by the effort of it all. She glanced around the empty cubicles worryingly. I stood in bemusement.

"Are going to tell me what on earth you're doing?" Cassandra hesitated, unsure where to begin. I trained my ear on the now quietened corridor and worried about missing the beginning of class. "Cassie?" I attempted to bring her back to reality, and she fixed me with a steady gaze. "You can't keep me locked in here all day, you know," I joked uneasily.

"Sophie. You must understand. People round here... they're not like where you come from. They... believe in things. Strange things." I didn't say anything. "Blackthorn's always been a superstitious village. My grandparents, their parents, my grandparents' parents' parents—"

"Yes, Cassie, I get it. Can you please just tell me what this is all about?" I interrupted, uninterested in Cassandra Nightingale's family tree.

She swallowed and looked me dead in the eye. "There's an old fairy tale. Everyone knows about it." I looked at her in exasperation. The toilets were stuffy, and I just wanted to get out of there.

"What fairy tale?"

"The Witches of Blackthorn." I snorted with laughter before catching sight of Cassandra's face in the cracked mirror. She'd gone from being rosy-cheeked to as white as a sheet in a matter of minutes. My smile faded. "I told you, Sophie, Blackthorn's a strange place with an even stranger history. The villagers here believe in all sorts of things."

I shook my head at her. "You can't be saying that people actually believe in witches that go around and cast spells on people..."

"I'm not necessarily saying that I believe it... but Blackthorn is associated with the practice of witchcraft, going back a long time." I bit my tongue to prevent a blunt remark escaping from my lips.

Cassandra was looking down at the ground now avoiding eye contact with me. I didn't want anyone to think I was crazy if I said I believed her. But then again, maybe I was the crazy one for not believing her. I deliberated for a few moments and then understood that Cassandra didn't have to tell me about this. She could have kept it hidden from me, but now I could begin to try and understand the villagers a little better. "Okay," I said with a sigh, and Cassandra looked up. "Tell me about this so-called fairy tale." I perched on the ledge of the sinks and resigned myself to listen to the ancient tale.

"Well, I don't know it off by heart..."

"Please, Cassie, just tell me what you know." She laid down her school bag on the ledge and sat with her back against the small window. I listened as the heavy drops began to fall outside and Cassandra began her tale.

"One hundred and fifty years ago, Blackthorn existed as a small market village. People from across the country would come to buy and sell their wares. Animals were led to market along with barrels of grain and wine. Trade deals were set in stone on this very patch of earth we're standing on. The villagers were happy. Their businesses were booming, and they had everything they could ever want in the most picturesque village in the country. But, one year, everything changed. A group of travellers – most thought they belonged to a circus at first – appeared out of the forest one evening.

"With their pale faces and long hair as black as the night they soon became the talk of the town. They were last seen disappearing into the trees never to emerge again. Villagers went looking for them – a strange group of women turning up out of nowhere and setting up camp in the woods would arouse suspicion. No one ever found them. Some thought they had gone away. Others were happy that if they were still there, they minded their own business. People stopped going into the woods and resumed their lives as before.

"But strange incidents took place the night of Halloween that year. People's livestock went missing, scorch marks were left on the ground in place of buildings, and trails of hay and animal blood led straight into the woods. In anger many of them took up kitchen knives, pitchforks, pokers – any weapon they could lay their desperate hands on – and stormed the woods, thirsting for revenge. Men, heads of their families, trying to protect those they held dear. Boys willing to prove themselves for a first love. None of them returned victorious. In fact, none of them returned to the village at all. Blackthorn suffered a great loss at the hands of those mysterious women in the woods. Heartbroken widows and distraught children became overwhelmed with grief and dread; they could not understand what they had done wrong in the eyes of God that would warrant such loss of life.

"People said that the women were evil, bloodthirsty witches that sacrificed people's animals. Some say they did it for fun. Others say they did it for strength – simply to stay alive at the mercy of whatever deity they worshipped. Blackthorn never fully recovered from that night. The village had to pick up their broken pieces, assemble their lives back together again and live as a cracked community, haunted by the past. Every Halloween was the same after that. Animals went missing. Sometimes they returned, most of the time not. Fires would burn until the early hours of the morning, and smoke could be seen rising from the village as a sign of the witches' power. The knowledge of their existence in Blackthorn was about as common as the fact that the villagers knew they were powerless to do anything about it."

At this point in her story Cassandra paused and spoke slowly. "That's how the story goes, Sophie, from what I can remember. People believe that it still happens now. That the witches still possess some influence over the village. Obviously not to the same extent. People's houses don't burn down, and no one's disappeared..." Cassandra faltered. Her wide eyes were awash with fear, and her lips quivered as she became unable to finish her sentence.

"Until now," I whispered. "No one's disappeared... until now." She nodded and lapsed into a mournful silence. The rain drizzled down the windowpane of the girls' toilets as people splashed their way hurriedly across the courtyard outside.

TWELVE

Cassandra's words played on my mind for the rest of the day. I had never been a gullible child growing up; I was always the first to question what I was told and weigh things carefully on imaginary scales in my head. But, despite my practical nature, there was something about Blackthorn and the curious tale I had been told that set me on edge.

How people could still believe in such things was a great mystery to me. The scale of belief in these witches revealed itself as the day progressed. I passed many a student talking in a hushed voice blaming the witches for the disappearance of the boy. Multiple theories and puzzle pieces of how they got hold of the boy started to emerge; most believed Michael to be still alive, but trapped, waiting for his moment of sacrifice on the night of Halloween.

I sat behind a group of chattering girls for my last lesson of the day just about ready to bury my face into a pillow and scream out all my frustration. I listened to their quick-fire conversation to pass the time, until the hands of the clock told me that I could go home. I drank in yet more superstition and fanciful tales of bloodshed and sorcery.

One girl leant across the table with wide eyes and uttered a hushed suggestion to put all the rumours to bed: "We could always just go looking for the boy... Take a torch into the woods and see what we find?" Her words were met with fearful faces and an eventual silence in the classroom. Someone dropped their pen a couple of desks along, and it made a deafening clatter as it hit the floor.

"Don't be silly," another one of the girls fired back. "We're not going into those woods, and you know it." Her aggressive dismissal of the idea was finalised by the ring of the bell.

I hadn't seen Cassandra since that morning and walked home alone, mulling her words over in my head. I felt like I hadn't learnt a single thing that day. Instead, mysterious phrases echoed around in the empty chambers of my mind: "an ancient legend... evil, bloodthirsty witches... haunted by the past... no one's disappeared, until now..."

There were two options: either this whole situation was ridiculous, and everyone was just trying to scare each other at Halloween, or Blackthorn really was a village under the influence of these strange women from the past.

I sighed and shook my head. It had to be fanciful tales made up by adults to scare children from wandering into the woods alone. But how could it be a coincidence that a boy had gone missing this close to Halloween? I had almost reached my front doorstep when I came to the sudden realisation that either way, a boy was still missing. Michael Burrows had disappeared from Blackthorn without a trace and, even more strangely, I hadn't come across any police officers out looking for him on my walk home.

The police were not actively searching for Michael or questioning his school friends about his whereabouts; it seemed that they already knew where he was. If they already knew where he was, and option two was the truth, they would have no desire to go looking for him. As I closed the front door behind me, I made great effort to ensure that my key clicked in the lock securely and we were sealed inside. Better safe than sorry, right?

"Sophie, where HAVE you been?" The smothering arms of my mother enveloped me, and I struggled to free myself from her embrace.

"I, er... what?"

"Your father and I had a phone call from the headmaster. Did you not think... worried SICK... walking home... when did you last check your phone?" Mum's broken words burst forth from her like an erupting volcano. Before I could begin to make sense of what she was saying, I caught sight of Dad in the kitchen with a look of great relief on his face.

"We've been calling you, Sophie," he said, in a calmer voice than his wife's. He put a comforting arm around Mum's shoulders. "It's alright, Anne. She's home now."

"I'm sorry," I said genuinely. "I didn't think to check my phone what with everything going on." Dad nodded slowly and then did the instinctive thing that would calm everyone down. When the kettle had boiled, we sat down in the living room and clutched the cups close to our chests.

"I can't believe it," Mum whispered. "How can this have happened? When we moved to this village... This is the last thing we expected to happen."

"This is the last thing anyone expected to happen." Dad frowned and leant forward to put his mug on the coffee table. "Are you okay, Sophie? This must be difficult for you – knowing he went to your school." I couldn't think of an appropriate reply as my headache set in.

"Anyway," Dad continued, "as long as we're all alright that's what matters. Mum messaged you when she couldn't get hold of you, saying she would pick you up from school, and then when you weren't there, your mother started to panic, and well..." He trailed off awkwardly, looking over at Mum sipping her tea with wide eyes. Dad sighed. "Just... please check your phone from now on." I nodded.

"I promise."

Dinner was a subdued affair, and we ate mournfully. It felt wrong to smile or to laugh in the wake of the day's events. Mum switched the local news channel on low and waited to hear anything about the boy's disappearance. I think we were all hoping that the whole thing had been a horrible mistake – that Michael would be found having innocently wandered off and got lost. A little whisper ran through my mind, a horrible, frightening thought: but how can a boy have wandered off and got lost at 11.30pm when he was sitting in his own bedroom? I closed my eyes and tried to get rid of this thought. My parents' concern and the effect the disappearance had on them only increased the impending sense of doom that had entered my heart since that morning. When the doorbell rang it came as a welcome relief from the silence that had set in through the household.

Mum got up and peeked through the curtains, dubious to let any strangers in, and then sighed in relief. "Oh, it's only Cassandra." I looked up in alarm. Why the hell would this girl be coming over after what she'd told me today?

"Is Wilhelmina with her?" I asked as Mum walked to the front door, thinking that I couldn't be bothered to deal with her fake niceties.

Mum looked slightly relieved as she replied, "No, just Cassandra, dear," and unlocked the door to the outside world.

"Hi, are you looking for Soph?" Before Cassie could reply, Mum cut in, "I've just thought. Please tell me you didn't walk here? Not after today."

Cassie stood awkwardly in the doorway. "Um, hello Mrs Lockwood. I, er—"

"Mum, please," I interrupted, feeling Cassie's embarrassment. "Let the girl in."

"Yes," Cassie added quickly. "We desperately need to finish that project, don't we? The one due for tomorrow on… marine animals."

Mum frowned. "Which of your subjects is that for, Soph?" And then, "You didn't tell me that Cassandra would be coming over."

"I forgot," I said bluntly, narrowing my eyes at Cassie wondering what on earth she was up to.

"Well, alright then." Mum closed the door behind her. "I'll leave you girls to get on and finish what you need to." There was a pause, and then she called up the stairs after us, "I'll be dropping you home after though!"

As soon as my bedroom door was safely shut, I turned to face Cassandra. "Marine animals? Really?" She shrugged and smiled.

"It was the only thing I could think of." The smile vanished. "The real reason I came over was to talk about what I told you today. I didn't want you to think I was unhinged or anything for telling you all that stuff. I know it sounds silly, but it's just what I've been told over the years." I sat down on my desk chair and span around thoughtfully, unsure of how to reply.

"I don't think you're crazy, Cassie. If anything, I'm grateful you told me the truth among all these rumours."

Cassie paced back and forth, running her hands anxiously through her mane of tangled black hair, biting her lip in frustration. There was a strange glint in her eye as she turned back to me – a mixture of fear and wild excitement. "But what is the truth, Soph? What if they never find Michael? Are we all supposed to live in fear every day, scared to leave our own homes wondering who will be next?" She sat down on the window ledge and watched the street below sorrowfully.

"They'll find him," I replied, not convincing myself as my voice faltered. "It hasn't even been twenty-four hours." An uneasy silence followed my remark as we both sat, deep in thought, a million different possibilities racing through our heads. I don't know what strange force had brought me and my parents to the village of Blackthorn but amongst all the myths and legends it couldn't have felt less like home to me. If we were going to live here happily and feel safe, I felt it was my duty to ensure that happened.

Maybe the village needed a new girl, an outsider, to break tradition and to see things for how they really were. Maybe it was my turn to grow up and do something to benefit everyone else. I don't know how much time had passed before I spoke the words that concluded everything in my head: "I'm going into the woods."

Cassie's head snapped up. I swallowed. "It's the only way the village will know for certain what they – what we – are dealing with. I refuse to live in a village where I don't know who could be lurking around the corner. I've only been here for a couple of days, but it sounds like these strange beliefs and tales of witchcraft have gone on for far too long. You're right, Cassie, I don't know what the truth is, but someone should find out before it's too late."

Cassandra Nightingale did not hesitate for a second as she nodded, a look of resolution befell her face, and she made the most important decision of her lifetime.

"I'm coming with you."

THIRTEEN

Cassie and I looked resolvedly up at the tree boughs that creaked in the wind. We talked ourselves into and out of the plan all day long; what we were doing was for the good of the village, but two girls wandering into the woods on the night of Halloween with a disappearance having taken place was in fact a very bad idea.

I thought back to that morning and shuddered. After Dad had dropped me at the school gates and whizzed back home, I was accosted by Cassandra's mother. Wilhelmina had made it clear that she did not want Cassie visiting me late at night. This was something she had also let my mother know, as she had told me upon returning home that Wilhelmina had uttered harsh words through her car window, despite her protestations that she didn't know Cassandra was visiting until she arrived on our doorstep.

The next morning Wilhelmina had gripped my shoulder with scarlet talons that dug into my flesh, and the words she had uttered had seemed more like a threat than advice: "I would hate to think you're leading my daughter astray, Sophie. A London girl like yourself... you'll soon learn the way of the village." I wished that instead of scurrying away to my first class I had confronted her about her nocturnal adventures. Her flashing white teeth that looked more like spikes as she spat her words out had made my flesh crawl. I had kept the exchange a secret from Cassie.

As the supernatural tales floated around the halls of Blackthorn High and showed no sign of slowing down, our annoyance, and perhaps our ignorance, led us to the entrance of the woods. Cassie and I achieved the miracle of evading both sets of parents. We blatantly ignored the rules about not leaving our houses come nightfall, and her wristwatch beeped a quarter past the hour as we took our first tentative steps along the forest path. Leaves crunched underfoot, and owls hooted way above in the treetops. Strange shapes loomed out at us from the dark. I fumbled for my torch and lit up the path in the hope that it would provide some reassurance.

Cassie and I had agreed that if we had not found anything by the time the clock turned midnight we would sneak back home before anyone discovered our disappearance. "I've never been this far into the forest," Cassie whispered after twenty minutes of walking in silence. "I didn't even know the path continued this far." No sooner had she spoken these words than a horrible thought occurred to me. A thought which I chose not to voice aloud: what if we couldn't find our way back home? We had tried to walk in as straight a line as possible and ignore the smaller and darker paths that forked off.

"Me neither," I replied. "There's probably nothing to find anyway. We'll just keep walking in this direction and then turn around."

Ten minutes later and we hit a barrier that made our plan near impossible. I stopped dead, and Cassie crashed into my back. "Shit! What are you—" She picked up her bag, rubbed her aching leg, and her words trailed off in her mouth. The path we had been so diligently following had ceased to exist. It ended without warning, and we were left staring into an abyss of tangled undergrowth that dared us to follow it into uncertainty.

"Well, I guess that's that then," I said, somewhat relieved that our journey had been cut unexpectedly short. We turned to go back on ourselves, and I lit up Cassie's face with my torch as she turned her head sharply to look back through the trees once more. Her face changed. The moonlight passed eerily across her features, and my heart dropped heavily into my stomach like a stone when she uttered her next words: "I think I can see a light in the distance."

I turned my eyes unwillingly in the direction of her gaze. It was faint and flickering, disappearing every second or so, and reappearing in the same spot through the black, spiky trees. Nevertheless, it was a light alright, a faint orange glow that made my blood run cold with fear. That light was not a light of hope or of happiness, but one of dread and uncertainty. We deliberated, fearing the worst, but as the seconds ticked by our hope of discovering an answer was quickly fading away. Cassie checked her watch anxiously. "It's quarter to midnight." I nodded, resolved to carry on and imagined that I was returning the very look Cassie had given me in my bedroom the night before. She pointed her torch in the direction of the light and endeavoured to make her way through the depths of Blackthorn Forest.

It was no easy task to accomplish. Thorny brambles tore at my hair and face bringing sharp stings and brief tears to my eyes. Tree roots lay in wait and attempted to trip me up with every resolute step I took. Small creatures scuttled off into the distance as we disrupted their home in the very heart of the forest. The trees were so thick and so black that our torches were rendered useless, as they could not permeate the darkness.

Cassie never took her eyes off the light and used it as a guiding object for both of us. I don't think I would have made it through that part of the forest without her. She was relentless in her will to reach the source of the flickering orange light. Without warning, there was a break in the trees, and we came to a clearing lit up by the moonlight.

Only, this was no ordinary woodland clearing, for in the middle stood a magnificently old house.

FOURTEEN

I squinted through the gloom and shone my torch across the clearing. The house had been forgotten by the world. Ivy twined itself around the walls offering up a protective barrier from the harsh elements. Uninviting circular steps twisted their way up and up towards the entrance. They created a maze of stone, challenging anyone who dared to enter.

The many windows that once reflected the shining sun were now boarded up and enclosed the secrets of the dwelling within. Ugly gargoyles stood guard stubbornly on either side, facing each other, mimicking a stand-off. Their stone eyes were glazed over as though in a trance from the strange magnetism of the house. A cat meowed in the undergrowth, and a black form streaked up the steps. The cat knew the safest places to ascend; it was no stranger to the house. Thick, invasive trees leant over as though trying to peek in through the cracks in the windows, permanently casting the house into shadow.

I scanned my eyes over the building and the glowing orange light that seemed to originate from the rooftop. I swallowed as my eyes finally settled on the entrance door. "I don't like this, Cassie," I concluded, not taking my eyes off that door.

Cassie jumped and let out a little scream. "There's someone standing over there!"

My eyes widened as I turned in the direction of her pale, shaking finger. "They're gargoyles, Cassie!" I hissed angrily at her for making my heart stop once more. "Come on, we can't stand here forever."

After having left our beds empty, disobeyed our parents and ploughed our way through the forest in the dead of night, it only made sense that we enter the house. We reached the bottom of the spiral staircase and looked up. The steps had clearly been built for a giant. It was impossible to mount the staircase any other way than by physically climbing up it.

We ascended slowly and carefully, avoiding the slippery parts of the stone and occasionally looking up to see how far we had left to the door, but never looking down to see how far we had come from the ground. On occasion we had to offer the other an arm for balance and hoist each other up the perilous entryway. The higher we climbed, the lower the temperature dropped; by the time we reached the entrance door I was shivering in my thick winter coat.

I grasped at the twisted door knocker, and my hand became caught in sticky cobwebs. The gigantic gargoyle's head had not been knocked in many years. I thought better of it at the last second; it was probably in our favour if whoever was inside this house didn't know we were here. I shouldn't have worried, however, as the creaky door swung open to my touch and we were invited inside.

My eyes were enveloped in darkness, and I grappled to find my torch. The moon had passed over to beyond the clearing; its shining white presence was no longer able to aid us. With the combined light from both of our torches, Cassie and I distinguished yet another staircase directly in front of us, which we proceeded to climb. The ascent was somewhat easier than the previous one, and I tried to stop my heart from pounding with fear as we reached the top. A low hum entered my ears as I found myself in the middle of a dimly lit corridor. Monstrous candelabras had been mounted onto the dusty walls, and the spiders had also made their home among them. Cobwebs stretched from one side of the dingy corridor to the other. They were lit; the house showed signs of life. The flames danced eerily in the draught coming from the entrance door and cast macabre shapes across the mothballed carpet.

"Can you hear that?" Cassie whispered. I nodded, fearing we would be heard by someone if we spoke too loudly. I could feel the blood pumping through my veins as I led the way down the corridor intent on discovering the source of the low humming noise. There were doors upon doors the whole way along, some which I could peek through, most which I could not. I kept turning around to check that Cassie was still behind me; I didn't want to do this alone.

My single beam of light illuminated the intricate framework that lined the walls. I peered closer at each frame and vaguely discerned the vast outline of mountains, the startling eyes of a deer and the deep green of a fairytale glen. I had no doubt that the paintings were once great works of art for the eager eye to marvel at. Now they were peeling, faded and obscured through a thick layer of dust. Nobody had taken care of these beautiful paintings for hundreds of years.

The further we advanced along the corridor the louder the noise became. The number of candles increased along with my sense of dread. A quick flash of black at the end of the passage caught my eye, and my heart stopped for a couple of seconds. There was someone else in this house. I pointed at the door, and Cassie's breath caught in her throat as black shapes passed across the tiny window. She looked at me in panic as if asking what we were to do next. I grabbed her hand and pulled her to the floor. "We have to crawl," I whispered, my voice barely audible, and we dropped to our hands and knees and slowly approached the door at the end of the corridor. The carpet was damp, dusty and stank like something was rotting beneath it.

We sat, crouched underneath the small window at the end, plucking up the courage to sneak a peek. There was no need for us to whisper, as the humming noise had now become a murmur of voices that masked our own. Cassie was braver than me. She raised herself up, inch by inch to get a good vantage point, praying that no one was looking out. I watched her face as she watched the room. A look of first confusion and then absolute horror passed over her features. Then her eyes locked on one point, and her mouth simply fell into an 'o' of terror.

There was something else. I read another emotion that I did not understand at first and only came to understand a little later.

Betrayal.

Cassie slid back down the door and made a soft thump as she reached the carpet once more. Her face remained in the same expression of fright. "Cassie, what is it? What did you see? You're scaring the hell out of me..." My voice broke as she shook her head in response. She could not bring herself to relate what was behind the door.

When I chanced a fearful look through the dirty window an image entered my mind: laboratory stools placed strategically in a circle... a black cauldron that bubbled and emitted foul-looking liquid... only, this equipment had not been stolen from the school store cupboard but had been purpose built for one reason and one reason only.

A group of women positioned themselves excitedly in a circle, clad in black from head to toe, their mouths opening and closing with the dreadful chant of their ritual. Every limb of my body went numb as I beheld Wilhelmina Nightingale in the centre of the circle, her once sleek hair now as wild as her daughter's, both hands raised upwards in worship to a deity we shall never speak of.

Witches did exist. And we had walked right into their lair.

FIFTEEN

Cassie and I sat side by side, arms wrapped around ourselves for warmth, our wide eyes reflecting the flickering flames of the candles. It all clicked into place in the depths of my brain. Wilhelmina Nightingale's late-night walks, how she seemed to repel the rain as if by magic, her fake niceties... they had all been subtle clues. I had just been too caught up in the boy's disappearance and Blackthorn's secrets to piece them all together.

I hung my head in my hands. Wilhelmina had visited that night. She and her big red smile had dropped by. Michael Burrows had been snatched from his home at eleven thirty the same night. It had been her all along. How could I have been so stupid? I should have mentioned my suspicions to Cassie right then and maybe none of this would have happened.

A loud bang came from a door to our right, and we looked at it in alarm. Two loud bangs, and then three, and four, louder every time. "Let me out!" a desperate voice screamed. I had never spoken to Michael Burrows before, however in that moment I had no doubt who the disembodied voice belonged to.

My heart skipped a beat. This was our chance. Cassie and I sprang into action. I called back faintly to Michael to reassure him that we meant no harm. Cassie combed her hair for pins and extracted one from her tangled mane. She worked furiously at that lock for five minutes, even though it seemed like a lifetime, and it clicked open and swung inwards. The poor boy was dishevelled. His clothes were in rags, and his face was streaked with tear tracks that had been there for many hours. "Who are you?" he whispered, wide eyes staring up at us, lip wobbling.

"There's no time for that now, Michael. The three of us need to get out of here. Now." I took his hand firmly, and he clung on for dear life. Half crouched down and half running, the three of us approached the top of the staircase.

I put one foot on the first step, ready to take them at a run, and felt a sharp pain sear through the back of my head. My hair was almost yanked from my scalp as I twisted around to face three women, three... hideous witches. Unlike Wilhelmina, their faces were gnarled and twisted, and they leered at us gleefully. Two of them had a handful of both mine and Cassie's hair. Their long fingernails dug in excruciatingly. Cassie's face contorted in pain as she looked at me in anguish.

I let go of Michael's hand, and he wobbled on the steps down from us. With my free hand I threw my torch after him, and he caught it in surprise. I fixed him dead in the eye. "Run." The boy did not want to leave us, but I am glad that he did. All I could do was pray that he would reach home and spread the news of this house in the woods before the witches reached him in Blackthorn Forest. I watched his rags disappear through the entrance door at the bottom.

"Find him," one of the witches snarled to another. "We'll deal with these two."

"Wait – I think this one is a Nightingale. You'd better be careful, Krista."

"Nonsense. If she's a Nightingale then she'll soon be one of us. She'll just have to learn the hard way, won't you?" Krista grinned derisively at Cassie with a horrible smile that made my skin crawl. The third witch vanished with a swish of her black cloak and reappeared at the bottom of the staircase. She leapt forward into the night to recapture their sacrificial lamb.

We were dragged backwards violently by our hair.

The room in which they had been performing their terrible ritual had an opening directly to the roof. The witches tightened their grip on us as we emerged onto the rooftop and gulped down the sharp night air. My hair whipped in the howling wind. We tripped over trails of ivy and were pushed down to the ground. We shivered in despair. We had nowhere to go.

The rest of the witches stood waiting for their instructions. The old house creaked in the wind as it strained under the weight of their blackened souls. One turned her head upwards, surveying the ever-darkening sky above. They swept across the roof of the house, their mysterious figures framed by the silhouette of the moon.

They surrounded us with their cloaks that billowed out into the night. The faint orange glow we had followed from the woods had been emitting from the rooftop; I now realised that it seemed to be coming from the witches themselves. "Why are you doing this?" I shouted from the bed of ivy, trying to buy us more time. There came no response, and I felt movement beside me. Cassie was lifting herself off the ground. She was standing up, and I looked up at her desperately.

"How could you do this? Have you been like this all along?" The questions spat from her lips. Her whole body sizzled and emitted waves of pure, red anger, increasing the temperature. They were directed at her mother, who stood, emotionless and as still as a statue. Wilhelmina Nightingale regarded her daughter simply as you might regard a stranger or a passer-by on the street. Her reply was as cold as ice.

"You will learn one day, Cassandra, that this is the only way to survive in this village. If you are truly my daughter you would not have interfered tonight."

The witches and I remained motionless, watching the exchange between mother and daughter, one as cold as a winter frost and the other preparing to erupt like a fiery volcano that had lain dormant for so long. "WELL, MAYBE I DON'T WANT

TO BE YOUR DAUGHTER ANYMORE!" Cassie yelled. A couple of birds in the nearby treetops departed their nests. Wilhelmina looked taken aback at this outburst; I was sure she had never seen her daughter so defiant.

What happened next seemed to happen in slow motion. I watched as bright orange sparks burst forth from Cassie's fingertips. They were brighter than anyone else's, and a few of the witches looked fearful. Wilhelmina took a step forward. "Cassandra. Be careful. You are only just recognising your true power. I can teach you. We can do this together." Wilhelmina's indifference turned into fear as she pleaded with Cassie to rein in her emotions. But it was too late.

Cassie's emotions got the better of her, and the orange sparks ignited into flames. I could feel the heat of them next to me and tried to shield myself. The witches began to panic. One of them had shut the door back down to the room, and they ran around trying to find a way down.

The fire spread as we were stuck on the rooftop. The dry ivy went up in flames and burnt the black cloaks around me. I picked myself up off the floor, looking for a safe place for Cassie and me to go, but there wasn't one. She was panicking now, trying to stop the sparks, but having no control over her magic.

There were screams and shouts, desperate and short-lived. One witch tumbled from the roof. Maybe she could fly. Or maybe not. I watched in grim horror as another clutched her swollen stomach desperately trying to protect her unborn child. The ancient house was burning, and the wild flames licked the sides of the walls as they made their way hungrily down.

All I could think about was the boy. I looked down from a great height and saw a yellow light bobbing in and out of the trees below me. It was heading away from the house and into the heart of Blackthorn Forest. It was a light of hope.

Run, Michael...

Run like the wind.

PART THREE

GEORGINA

SIXTEEN

Gnarled faces in the twisted knots of the tree boughs stared back at me as I hesitated on the trail. I arrived at a fork in the path. Scanning the shadowy outline through the trees, I squinted and deliberated which way. Each trail looked as sinister as the other in the quickly fading light. The trees have eyes. Who was it that told me that many years before? Quickly now, there was no time for reminiscing in Blackthorn Forest.

I took the left trail but soon regretted my decision. The path shrunk away, and I found myself battling through tangled undergrowth that hadn't been trodden by anyone in many years. It was too late to turn back; I might not make it through the trees. Losing your way in Blackthorn Forest is a tale only to be told around a dimly lit fire on a spooky night about times long ago. It doesn't happen now. It's not supposed to. At least, that's what they say.

Grandmother's thinly knitted jumper was not enough to protect from the biting cold and my feet… my… bare feet? Why were my feet bare? A feeling of immense dread wormed its way into my stomach; I was barefoot and had unwittingly wandered into the forest alone. I wasn't in the middle of a jog as the sun went down. I had no dogs to walk, no photographs to take, no flowers to pick.

Flowers did not grow in Blackthorn Forest. The trees were thick, spiky and as black as a raven. I ploughed through the darkness not knowing where I was going or what I was looking for. I looked up at the darkening sky as the owls commenced their hooting. I clutched at my chest. I started to panic, gasping for air, as my throat tightened and constricted my airway. I bent over, my vision blurry, struggling to regain composure. An object collided violently with my back, and the wind was knocked out of me. Gasping, I twirled around on the spot like a clumsy ballet dancer. The world became motionless. The owls ceased hooting, the wind caught in the boughs died down, and the woods fell deathly silent.

Squinting through the darkness I managed to discern a few details; it was bound in black leather with gold fastenings, and an intricate padlock fell to one side as it hit the forest floor with a thump. I picked it up and examined it further. It was old. So old I was surprised it had remained intact from the fall. The fall. From where? From heaven? The sky?

I held the book in my hands. The weight of its contents pressed down upon my shaking palms. A sudden wind rushed past my exposed ankles, and I shuddered. The light had completely vanished now. The cold, metallic feel of the padlock travelled through me, chilling my blood. I was enveloped in a swirl of blackness and hit the floor of Blackthorn Forest in a faint, the book lying inches from my desperate, outstretched hand...

My keyboard was buried beneath stacks of articles and papers I had scrutinised repeatedly. Swirling my mug of strong instant coffee, I sighed and rubbed my sore eyes. Sleep had evaded me for days. I'd been having bad dreams recently, and last night was no exception. I was in the woods, wandering and alone. Then I had woken to normality in my little bedroom in the tiny village of Blackthorn. The streaming sunlight filtering through my curtains had eliminated my night-time fears. Nonetheless, I still felt a pressing feeling of intrigue, and my bedroom floor was now littered with articles featuring snapshots of missing faces and timelines of disappearances.

Blackthorn Forest had been a source of mystery and fear to the villagers for as long as I could remember. The trees had swallowed up multiple victims, and their bodies had never been found.

I was just twelve years old – a schoolgirl happily skipping to the gate in her summer dress expecting to be enveloped by the smothering arms of her mother. Instead, I was met with the deadpan faces of two police officers and the distraught face of my father at their side. They said she was 'missing'. 'Lost in the woods', but there was an 'ongoing search', and we should hurry home before it got dark. The one thing I cannot forget about that day was the feel of my father's ice-cold hand as he ushered me home to safety in the beating heat of mid-July. Father was never the same after that; he didn't like to talk about his wife's disappearance, he didn't like to think about it, and most of all, he didn't like my ongoing quest for answers.

The research began when I was fourteen. I soon learnt that Blackthorn Forest was something of an elephant in the room for the locals. Schoolchildren, teenagers and adults alike had all been lured in by the trees. The most shocking part was that the woods had been claiming victims dating back a hundred years. All these people had vanished without a trace, just like my mother. No clues, no hints, nothing. It was like they had never existed. In Blackthorn, you could walk down the road and recognise everyone you met. You could go down the pub for a pint and talk to someone who had lived there for eighty years. You could go for Sunday lunch and be in the presence of your neighbour and your neighbour's daughter's daughter. So how people could go missing in this tiny village where everyone knew everyone began to make people question how well they knew their neighbours.

Villagers began to keep themselves to themselves, venture out less, divulge information about their families not so easily. Eventually, Blackthorn put it down to a curse. The forest was simply cursed, bad luck, and it was sealed off to the villagers. But the woods had a secret. Something lurking behind the trees and waiting in the undergrowth. Something worth investigating.

My research became unhealthy. It evolved into an obsession that haunted me night and day. I couldn't walk down the road without thinking I was being followed or scrutinising everyone I passed. Eventually, my father forbade it. He said it was making me ill and that I needed to stop. So, I did. I couldn't bring myself to throw everything away, so I stored the stacks of paper in the back of my wardrobe, the place where all bad memories go to hide.

Noting the dark circles under my eyes in the black screen before me, I sighed and ran my hands through my hair in frustration. The printed words swam before my blurry eyes, and I blinked back up at my laptop screen. My father always said I was the spitting image of her. With our matching black hair that curled loosely to the shoulder, emerald green eyes and face dotted with freckles that spanned the nose and cheeks, there was no doubt that I belonged to the Artruth family.

I looked older and wearier than I had ever before – a face that reflected my inner troubles. Fears from the past had swum back up to the surface after last night's dream. Two years had passed since the research had been hidden in my wardrobe, and unearthing everything today had not given me a feeling of optimism as I had hoped, but had led me further into despair, a wave of hopelessness crashing down upon me. I exhaled slowly, thinking I could not bear to broach the topic again with my father.

The villagers believed that Grandmother's cottage was too close to the woods. Too close for comfort. The comfort they were referring to was clearly their own. With her tarot cards, crystal balls and supernatural beliefs, they had at one point blamed her for the disappearances. They said she had cursed those woods, that there was something not quite right about her, she was bad for the village. Despite their ill feelings, nobody bothered her. I think on some level they're still afraid. They question how she can live on the border of something so unnatural. I know better. I know that she has always felt some strange pull towards Blackthorn Forest. She feels at home close to the trees. I resolved to pay Grandmother a visit in the hope that she could offer some consolation.

SEVENTEEN

Avoiding the questionable stare from my father, I slipped past the kitchen table, buttoned up my red winter coat and headed outside into the cold. Heavy raindrops plummeted from the sky. I braced my body against the lashing rain, my hood pulled tight about my face, and hurried on to Grandmother's cottage.

Bold headlines and printed snippets surfaced in my mind's eye as I passed the village square with urgency. I fumbled with the latch on the cottage gate and glanced at the vegetable patch drowning in the rain. The door swung open before I could knock. Grandmother always seemed to know when I was coming.

I stepped through the tiny door. She hung my coat up on her rickety wooden hooks before reprimanding me gently. "I expected you ten minutes ago, Georgina." She bustled to the kitchen, and I watched fondly as she pottered about the stove brewing up her herbal tea.

"It still amazes me how you expect me at all," I replied, smiling. Grandmother Pebbleton did not embody the typical preconceptions that one might associate with a grandmother. Tall and thin, with hair that was still dyed as dark as it had been before the grey set in, her appearance defied the expectations of the villagers.

They would mutter under their breath that she ought to be thinking about dressing her age, stop dyeing her hair, or give up on the pink lipstick she always carried around with her. Grandmother was too much of a tough cookie to let their distasteful comments upset her. Despite her spritely image she had been burdened with a heart condition, something which my father was very quick to remind her of when he thought she was overdoing things, which was often.

Over the years I had come to associate the curious taste of her tea with comfort and understanding. "Come," she said wisely, watching me deliberating in the doorway. "Let's sit by the fire. You'll catch cold and something's bothering you." I received her teacup in my hand with thanks and began the precarious crossing from the kitchen to the blazing fire in the living room. Stepping over a pile of books teetering on the edge of a coffee table, dodging around a stack of cards piled high, I succeeded in my mission all without spilling one drop of tea. I sank into my favourite armchair by the fire and Grandmother occupied the one opposite with a sigh of relief. She fixed me with her familiar stare.

I looked away and watched the flames leap and flicker in the grate. Grandmother's stare was difficult to withstand on a normal day, let alone after my dream last night. I felt like she was staring into my soul, probing deep beneath the surface, and there was nothing I could do about it. I cleared my throat and met her eyes after a few minutes. "I had a dream last night." She remained silent and sipped her tea through pastel pink lips. "It was about the woods." She narrowed her eyes and shifted in her armchair. "I was lost, looking for something… or maybe someone." I paused as the fire crackled. "It felt like… the trees were watching me. Like they knew something I didn't. Then I fainted and woke up in my own bed. It all seemed so real."

There was a chink of china as Grandmother set her teacup down. "Georgina, I thought the nightmares had stopped. After you stopped your research."

I looked up guiltily. "They did. I just can't shake the feeling that I'm missing something."

Grandmother sighed. "You know I have always understood the need to search, to question. Ever since you were a little girl you used to be obsessed with your father's riddles. But maybe it's best for now to just… let it alone?" My heartbeat quickened. How could she be saying this?

"Let it alone?" I repeated, unable to obey her instruction. "But, Grandmother, what do we really know about the forest? All the disappearances and the stories… You've grown up in a village plagued with strange goings-on, how can the forest not interest you anymore?"

"Oh, it interests me, Georgina. Always has, always will. I know what everyone thinks about me. Just because someone is different doesn't mean they're cursed, for heaven's sake! I just don't want you to get sick again. You know that." She sighed gently. "I think it's perhaps time you stopped thinking about it… it's not good for our family." She heaved herself out of the armchair. "I'll get the bread out of the oven."

I sat there, sopping wet, clutching my teacup to my chest and staring into the fire. Grandmother's words came as a shock to me. She knew better than anyone that I needed answers. I shook my head and stood up, following her into the kitchen. I knocked over a few cards, and they drifted to the floor in my wake. "Don't you care about what happened to Mum?" I regretted the words the moment they left my lips.

Grandmother stood with her back to me. Her shoulders drooped, and she rotated her head to look at me. "Georgina… never accuse me of giving up hope, because I never will! This family has been through enough, and I think it's about time we left the woods well alone. It's dangerous, it's unhealthy and I don't want anyone else getting hurt." I turned away.

The rain beat on the windows of the cottage, and the wind howled in the chimney. The whistle of the kettle on the stove aggravated me, and I knew there was nothing I could say to her that would change her mind. She set about kneading some more dough, and I resumed my position next to the fire to try and dry off.

I didn't understand where all of this was coming from. Why couldn't I shake my obsession with uncovering secrets? Why was I so drawn to the woods when I knew its danger? I rested my head back in the armchair and felt a pulsing headache creeping up on me. The clutter of the cottage darkened my mood; it was littered with objects, leaving little room to move about properly, let alone to think with a clear head. My eyes scanned over the piles of books jumbled up on the floor, and I wondered what strange spiritual secrets they hid.

That was when I saw it: black leather, gold fastenings, shiny padlock. I sat up in my armchair with a creak. I'd remembered the whole dream apart from the book that had fallen from the trees above. My blood ran cold. How could it be possible that the book from my dreams just happened to be stacked haphazardly in Grandmother's cottage? There was no mistaking it. I had to look inside.

As I stood up a wave of nausea overcame me. I clutched the edge of the armchair for support as the dizziness blurred my vision. I don't know what made me do it. Maybe it was the sickness, maybe it was the anger, or maybe it was the disbelief of what I was witnessing. I lunged for the book and knocked over the pile with a crash. "Georgina?" Grandmother called.

I blinked, crashing into a nearby lamp as I stumbled across the room. I could smell her freshly baked bread. I didn't want to talk to her. Didn't want to hear about my obsession or how I should stop asking questions. I threw on my coat and stuffed the book underneath to shield it from the rain. I tore open the door of the cottage and tumbled out onto the slippery path. Grandmother called out faintly, but I had already disappeared into the downpour.

EIGHTEEN

I sat anxiously on my bed biting my fingernails, watching the hands of the clock tick by, signalling the passage of time as evening arrived and departed. I still hadn't retrieved the book from beneath my pillow.

Repressing my incessant need to look, I left it there hidden away and pictured the scene of the crime. I had become a thief and could not return the book without Grandmother knowing. The state I had left her cottage in – lamps had been overturned and papers kicked over the floor – meant that she would soon realise something was missing. I sighed and relived dinner with my father a few hours before. We were no stranger to the long silences and grunted conversations over the clinks of our cutlery; once the police had finished with their investigations, silence became a welcome gift in our household, and it had since remained an occupant around the dinner table.

Benjamin Artruth's wavy hair, once a deep chestnut and the object of many ladies' attention in Blackthorn, was now streaked with silver and flopped over his forehead as he ran his hands through it. "I expect your grandmother will bake something special for her stall," he grunted in reply to my enquiring about the village fete the next day. I looked down at my dinner plate and prayed he would not ask if I had seen her recently.

He didn't exactly see eye to eye with his mother-in-law; an incident involving a crystal ball and a drunken night spent in Arthur's Tavern had got him into great trouble with my mother once. He didn't ask about Grandmother. In fact, he didn't say anything after that. The countless questions and accusations from the police had resulted in my father running out of words. Spending a year being the police's primary suspect in the investigation of his wife's disappearance had never quite left him. He carried it around with him, a heavy weight upon his shoulders, sagging down a father who once carved intricate puzzles and formulated challenging riddles for his daughter; a father who used to play happily with his little girl. A little girl who once thought him to be invincible. I excused myself from the table.

I switched on my desk lamp. The sky had turned black by the time I held the book in my hands. I had no doubt it was the same one from my dream. This time, the tiny key had been left in the padlock, and I turned it slowly until the lock clicked open. My heart hammered in anticipation as I prised open the pages. Taking care not to damage the contents, I grabbed the lamp next to me and shone it over the scrawls, narrowing my eyes.

The pages were handwritten... I recognised that loopy handwriting. It was a diary. I had stolen my own grandmother's diary. I swallowed. A pang of guilt prompted my moral dilemma. Was it acceptable for me to comb through her innermost thoughts? Would I ever be able to look at her the same again? Reading a person's diary could uncover well-guarded secrets of the soul. There was no going back from that. I hung my head in my hands and groaned. I was nothing but my father's daughter; it was impossible for me to leave this riddle unsolved.

A lot of the diary was filled with Grandmother's recipes, book reviews for her reading group, and her predictions for the weather next week according to the position of the planets. I turned the old pages, scanning her entries, growing impatient at the lack of answers it offered. I was about to close the book and accept that I would simply have to return it when I came across an entry dated from one month ago.

I couldn't help myself. It's been plaguing my dreams for months. I set off slow and steady and stuck to the paths I knew from years ago. They were watching me, the trees; they have eyes.

If Benjamin could see me now, he'd have a fit. His silly mother-in-law venturing into Blackthorn Forest alone. Doing exactly what the police forbade. After today I'm surprised I have enough strength to recount these events, but I must do it; I can't risk forgetting.

I came to a fork in the path and chose the left trail, my breathing even, and my steps firm. I wanted to reach the heart of the woods. My instincts were telling me that if I reached the very centre, I might find some answers. But the closer I got, the worse I felt. My vision blurred... my head span... I was completely disorientated. I could barely distinguish the thick trees from the path.

I turned back. If I were younger, fitter, I might have been able to carry on for longer. I retraced my steps and the dizziness wore off. I cursed myself. There is something about those woods. Something at the very centre. Something dark, something dangerous.

Don't go into the woods alone.

I snapped the diary shut. She was right; if my father knew about this he'd probably have a fit. I shook my head in disbelief. This was why she warned me off any more investigating. She knew it was dangerous. I grew concerned for her safety – what if she tried to reach the heart of the trees again? What if something happened to her next time? I deliberated going downstairs and revealing the diary entry to my father, but no, that would only make things worse between them. I didn't need him worrying about that right now. I clutched the book to my chest. I would have to keep this one to myself.

I kept returning to my dream from the night before. Closing my eyes, I visualised as much as I could remember, trying to understand what it meant. I must have seen Grandmother's diary tucked away in her cottage before and somehow incorporated it into my night-time adventures; the brain conjures strange tricks sometimes. It was too much to believe that the book from my dreams had magically appeared beside her fire, taunting me to open it, a manifestation of my dream.

But, I thought as I pulled my pyjamas over my head and clambered into bed, was it just a remarkable coincidence that in the dream I had played out my grandmother's words? I too had been searching for something in the forest, growing dizzy and sick, unable to continue my journey.

As I lapsed into a deep slumber, Grandmother and I became one as we wandered helplessly through the foggy trees, fighting our way through a visible haze of uncertainty that glimmered in the darkness.

NINETEEN

On one day of the year the inhabitants of Blackthorn emerged from their shells and ran amok along the cobbles. Tables groaned under the weight of baked produce, arts and crafts and bottles of ale lined up for sampling. Brightly coloured stalls and large marquees had all appeared overnight and struggled to cope with the multitude of bodies that fought to peek at their wares. The smooth grass on the village square had been trimmed, and its deep hue of green sparkled like emeralds in the rare sunshine.

As we jostled our way through the crowded stalls, I caught snippets of hushed conversation from a huddle of women sampling blackcurrant wine. They made little effort to conceal their suspicious glances. "Artruths... Benjamin... couldn't show my face... that poor girl..." Their thirst for gossip had only strengthened over the years, and I steered my father away, throwing angry glances over my shoulder. "Come on, let's get some tickets for the tombola," I suggested cheerfully.

Our coins were exchanged for flimsy paper tickets by the elderly man sitting at the raffle table. I thanked him and proceeded to zip them up carefully in my purse; I knew what my father's organisation was like these days. Grandmother's stall teetered precariously on the edge of the village green as though trying to make a getaway from the hustle and bustle. Father made a beeline for her. I hesitated, having a flashback to her diary waiting expectantly on my desk, and approached the table apprehensively.

"Benjamin." She nodded curtly, rearranging her shining amulets. "Georgina! How are you both?" She cracked into a smile, cocking her head on one side, trying to discern if I had told my father about our exchange yesterday.

"Oh, not bad thanks, Ivy…" He eyed the villagers with distaste. "You know what it's like."

"Indeed." She nodded wisely, watching a family pass by. One half of her table was laden with homemade cakes and pastries, a couple of gaps showing where villagers had spotted something they fancied. The other half displayed coloured amulets that reflected the rays of sunlight with such a twinkle that a mini light show seemed to be occurring on her stall. Grandmother professed that they contained magical powers.

The three of us conversed in the midday heat, and watched as most villagers swerved to avoid her, leading their children away in fear of catching something from the strange lady. There was no mention of the diary.

One of the women I spotted prattling earlier about our family now had a child in tow, and her mouse-like features stopped by Grandmother's stall briefly before registering who sat behind the table. She paused as a look of horror overcame her face. "Come on, Tommy," she barked as she dragged the child away quickly. "What a load of rubbish. We don't want her counterfeit goods." Grandmother narrowed her eyes and fiddled irritably with the lockets. My father sighed and watched as she managed to distract her child into a marquee offering to face paint the boy's confused features.

"Well, you can't be surprised, can you?"

"What's that supposed to mean?" Grandmother fired back, her pink lips moving at high speed. My father cleared his throat, fumbled with one of the necklaces, and picked it up from the table with his eyebrows raised.

"I just mean, you don't exactly help yourself, that's all. Setting up your stall right on the edge… selling these… whatever they are, it just makes us look bloody weird…"

Grandmother Pebbleton did not often succumb to anger, but my father's latest comments sparked a fuse inside her, and she rose swiftly from her stall. "I will not bow down to the tittle-tattle of bored villagers that have nothing else to do with their lives, thank you very much."

Father looked at her indignantly. "Look, Ivy, I'm not trying to cause an argument here, but don't you think we have enough rumours about us circling around without you trying to sell supernatural objects to everyone?" I took a step back from the igniting fuse.

Grandmother exploded with anger. "I will not be dictated to! If I want to sell my amulets, I will do just that. I can't help that the villagers don't like our family, it's not my fault that you were under investigation; like it or not there will be rumours and gossip with or without my amulets, Benjamin!"

Father struggled to swallow the truth and turned on his heel, grabbing my hand. "At least I don't live on the edge of the woods as well!" he shouted over his shoulder attracting a couple of shocked stares. "Come on, Georgie, we're better off at home than at this shit show."

I looked at Grandmother apologetically, who was bending down to pick up one of her amulets, scowling at the back of Father's wavy hair. I was ushered home not half an hour after arriving in the village square. It was not very often that I heard my father swear, and knew that something had really riled him up. I sighed as he barged through the front door and dumped our paper bag of sweets on the kitchen table. The bag overturned and the contents rolled out over the side, scattering the table with fluorescent wrappers.

He sat down silently and ran his hands through his hair, staring at the sturdy oak surface, a look of regret on his face. I hovered in the doorway awkwardly. "It's not going to help, you know." He looked up at me blankly. "Arguing with her – it's not going to change anything."

He took a few deep breaths. "I know. I'm sorry, Georgie…" He shook his head and smiled at me weakly. "What would your mother think, eh?"

I felt a great pang of longing, and in that moment, I would have given anything for her to be sitting at that table with him. For them to be laughing and joking as they used to, hand in hand; for her to pick up the fragile shards and piece by piece carefully fix a broken man. Blinking a few times, I reached for the kettle and flipped the switch, busying myself retrieving items from the cupboard. Father smiled gratefully when I set down the steaming mug in front of him. We sat for a while and chatted as I tried to take his mind off that morning.

Who was I kidding? I thought as I climbed the stairs an hour later. We could never be a normal family. Not now. I sat down on the edge of my bed and stared at the diary on my desk. My mother's disappearance was the real reason why they were at odds with each other. They both missed her so much that their grief manifested itself in spite and anger, when all they really wanted was to go back four years, before our lives were changed forever. I allowed myself a rare moment of weakness and felt the tears roll down my cheeks. A barely legible line of handwriting surfaced in my mind's eye:

"If I were younger, fitter, I might have been able to carry on for longer."

A fragmented idea began to form in my mind. An idea so forbidden it scared me.

TWENTY

I knew it was wrong. Teenagers didn't wander off into the woods in the dead of night to return home safe and happy. My father would never forgive me. His blurred face when we received the news from the ashen-faced police officers haunted me still, but I shook my head and closed my eyes, locking it away. I waited until dark, avoiding him for fear I would change my mind, and packed a backpack with Grandmother's diary, a torch, some food and water. Unlatching my bedroom window as I had done many times before, I dropped onto the roofing below, and shimmied my way down until I reached the pavement. I slunk away.

Blackthorn was sleeping. Children were safely tucked up beneath the covers with their heads full of happy fairy tales. What few lights were still on flickered off as I passed house after house, as though I were sucking all the energy out of the village. I shifted the weight of the backpack on me. The diary was weighing me down, Grandmother's warning dragging me back from my foolish plan. The silence was unnerving. I did not pass another human soul, and I soon neared the border of the village and the entrance of Blackthorn Forest.

It was different to what I remembered. The iron gate they had erected all those years ago had grown rusty and crooked with age. It was easy to find an opening. I swallowed as I looked up at the dark trees looming above and contemplated turning around. I thought of everyone fallen victim to the woods and how their families deserved an explanation for all the lost time.

I scrambled through a small gap in the twisted iron barriers with some difficulty and emerged on the other side. I felt as though I had stepped foot into my dream. I drifted along the forest path, the slight wind sweeping my hair back behind me, the book feeling even heavier than before. The branches emerged from the darkness, catching me unawares a couple of times, my heart thumping against my chest. They seemed to contort and twist of their own accord, casting strange shapes in the moonlight. I fumbled hurriedly for my torch. The beam of light made little difference considering I didn't know where I was going. After twenty minutes or so of wandering blindly amongst the trees I arrived at a fork in the path and hesitated. I was sure I should take the left trail; unconsciously I had been here before.

The path narrowed, and I fought through thorny undergrowth and prickly branches that scratched me harshly and stung my eyes. My breath caught in my chest, and I tried to grab at a nearby branch for support. At my touch, the trees seemed to melt into the ground, and my legs failed me.

Blackthorn Forest circled me like a merry-go-round, and I heard the thump of my backpack hitting the ground before I felt it. The floor felt spongy like I was being sucked into it… I was enveloped by the deep earthy smell of mulch blanketing the ground. My hearing grew muffled, and my breathing ceased. I was dragged down by the roots.

TWENTY-ONE

A bell tolled in the distance. I counted the hour groggily as my eyes fluttered open. Midnight. But midnight where? I felt as though I had been sucked down a plughole and emerged on the other side of the world. The feeling came back to my limbs, one by one, and I inhaled a sharp gulp of putrid-smelling air. The hard floor was damp, and I shifted my position to an upright one as my head span.

I sat for a few moments until my vision cleared, and I was able to raise my eyes up off the floor. I blinked several times and adjusted to the gloom. The forest had vanished. I heard the continuous drip and splash of some foul liquid that I hoped was causing the awful smell. But no, I thought, struggling to heave myself up off the floor, that smell belonged to something rotten, something decomposed. It smelt like bodies. Like human corpses. I retched.

My hand grasped on to a cold, sturdy bar, and then another, and another… I was trapped. A deep pit of dread formed in the bottom of my stomach as I managed to stand. My head almost touched the top of a suffocating low-walled cell. I was a prisoner inside a dank, festering dungeon.

My knees buckled as I sank back down to the floor. How could this be happening to me? I took deep breaths, in and out, trying to fathom how I had ended up inside the horrific cell. The last thing I remembered was the feel of the forest floor and how it had shrouded me with its mossy arms, dragging me under, and then blackness. Had I somehow ended up underneath the earth? Had this cell been constructed and hidden underground? I shook my head and wrapped my arms around myself, shivering. I looked up at the tiny crack in the wall above me, but all it showed was pitch black outside. I couldn't tell if the forest still existed. But I had heard a bell tolling; there was no bell tower in Blackthorn Forest as far as I knew. The pit of dread inside me grew larger. I had an uncanny feeling that I was very far from home.

Something slimy scuttled across my feet and I jumped. I followed the pitter-patter of its long claws across the floor and watched as the rat slipped through the bars and scampered out of sight into a dark patch on the floor. It was only when I raised my eyes and saw the dark shape looming out of the dungeon corner that I realised I wasn't alone. A pair of red, glowing eyes belonged to the tall figure who had been watching me the whole time. I scrambled to my feet and backed against the wall behind me. The hovering red eyes did not move, or blink, and all I could hear was the hammering of my own heart against my chest. The silhouette remained motionless and gave not one sign of life apart from those awful eyes that never removed themselves from mine. A strange notion gripped me; this sinister dungeon guard was somehow inhuman.

A hasty clink of coins disturbed the silence, and I heard distinct shuffling from outside of the dungeon. A woman's voice murmured and echoed in the deep recesses of the walls. "Please, I have the extra you asked for." A deep grunt and an unintelligible muttering met her imploring words. "What do you mean you can't keep doing this?" The woman raised her voice slightly, and a pang of vague recognition struck me. The red eyes had turned their back on me now and were instead focused upon the woman who was still out of eyeshot. "We had a deal: I keep my end of the bargain and you keep yours." She paused, considering her next words. Her voice faltered slightly

but she continued, "You can't go back on that now. If you do...
I'll be forced to tell her."

The drip of liquid splashing onto the floor resumed as a minute's silence followed. "She'd punish you if she knew," the woman whispered. The red eyes blinked, and whatever they belonged to grunted once more, longer and higher pitched than the last. A second, much smaller figure hurried past the imposing guard, clearly taking this as permission to proceed. I wasn't sure the guard could speak.

My cell was the third one along on the left, and I watched as the woman's shadow peered into every one. I wondered who she was so desperately searching for. She eventually approached the bars in front of me, and I hastily retreated in fear. Her face loomed eerily out of the shadows as her eyes widened in the gloom. Her long black dress draped heavily about her frame, and she wore a frilly white apron on top that had grown grimy. Her emerald green eyes looked like lanterns in the dark as they met mine. A white cap encased her hair, and strands of jet black had escaped and fell around her face, framing her freckled features. "Georgie?" she uttered. My legs gave way beneath me as I abandoned all reason and collapsed at the feet of my mother. Her hands fluttered back and forth in between the bars trying to get hold of my own. I wept. I had not seen her features for four years. "I can't believe it's you," she kept saying, over and over again, running her hands across my face, wiping away the tears.

"Mum?" I croaked in disbelief. "What's happening? Where are we?"

A grave expression overcame Lily Artruth's face and she sniffed, as though pulling herself together, and took my face in her hands. "We don't have long, Georgina." She looked behind her at the dark shape still standing in the entranceway. Her voice dropped to a whisper, and I forced myself to control my sobbing to hear her words. "We can't talk properly here. Meet me tomorrow underneath the willow tree in the gardens at midnight. Do you understand, Georgina? Under the willow tree at midnight, not before." I shook my head, struggling to comprehend.

She reached for something in the long folds of her apron pocket and crumpled a piece of paper into my hand. "You must always keep this with you, Georgina, are you listening? You must not lose that piece of paper." The red eyes approached slowly. I grabbed at the long fabric as she stood up and looked over her shoulder. "At midnight," she hissed with urgency, "under the willow tree." She pointed to my hand. "Don't let anyone else see that." Turning to the dark figure she retreated from the bars hastily. "Yes, I know, I'll be on my way now."

I watched as her dress trailed across the wet floor and she turned around on the spot. The smile I had only dreamt about for the past four years spread across her features. "God, I've missed you."

She exited the dungeon.

TWENTY-TWO

The dull toll of the bell rang out at three o'clock in the morning as I sat huddled in the darkness. My mother's face swam before me, and I rubbed at my temples with a grimace. Still keeping one eye on the guard, I peered out of the thin rectangular gap in the wall, waiting for the sun to come up. I had half convinced myself that this was all a dream. That I had, perhaps, hit my head a little too hard in the forest, and would wake up in my own bed with my father bending over me in concern. He was going to wake up soon and realise that I was gone.

I was overwhelmed with guilt; which was the lesser of two evils? Here, with my mother, in an unknown place trapped in a cell… or at home, with my father, where we could safely mourn the memory of her? I looked down at the piece of paper I clutched between my finger and thumb. It had been dripped on, and the ink had faded in places, but it was still legible:

Midnight. Underneath the willow tree.

Make sure you aren't followed.

Before I could begin to fathom what these words meant, I heard footsteps again and stuffed the note inside the deep pockets of my coat. She had also told me not to let anyone else see it. I struggled to my feet, the heavy cloak of night still weighing me down, and put both hands on the bars. I squinted through the shadows and saw the outline of another human reflected in the immobile red eyes. "Now," a young woman's voice called out brusquely. She sniffed distastefully. "She wants to see the newcomer now." The guard grunted in the affirmative, and I realised with horror that it was approaching my cell. Two red circles progressed quickly towards me, and I recoiled behind the safety of my bars. I heard the unmistakable jingle of a set of keys. As the bars swung open with a great groan, my breath caught in my throat. I had been right to assume that this thing was not human.

It was seven foot tall and encased in black armour from head to toe. Great clunky boots hit the wet floor with a violent splash with every step it took. I was sure that the lower part of the breastplate, which was directly level with my eyesight, would not dent even if a thirty-tonne lorry smashed into it. Even its hands had been hidden in black gloves, which, to me, did not look like they had the right number of fingers.

I looked up at the towering figure in fear. Black feathers protruded from the helmet giving it the impression of a monstrous bird. All that could be seen through the oblong gap in the plate was those red eyes that burnt into my own. As it stooped awkwardly to avoid the low ceiling I caught sight of a strange emblem blazoned across its chest; what looked like a golden letter 'D' with delicate embellishment inside it flashed in the darkness. At its side hung a foreboding-looking double-edged sword, and I thought for one second I might end up being impaled on the other end of it.

The woman bustled into the cell. She wore the same sort of attire that I had seen my mother in: a long dark dress with an apron over the top. "Come on then," she barked. "Out you come." Her thin upper lip curled as she arranged her pointy features into an unpleasant grin. "Unless you want to be thrown out, you'd best find the use of your feet." She grabbed my wrist, and I felt a long set of nails dig into my skin. "You don't want to keep her waiting." I was marched out of my dingy corner and stumbled across the dungeon floor. "Pathetic," the woman hissed at me with disdain. She possessed a haughty demeanour of self-importance that clearly came as a benefit of the job.

I straightened up and threw her a filthy look. I would not be made to feel like dirt underneath her polished boots. I followed the guard out of the dungeon with my head up high. Being summoned by whomever she was had to be better than being trapped behind bars at any rate. That is, only if she didn't mind being disturbed in the early hours of the morning. I contemplated what the effort would be to fight them both off and escape. The guard's sword swung lazily in its hilt in front of me. It would not be worth it.

I followed the colossal bird out into a corridor and adjusted my eyes to look at the blazing torches that lit the way. The ceiling seemed to have been adapted to enable the guard to walk freely, and as we advanced along the corridor I realised there was more than one of him. Multiple pairs of glowing red eyes spied on us as we walked. They lined the corridor, and I tried not to make eye contact with any of them; I had no doubt one of them could crush me with its little… finger?… if it wanted to.

Avoiding putting my hand into my pocket to check if my mother's scribbled note was still there, I looked straight ahead of me, and suddenly felt as though we were travelling upwards. We were certainly on an incline now, and my guess was that I was being taken up into wherever the main occupants of this building lived. Eventually we came upon a great wooden door. With a simple flick of the hand the guard prised it open. A rustle directly behind me indicated that the horrible woman was still in my wake. I shuddered. I didn't fancy extracting her fingernails from my skin again. I was shoved through the door and blinked repeatedly in the unexpected bright light.

A high ceiling stretched way above us, and as I gazed above I felt as though I could finally breathe fresh air again. Despite the lateness of the hour, multiple torches had been lit in their brackets, and their orange light illuminated the features of the grand room. The ceiling had been magnificently carved; strange wooden shapes twisted their way around each other in a ceaseless pattern. We had emerged into a vast entrance hall, and looking hurriedly to my right, I spied a gigantic door locked and bolted, complete with two guards on either side. That was my way to the outside, but how could I possibly get through it now with that evil woman at my side and those inhuman shapes that stood guard?

I turned my attention to the left, trying to ascertain as much information as possible about my new surroundings, hoping this would help me later. A great rectangular table laden with chunky goblets and wooden serving plates and spoons stood proudly at one end of the hall. It was positioned in front of an enormous fireplace which, although unlit now, was certainly capable of warming an entire room full of people. Empty suits of armour frequented each corner of the hall, some standing seven foot tall, others suited to a more normal size of warrior.

"Stop dawdling," the woman hissed in my ear, and I recoiled at the closeness of her ugly features. She steered me in the direction of a darkened corridor to our left, and we exited the comforting orange glow of the hall. The corridor led to a twisting staircase, which the guard in front of me began to mount with some difficulty; the high ceilings had obviously been adapted, but these tiny steps provided something of a challenge. I was sandwiched in between his hulking figure and the rasping breaths of the pointy-faced woman behind me. I was clearly being taken to see her.

I stumbled up the steps, trying not to crash into the guard, and we eventually reached another corridor. This one was wider and more accessible than the last. As we hurried along it, I didn't have much time to glance at the doors on either side of me; I got the impression they were trying to deposit me at our destination as quickly as possible. We neared the final door on the right-hand side. The guard raised his fist and knocked purposefully thrice on the door. "Enter," a cold voice said almost immediately. We stepped inside.

TWENTY-THREE

The room was warm, yet not as inviting as the entrance hall we had left behind, and I shuddered despite the increase in temperature. Candles flickered eerily in their holders, and wax melted into grotesque shapes that cast shadows on the wall opposite. The room contained a large four-poster bed, a couple of hard-looking wooden chairs, and a dressing table in the centre directly opposite me.

A stool had been placed in front of the mirror, and two girls stood on either side of it, hairbrushes in hand, gently combing the hair of the third girl who perched atop it. They both wore blank expressions and took no notice that we had entered the room. We stood there for a few minutes and watched as they rhythmically moved their hands up and down the bright blonde hair that fell to the waist of the third girl. They were so gentle they could have been holding a baby, and they only paused their synchronised brushing when a throat cleared and said, "Enough." They set down the delicate hairbrushes and retreated into the shadows.

She sat poised and let her poker-straight hair cascade down her perfectly postured back. Her face was slightly upturned, as though she were trying to balance a small object on the end of her nose. She stood up slowly and walked around to the opposite side of the stool so she could face us. I gulped. As she sat back down again, her blood red gown puffed up against her body, and she rearranged her skirts, narrowing her eyes. "Leave us, Raven." The cold voice struck again. I only realised she had been addressing the guard when he turned his back upon the room and left, closing the door behind him with an ominous creak. I didn't have a clue if Raven was his name, his rank, or something else entirely, but this description made sense somehow as I imagined the feathers atop his helmet touching the top of the corridor as he dutifully made his way back to the dungeons.

"How lovely you look tonight, miss, that colour quite becomes you." The ugly woman tripped over her words in her haste to pay the girl a compliment, but she simply held up her hand to silence her. The girl maintained the outward demeanour of a cold and barren glacier. The impenetrable fortress with which she surrounded herself manifested itself in her cold expression and empty blue eyes. As they met mine, a shiver ran down my spine. She could have once been considered beautiful, but something about the slight point of her nose or the jagged edge of her jaw ruined that beauty.

An expression my mother once told me came suddenly to mind: if a person thinks ugly thoughts, then everything about them will appear ugly too. She tossed her hair impatiently behind her shoulders with a small sigh and pursed her pink lips. I understood why everybody seemed to fear her; I felt as though she were about to deliver a life sentence. "Now what am I going to do with you?" Her voice was steady and deliberate. I should have taken this for a rhetorical question, as my answer seemed only to amuse her.

"You could tell me where I am, or who you are?" My heart pounded in my chest as I replied bravely. She laughed, a cold, high-pitched sound that was reminiscent of out-of-tune violins scraping inharmoniously.

"It's always the same questions." Her mouth curled into an unpleasant sneer as she shot the other woman a look, who returned it appreciatively. "Who are you? What do you want?"

"Where am I?" the other woman interjected with a snarl as she joined in teasing me. The girl laughed icily again and the woman, who I now understood to be her maid, looked pleased with herself.

I shifted restlessly from one foot to the other, growing exasperated at the lack of answers I was being given. I waited impatiently as they stopped their hideous laughing and turned their attention back to me. "You're a pretty one, aren't you?" the girl said matter-of-factly as she rose from her dressing table stool. She was taller than me, and I estimated a couple of years older too. Her hair looked like spun gold in the candlelight.

"I don't like the pretty ones," she said suddenly, looking down at me. "They cause trouble." She hummed sinisterly as she swept her long skirts about the room. "Shall she remain a maid?" the hook-nosed woman said as she fumbled with her apron. "That way we can keep an eye on her—"

"I have too many maids already," the girl snapped. "They become extremely annoying after a while." She turned to face the pitch-black window as a great gust of wind swept past and extinguished a candle on the ledge as it crept in the room through a tiny crack.

She cocked her head on one side and revolved slowly on the spot, exposing her pointy teeth in a blood-chilling grin. "Yes... I've got it. That's perfect." She walked once more around the bed and stood directly in front of me. She raised one hand up to my face and pinched my right cheek sharply. I tried to struggle out of her grip, but my hands were restrained behind my back by her faithful maid. I looked defiantly into her eyes. "It's the stables for you, girl." My heart sank. Whatever that meant I could tell it wasn't good.

She let go of my cheek, and I felt it sting as she delivered my sentence. The maid clapped her hands gleefully and said, "But where shall she sleep?"

"With the pigs, of course," the girl replied. Her smile vanished immediately as I stared at her desperately. "Take her away. Her face is making me feel sick."

The maid curtseyed politely as she grabbed my arm. "As you wish, Miss Letha, as you wish…" I was steered forcefully out of the room.

The door closed behind us with a snap, and two of the ravens reappeared instantaneously, their elephantine figures having clearly been standing guard outside Letha's chamber. I was certainly glad to see the back of her and prayed that we would never meet again. I was given no choice in the matter but to be led back along the corridor and down the little staircase into the shadows. All sense of time abandoned me. We did not turn right back towards the entrance hall, but instead I was frogmarched outdoors into the elements. The warm night air surprised me; the dungeon was cold and slimy, and I had expected it to be a bitter night. But a bitter night where? I asked myself as I swivelled my head around, trying to get a better look past the shadows of my unwanted companions.

Uneven cobbles rose up underneath my shoes, and I stumbled. The set of sharp fingernails clawed at my wrists again. The ugly woman snarled at me once more, and I was instructed to keep walking or else lose an unspecified limb. I gulped and stared straight ahead of me, wishing to remain intact tonight. The three of us walked in a large courtyard at the back of the main building. In other circumstances, I would have thought it beautiful.

I would have longed to sit deep in thought at one of the benches either side of us, existing in peaceful harmony next to the orange and lemon trees that lined the walkway. I would have turned my face up towards the sky and sniffed the sweet perfume of the fruits. I would have been enticed to take a walk in the orchard that lay beyond, that I could just about discern with the help of the lit torches in the distance. But not tonight. Tonight I was a prisoner inside this magnificent setting, or rather outside, I corrected myself as we swerved around another building smaller than the main one.

I looked back quickly while the evil woman was busy instructing the two ravens what to do with me next, and gasped. The sheer magnitude of the building we had exited hit me, and I gazed up at its impressive stone walls. It looked like a gigantic house with buildings and outhouses attached, but it was more than simply a house. It was grand, expansive and clearly housed many occupants and hosted numerous guests going from the regal entrance hall it boasted. The house clearly belonged to somebody wealthy, somebody pompous like Letha, or perhaps a parent figure. She struck me as the daughter of an affluent family, and I would have bet all the oranges and lemons in that courtyard that was who owned the house.

"I trust you can take it from here?" I snapped back to my current circumstances. "I trust you ignorant fools can manage to escort her two minutes from here?" the woman repeated impatiently, and the ravens grunted in response. "Lovely." She bared her teeth at me in what I supposed was a sinister grin. "I'm going back to the manor. Sleep well." She released me from her grip, swept herself away and disappeared behind the trees. I looked up expectantly at the two guards, and they turned their backs on me and continued walking away from the house.

I stood frozen. How could they be so sure I wouldn't run away? I looked around me bitterly and answered my own question. There was nowhere to run. The courtyard and gardens were walled, hiding the world outside of this manor house and the answers I sought. "Come." A low, deep voice sounded from out of the darkness and I jumped. They could talk. I shivered in the warm air. My punishment for running away and getting caught five minutes later would be far worse than spending a night in the stables. I swallowed my pride and obeyed the gargantuan birds.

The stables turned out to be smelly, full of pigs, and my bed for the remaining few hours of the night. Ignoring my protestations that I would much rather be kept in with the horses next door, the ravens left me to make a bed of straw in a corner not tainted by droppings, and settled themselves outside to stand guard for the night. I sighed as I scooped up bundles of the dry bedding and ignored the inquisitive stares from the pigs, who were disturbed from their slumber. At first, they thought I was coming to feed them and made a great racket of noise, bounding up to me and almost knocking me over. Upon realising they were a few hours too early for feeding time, they grunted at me and left me alone in my corner to dwell upon the night's events.

I sighed and sat atop my makeshift bed of straw, knees drawn up to my chest, arms wrapped around myself. My brain was buzzing. I had sunk down beneath the earth and landed in nothing less than a medieval dungeon. I had been taken to a foul girl who it seemed had the right to choose who I was in her gigantic dollhouse – not a maid, as she had too many of those, but a lowly stable girl. Grotesque birds prowled around in the shape of giant humans that appeared to do the bidding of those in charge. I had seen my mother again for the first time in four years, yet was none the wiser as to what on earth was going on. Would I have any choice in my fate here, wherever here was?

I fumbled with the crumpled note in my pocket. It was the only piece of her that proved she hadn't been a figment of my imagination. It seemed I would have to wait until midnight the next day to get any answers. Had my mother been here for the past four years? I looked up at the stars above and felt tiny underneath their expanse, wondering exactly how far from home I was, and if I would ever be able to find my way back. I blinked at the sparkly black canvas that stretched above me and yawned. As I thought of my father waking up soon and discovering I was missing, I felt as though I were looking up at a different sky, in an entirely different world to my own.

My musings were suddenly disturbed by a faint noise in the distance. I strained my ears above the grunting of the pigs and looked out into the darkness. I couldn't see anything, but the noise became louder. Not noise, I thought, as it grew in clarity, but music. Sweet music plucked from a string instrument. It was delicate, like a lullaby, and I found my eyelids drooping.

The music filled the courtyard and bounced off the stone walls that encased the manor house. It drifted into the pigsty, and I hummed along pleasantly. It reminded me of long summer days and warm sunshine underneath a bright sky. I lay back sleepily in my bed of straw and smiled. This wasn't so bad after all. Being played a lullaby beneath the stars... the straw was surprisingly warm... the sound of the instrument so melodious...

The shining emblem across the guard's chest struck a chord in my mind, and right before I was put to sleep, the lucid image of what I had thought to be a letter 'D' transformed into a golden harp.

TWENTY-FOUR

I woke a few hours later following a sharp prod in my arm. I sat up quickly and groaned. My back was stiff from lying on the ground, and my muscles sore and aching. I raised my arms above my head to try and stretch out and screamed when I realised there was a person standing above me. "Don't be so dramatic," he snapped, turning his back and beginning to shift the piles of straw I had moved in the night back to their proper positions. "You're late for duty."

I rubbed my temples, my head groggy. "What did you say?"

"You're late for duty," he repeated, his back still turned. I looked about me in confusion. Why was I lying in a pile of straw? Was I in a stable? I cleared my throat and looked down at the change of clothes that had been thrown in my lap. "Well, come on then!" the boy shouted. I looked up at him in sheer bewilderment. He wore a long brown tunic tied at the waist, with thick stockings and clunky boots adorning his feet. I guessed that he was about three years older than me. "You'll have to change quickly, and here..." he handed me a massive jug filled with water, "wash your face and hands with this." I took the ewer with fascination. He stared at me when I didn't move, an annoyed expression in his dark brown eyes. "Are you a mute or something?" he said rudely, bending over me again and staring me in the face. I shook my head silently. He rolled his eyes and picked up a bucket of pig feed.

I scrambled to my feet, sloshing water everywhere. "Who are you?" He poured the feed into two troughs and there was a great scuffle as the pigs fought for food. He turned to face me, eyeing me up and down as I clutched the clothes he had tossed me in one hand and the ewer in the other, my mouth open in an 'o' of befuddlement. A brief look of pity passed across his face, and he ran his hands through his curly hair and sighed.

"Nathaniel, who're you?"

I paused. "I'm, er..." Why couldn't I remember my own name?

His eyes widened, and he looked at me in annoyance again. "Yes?"

"Georgina!" I nodded enthusiastically.

"Right..." he said slowly, picking up the empty buckets. "Well, we're going to be working together from now on, Georgina. Get dressed while I start getting the horses ready. She'll be here any minute." He left me with the now occupied pigs, and I looked down at the grey tunic in my hand. I couldn't remember who I was or why I was there, but it made sense somehow for me to get ready having been given the necessary implements to do so. I washed and dressed hurriedly, humming a strange melody that had got stuck in my head, and left the pigs to their breakfast.

I found Nathaniel in the stable next door brushing a beautiful chestnut horse with a sleek coat. The horse was obviously regularly pampered and gave a snort when I entered the stable. "Careful, he's not too good with strangers," Nathaniel warned. "If you take it slow, I'm sure he'll let you stroke him though." I approached the creature tentatively, knowing little about horses, and reached out a hand. He threw his mane back at first but then let me touch him after some encouragement.

Nathaniel smiled. "See, he's lovely really." I smiled in return. I didn't know who this boy was, but he had a dazzling smile, until a dark look passed across his features like a thunderclap and he hissed at me under his breath. "Quick, stand back, she won't want to see you touching him." I stepped back immediately, and another beautiful person entered the stables. She was dressed for riding, and her long blonde hair had been pulled back into a slick ponytail that trailed way down her back. I recognised her instantly. Letha. I had met her before, but I didn't much like her, I thought.

Letha strode purposefully across the stable towards the chestnut horse and threw back her arms as she revealed her pointy teeth. "My beautiful boy." She stroked the horse delicately, shooting Nathaniel a sly look as she did so, who blushed and cleared his throat.

"Are you ready, my lady?" He gestured for her to take a seat upon the saddle, inclining his head in a slight bow.

"I'll mount him when I'm ready," she snapped, tossing her ponytail over her shoulder.

I felt as though I may as well have been invisible for all the acknowledgment she gave to me. She rearranged her features into a simpering smile and flashed her teeth again at Nathaniel. "Let's go. Come on, Thorn." I frowned. Why would she call such a beautiful animal such an ugly name? She expertly manoeuvred her way into the saddle as I played with the hem of my grey tunic. I felt somewhat inadequate as she trotted out of the stables and into the morning sunshine. Nathaniel was already in her wake, a look of amazement upon his face, willing to do anything she asked of him. I sighed and followed them, wondering what on earth I was supposed to do now.

In answer to my silent question, Nathaniel turned over his shoulder and pointed back inside Thorn's stable. "Clean that out!" he instructed, and turned back to look at Letha, leading her horse towards the direction of the orchard I had spotted last night. I frowned again. I changed my mind; I didn't much like him either. I looked around the empty stable in disdain. Although Thorn might be an attractive horse, he sure made a lot of mess. I eyed the buckets of upturned feed, droppings, and grooming tools that had been strewn across the floor. My head still felt groggy and a little confused. Not quite sure why

I was willingly doing as I had been told, I began clearing up and scrubbing down, waiting for their return. Cleaning the stable was not light work. It was smelly, dirty work that took a long time, and I often looked out into the sunshine thinking longingly of those orange and lemon trees in the courtyard. I was so hungry. But I wasn't allowed to go there, I thought. No… not allowed.

A couple of hours later, Letha and Nathaniel returned to the stable, and she dismounted the horse with ease, stepping back lightly onto the ground. "Who on earth has been in here?" She looked about Thorn's living quarters in shock. Nathaniel mumbled something under his breath. "What was that?" She addressed him sharply, and he looked up from the floor.

"This is Georgina, the new girl." He looked at me apologetically.

I shifted on my feet, knowing I shouldn't say anything, and was a little disappointed that she hadn't been pleased with my handiwork; the stable was much cleaner than it had been three hours ago. Letha strode over to me, her head held up high, as Thorn settled himself down happily in the hay behind her. "Well, she's moved everything, haven't you?" Her cheeks were flushed as she eyed me with anger. "Everything's in the wrong place!" I gulped, and tried to defend myself.

"Well, nobody showed me where to put things," I gestured around, "so I just tried to clear things away a bit and—" I gasped as the pain came. I raised my hand up to my face in shock. She had slapped me, hard. I looked at her, lost for words, my cheek smarting. I witnessed a crack in the icy glacier as she lost control, but then she exhaled and pursed her lips, looking pleased with herself.

"I told you the pretty ones cause trouble."

I stood with my hand still pressed against my cheek and looked at Nathaniel expecting him to react to this injustice. He looked confused for a moment but then hung his head sheepishly and remained silent. "I have more important things to be doing with my morning than reprimanding foolish little girls." She turned to him. "I expect you to clean out all the outhouses by the end of the day – the chickens, the cows, the horses…" she eyed me and grinned, "and the pigs." Letha turned on her heel and exited the stable in a cloud of indifference.

When I was sure she was out of earshot I turned to Nathaniel angrily. "Is she always like that? What's wrong with her?" I rubbed my cheek with a grimace. "That was so painful." He stood awkwardly for a few moments as though about to say something to me but then shrugged.

"She's not so bad." He too left the stable to go and do Letha's bidding. I scowled and plonked myself down on the last remaining upturned bucket, thinking that if I were to clean out the chickens and the horses, Nathaniel could at least do the pigs.

TWENTY-FIVE

LILY

I hurried past the orange and lemon trees, casting my eyes into the dark corners of the courtyard, ready to come up with some cock and bull story about Letha needing something from the kitchens if a pair of those red eyes appeared. My skirts swept across the cobbles as I passed through the shadows unnoticed. My pulse quickened. I was going to see my daughter again. My beautiful, grown-up daughter. Oh, Georgina, you have no idea how much I have missed the two of you.

I slunk underneath the arch to the walled gardens and checked I was still alone. I was safe, for now. Those bloody ravens.

Four years. Four miserable years I had been trapped in this godforsaken manor, at the beck and call of that awful girl and her father, Etimus. Etimus Villinor, the Baron of Blackthorn. The name alone made me shudder.

I pulled my shawl tighter around me and headed in the direction of the willow tree whose feathery arms would provide us with the secrecy we needed. The night air had grown cold. How on God's green earth was I going to explain to Georgie what was going on? I had practised fictional conversations in my head but there was no easy way of doing this. I spun quickly on the spot. Still alone. Still safe.

How was I going to tell her that we were in a different time to the one in which ours existed? That when she found the

112

entrance in the woods, as I did four years ago, she fell through, travelling back in time, to here. That here was a foul place, run by foul people who reaped the rewards of the brainwashed peasants until they fell back drunk and ignorant?

The baron and his ravens were what nightmares were made of, but she was even worse. I raised my arm behind my back to check if the scar was still there. Of course it was; I had endured many a bruising at the hands of Letha, but that day was something else with the riding crop. I was only trying to find you, Georgina… paying the dungeon guard so I could check every night who had fallen through… Where are you, Georgina?

I came upon the willow tree, but my daughter was not there. I snuck under its protective barrier and prayed that she would show. I would explain everything to her. All about the harps, the music, that that's how they control us. That the music makes you forget who you are… but that they do not last forever… the magic only lasts a few hours… but then the minstrels appear and make you forget all over again… so the baron can keep getting rich and we can keep being poor…

I wrung my hands out in my haste for her to appear; any minute now, her freckled face would greet mine once again.

I paced underneath the willow tree as the seconds ticked by. I would tell her all about how I had a plan. To find him. If I could just find the sorcerer who made the harps in the first place I could get him to reverse the magic, and we could all find a way out of this world we were trapped in.

I clasped my hands together in frustration, still waiting. (Where was she?) It had taken me four years to gather all this information; it came in handy being one of Letha's maids. I could listen in to conversations; make notes for later, clues for myself to remember… If only I had help… I could go home.

I was running out of time; the minstrel would arrive soon with his harps, and we would all forget again…

A rustle next to me made me jump, and my heart soared. Finally, she was here! We would be reunited and get out of here.

It wasn't my daughter who appeared from beneath the arms of the willow tree.

The raven looked at me with its dead eyes. Without a second thought I turned on my heel and ran. I got halfway across the gardens before it caught up with me and dragged me to the ground. My heart sank as I ignored its rattling breath and looked instead at the shadow on the wall next to me. The minstrel with his pointed shoes and curly hat was back. He carried it with great delicacy, and the sweet melody rang around the manor once more as he plucked at the harp strings.

I looked up at the stars in the night sky. I will see you again one day, Benjamin, my love.

CONRAD

Shrinking from my cloak, I took flight into the night as she wandered helplessly back to Blackthorn Manor. I perched my small body amid a treetop. I preferred this form. But I was trapped like everybody else. I could not leave. I was told they would all die if I didn't serve. My brothers, my sisters… I must serve to protect.

I ruffled my feathers in the light breeze, contemplating the lifetime of servitude before me, and surveyed the manor grounds from above through my red eyes. Don't they know that ravens don't have red eyes?

PART FOUR

LUNA

TWENTY-SIX

INSIDE THE FORTUNE TELLER'S SHOP

The shop was engulfed in shadows, lit only by the pale light of the moon high in the night sky outside. Milky white light bounced off the domed surfaces of the orbs that lined the windows. For those who could read their secrets, their complexity revealed a great many wonders. Instruments of measurement scattered the shop – instruments capable of gauging what the human eye cannot.

Talismans promising great power, protection from otherworldly influences and healing properties dangled from the shelves above. On a blustery day, the wind would rush through the shop, and they would tinkle and dance, enticing you into the promise of the unknown. A fragrant trail of smoke wafted its way into her nostrils; she inhaled deeply, breathing in the incense that burned continually away.

Her shawls glittered and draped across the table as she sat upright in her hard-backed chair and dealt out her cards with grim expectancy. She knew a change had arrived that morning. She could feel it in the air. The others knew it too, but they were afraid to explore the darkness. She had been putting off this reading for many hours, but the time had come now to unearth what the fates had in store.

She revealed the cards slowly, purposefully, and with every one came a great pang of emotion. She felt it all. Loss, love, betrayal, anger and finally... the tarot that is feared the most.

The image that every mortal soul prays they do not encounter until it is due. The reaper, with silver scythe in one hand and hourglass in the other, was a stark reminder of the inevitability of death.

"He will come," she whispered into the night, shuddering at the sudden cold around her. "The boy will come to me."

MEANWHILE, DEEP IN BLACKTHORN FOREST

Heavy droplets fell from the grey canvas that stretched above me as the clouds lingered over the village like unwanted guests. I reached up for my hood and tried, struggling, to protect my basket from the downpour with my cloak. A twig snapped. I scanned the path behind me quickly and narrowed my eyes. No sign of life. An animal, probably, hurrying for shelter.

Turning my back on the path behind me I shook my head at my skittish behaviour. I picked up the pace, my feet sloshing in puddles that had already formed, feeling the wet soak through. In my haste to complete my task, I stumbled upon the path I usually avoided, and looked mournfully at the now mossy tree stump before me. I paused for a second as two bright shining faces flashed in my mind's eye. I glanced down at my basket and ploughed through the forest.

The little wicker basket was almost full. I bent down to pick up some smaller branches that had fallen recently in the storm. As I gathered my supplies from the forest, a padded footstep sounded behind me, and I pricked up my ears. Someone was following me. I rose from the forest floor and slipped on its muddy blanket. As I crashed to the ground, I saw it. A figure not three metres away from me, poised in the headlights of my stare, an animal caught in a trap.

He was tall, wore dark clothing, and the elements had plastered his raven-black hair to his forehead. He turned his features towards my fallen figure as he blinked away droplets from his electric-blue eyes. He hesitated on the path, staring at me with a strange expression, as though suddenly angry he had been disturbed by the presence of another human being. I remained where I was on the ground. My crimson cloak was now caked in mud.

The man's eyes darted to the upturned basket of firewood lying askew next to me and then down at his own hands. He carried an odd contraption that enabled him to slot glass jars into neat little sections. From what I could discern, each bottle contained something different; what looked like berries, plants and flowers had all been picked and deposited in each individual jar.

I adjusted my position, attempting to stand up, when a great gust of wind blew my hood off my head, and the raindrops changed direction. Half bent over, crouched against the wind and squinting through quickly declining vision, I watched him turn his back. "Wait!" I shouted. My cries became one with the shriek of the elements, and he was gone.

Cursing, I retrieved the basket of wet firewood off the forest floor and picked myself up from the mud. Time to abandon ship. It was pointless to try and wipe the mulch off myself now; the worsening storm had already soaked me wet through. It would have to wait until I got back to the cottage. I wended my way in between the spiky trees and retraced my steps until I reached the edge of the woods. The wind howled desperately at the panes, begging for entry, as I fumbled with the latch on the cottage gate. The wooden gate almost got torn from its bracket as a mighty gust swung it open on its hinges. I juggled to keep hold of my basket, my flapping cloak, and the gate trying to make its escape into the vegetable patch. Blackthorn had not seen a storm like this in years.

One year to be precise, I thought bitterly, reimagining that fateful tree plunging to the ground. I stepped through the door and hung my cloak up on the hook. A pool of water formed on the floor beneath it, and I tossed it instead into the kitchen sink ahead of me, making a mental note to wash it out later. Luna padded down the rickety stairs, bottle-brush tail in her wake, clearly just having awoken from a slumber in the window seat upstairs. I bent down and scratched her tabby head before walking into the living room and upending my basket into the larger one by the side of the fire.

"I'm not sure if these are going to light now," I said absentmindedly, half to myself, half to the cat. The firewood fizzled pathetically before burning out. I tossed my hair behind my back and rummaged deeper in the wicker basket. I unearthed a couple of dry logs, which soon fizzled and popped invitingly in the grate. Luna's eyes widened in the glare, and I watched the flames leap and dance in her curious shining orbs before going upstairs to grab a towel.

Ten minutes later, I had settled myself under a blanket in the large armchair in front of the fire, and the shivering eventually ceased. Luna stretched out her long body in front of the fireplace, content with her lot. I looked around the cottage and sighed in what I suppose was a gratifying way. It wasn't much, but it was home. My home. I gazed out the window and thought that I ought to be more careful on evenings like this; Grandmother had warned me not to venture into the forest when it was stormy.

Once upon a time, Grandmother, Mother, Father and I all lived in the cottage together. Undoubtedly it was cramped at times, but we learnt to live with it, and each other. I took a sip of my herbal tea and scalded my tongue. I exhaled quickly and set it down on the tiny table beside me. I had tried to avoid thinking about it all day. I had seen Grandmother that morning, albeit a morose visit compared to usual, baked bread that afternoon and taken a trip into the forest, which may have been my subconscious telling me to think about it. I rested my head back into the armchair and let my mind wander. Today was the one-year anniversary of my parents' death.

TWENTY-SEVEN

It had been a horribly stormy night, and it was as though the elements had mustered all their energy one year on in memorial, gusting up the violent turbulence of the past. I remember it as though it were yesterday. It was Grandmother who had found the bodies. They had gone out walking one evening; I had been in a mood and did not want to go, and Grandmother said she had a dark feeling about that night. Grandmother's 'dark feelings' usually did not end up devoid of reason.

They had set off early evening, but the storm soon made its presence known. Luna and I had sat watching the sky turn grey long before sundown was due. Full of concern about their safety, Grandmother had braved the gale against my protestations of going instead, or at least with her, and I was left to worry on my own. I never saw them again. Grandmother had spared me the gory details, but my imagination had not. She stumbled across them both, crushed by a fallen tree, knocked dead on impact. Their white faces cropped up in my nightmares on the bad nights, their limbs askew, their mouths open in a silent scream of terror they never had time to voice aloud.

I had to think about it, had to accept it, but it was not any easier one year on. Grandmother took it harder than me. She said she couldn't live in the cottage anymore and gifted it to me on my twenty-first birthday, shortly after their death. She said it finally gave her the excuse to do what she had always wanted and set up a shop in the village that she could maintain and live above. She even left her cat behind. I sighed. I had been left everything. The cottage, the cat with which I shared my own name, and the accumulation of memories we had gathered over the years.

There were traces of it throughout the cottage: blankets my mother and I had sewn together, books my father had bound and read to me, the little dinner table we sat around every evening sharing our ideas, hopes and dreams. I had kept very little. The odd trinket here and there, the cloak my mother had made for me, and a silver half-moon amulet my father had presented to me on my eighteenth birthday. It hung loosely around my neck, and I fiddled with it as I picked up my tea again, thinking about faraway times. I had learnt to fend for myself in the sudden deluge of independence I had been unceremoniously drenched with.

A sudden squall hit the side of the cottage and Luna scarpered. I spilt my remaining tea over myself as she leapt across the arm of my chair and headed for the kitchen. It was cold. The glowing embers of the fire died out in the grate. I must have sat for longer than I thought. "Come on then," I said with a sigh. "It must be your dinner time." I had grown used to talking to myself and hardly realised I was doing it nowadays. Something had to fill the silence.

Once Luna was fed and watered, I washed my cloak out in the sink and hung it up to dry. She followed me up the stairs and watched as I folded away blankets. I threw a particularly fluffy one over myself and settled myself down in the window seat overlooking the treetops. I squinted through the darkness and saw blurred shapes being tossed about by the wind.

My thoughts turned to the strange man. I raised my eyebrows as Luna perched in front of me on the ledge; I hoped he wasn't out there now in the storm. I yawned and pondered upon the chance encounter. He appeared to be gathering from the forest much the same as I; with his glass jars slotted in sections, it looked as though he were collecting samples. I didn't usually see another human soul in Blackthorn Forest; the villagers' fear of the old haunting tales meant that their children would grow up never to know the beauty of the trees.

My eyes grew tired of peering into the pitch black, and when I could no longer discern shapes in the shadows I clambered into bed. Luna curled up her furry body at the end and warmed my feet comfortably.

The tempest raged for most of the night. I tossed and turned in an agitated state as the cacophony of noise outside grew louder. Throwing the covers off me restlessly, I forced myself back into sleep; it would not be another night of insomnia.

My dreams were punctuated with violent visions of tree trunks as their roots became dragged out of the earth and a pair of electric-blue eyes, blinking curiously at me, emerging out of the gloom.

TWENTY-EIGHT

A sharp set of claws sank into my back, and I yelped. A weight lifted off the bed, and a heavy thump hit the floorboards. I groaned and rolled onto my front. "Thanks, Luna." I rubbed my bleary eyes and pushed the bedcovers off. My rude awakening was a result of having slept past Luna's breakfast time. The sun streamed through my curtains, and as I stretched my way over to the window, I saw that all traces of last night's storm had disappeared and the forest lay still. I had half expected the man to come knocking on the cottage door in the middle of the night to seek refuge from the storm. But there had been no sign.

I sighed and checked the clock. Cursing, I sprang into action; I only had ten minutes before I was supposed to be helping Grandmother open the shop. I pulled some clothes on, and the wardrobe doors banged shut after me as I left the bedroom. Following Luna down the stairs, I managed to slop half her breakfast onto the floor, whilst noticing that my cloak was still sodden, and had to hurry to find another warm garment in the cupboard under the stairs. I left the cottage in a disorganised hurricane, and Luna's amber eyes scowled at me as she went to retrieve her late breakfast from off the floor. She was quite picky for a cat really.

I headed along the narrow trail that soon led onto the cobbles and into the village square. Birds sang in the sunshine, their colourful bodies streaking across the blue sky above me, waking up Blackthorn to a bright Saturday morning. Arthur's

Tavern, the fishmonger and the greengrocer's passed in a blur as I greeted various proprietors setting up their shop fronts. They half waved and gave a sort of sad smile in my direction. The kind of sad smile they had conjured one year ago and ever since.

Grandmother's shop stood next to the abandoned jeweller's on the right-hand side, just after the darkened alleyway that I rarely ventured down. But the jeweller's didn't look abandoned this morning; there were people inside, and battered old furniture had been strewn across the cobbles in front of the large glass windows at the front. I didn't have time to look now, I was already late. I stopped short as I approached Grandmother's shop and was taken aback for a second as I realised who was standing outside.

George and Betty stood awkwardly conversing in quiet tones, a wry smile playing around his lips as she twirled her golden hair embarrassingly round her fingers. Only a vague pang took place inside me as it tolled dully in the pit of my stomach. George Fallow was the son of the village blacksmith, and our acquaintance originated from when we could first walk and talk. Our parents had been great friends and the Fallows were like a second family to me.

Subsequently, George and I had spent a lot of time together growing up as we rolled our eyes at our parents' conversations and spent lazy summer evenings whiling away the time in each other's company. Naturally, our relations progressed into something more than friends, to the delight of both our families. I became the envy of most girls in the village; George's backbreaking trade and constant perseverance with hammer and hot iron had gifted him with pronounced muscles, and he often cropped up in the tales of gossiping gaggles of girls. Not to mention his natural charm and kindness for others, it was easy to spend time in his company, and we were happy. At the age of twenty and twenty-one there was talk of our marriage and the union between the Redlocks and the Fallows; we had been together for three years, after all.

Had it not been for my parents' death I believe our marriage would have taken place. It's not something I blame them for, in fact it made me realise that George was perhaps not everything I had thought him to be. Our relationship fell apart two months after they passed away. I became withdrawn, more cynical about life and difficult to talk to. At first, he was kind and understanding, bringing me cups of tea as I sat gazing into the fire at some far-off point in the past, trying to come to terms with my loneliness. He would sit with Grandmother and me until I wanted to talk, leave the cottage with me when I could bring myself to, and swerve the awkward conversations with villagers when anyone brought up the topic in front of me. In short, he was brilliant, and I don't know why I expected his uncommon display of compassion to last.

George grew impatient at my lack of interest in the world. He was irritable around me, would tell me to snap out of it after one month of mourning, take long walks in the forest by himself and return none the calmer. His frustration with me was the wakeup call I needed; after one month I started to pull myself together again. Grandmother had given me the cottage, so I tidied and organised it into the way I wanted it, making a comfortable home for our potential future. We met with our friends again, caught up with our old life and got back into the swing of things.

Yet George's frustration with me never seemed to leave, only bubble away below the surface, erupting in more frequent outbursts of unfair accusations. He had been at my side and consoled me for one whole month of his life, and in return I got the impression that he thought I owed him for this. I thanked him endlessly for his loyalty, ensured I was kind to him every day, let him live in the cottage with me whilst I cooked and cleaned for him… None of it was ever enough. He would never know the extent of my eternal gratefulness for him in the wake of my parents' death, because in his eyes it was something that I would never be able to pay back.

After ten months of being on my own I had more than enough time to contemplate the events of the past year. I didn't blame myself for mourning them and for acting the way I did, and I didn't blame George for his behaviour and his eventual acceptance of the fact that we were never going to get back to who we used to be. It was simply just not meant to be. I shook my head out of the past and smiled despite these sad memories. George returned my smile with a "Morning, Luna," and made his excuses for returning to his father. It was no longer awkward between us after all these months, and I surprised myself at how little emotion I felt as he walked away, running his hands through his blond, unkempt hair.

I turned to Betty, who stood hanging her head and peering at something evidently very interesting on the cobbles. Betty also helped my grandmother in the shop, and I patted her gently on the arm and gestured inside Luna's Luck. "Shall we go in?" She nodded, still avoiding my gaze, and led the way inside. The bell tinkled as we stepped over the threshold, and Betty immediately busied herself behind the till. I would have to talk to her about this.

TWENTY-NINE

Grandmother tutted playfully at us. "It's a good job I'm not like a normal employer, isn't it, Betty, or else you'd be fired for always being late… or do I have Luna to blame for that one?" She winked, a mischievous twinkle in her eye. I felt a little awkward for Betty as she avoided the question with a small apology. For the sake of her blushing face I decided not to bring up the topic of who was making her late.

I lit the fragrant incense sticks dotted about the shop and pondered on Grandmother's words. She might not think herself scary, but to some villagers she represented everything they feared. Fortune-telling was not something that had ever interested me; why would you want to know what's going to happen next Tuesday when you could just live your life as normal? Nevertheless, I admired Grandmother's gift and would often observe in reverence as she deciphered the mysterious swirls of the crystal balls or uttered everyday predictions that always turned out to be true. Grandmother had always had the gift, and it was only until recently that she decided to make some money out of it, and I didn't blame her. It gave her a purpose and had taken her mind off what would have been a very difficult year losing her daughter.

Those who knew my grandmother wouldn't look twice at her appearance; however, those who may happen to stumble upon Luna's Luck (she said the name came to her in a dream, however I think it may have been an unusual lack of originality on her part) might be a little startled by what they saw. Grandmother's hair was as black as the night, and not one strand escaped from the harsh tyranny of her sleek bun. Her lips were always painted blood red and her startling eyes, the blue and green flecks ever swirling like a hazy sea mist, were two different colours. She draped her slight frame in glittering shawls and shining materials that danced and mesmerised the client sitting opposite her, their disbelieving eyes growing wider in the candlelight. To me, she was simply Grandmother, an all-knowing and sometimes slightly unsettling one, but still just my grandmother.

I looked about the shop, finding myself a job, and my eyes rested upon a table scattered with strange-looking spindly instruments. I peered closer and tried to figure out what they were. They looked like odd little metal animals with legs, and I thought I had seen one on a shelf a couple of months ago as it whirred and ticked, different parts spinning around. "Be careful with those, Luna." A sharp voice sounded right behind me. I hadn't even noticed Grandmother approaching. "They're a new shipment delivered this morning, but if you're going to polish them all and arrange them on the shelves, I want you to wear proper gloves. I don't think they should be touched for long periods of time."

I hastily accepted the pair of leather gloves. "What are they? They look like little creatures."

Grandmother shot them a mistrustful glare. "They're supposed to warn when dark spirits are near – so you'd best pray they keep still." She winked at me again. I cleared my throat apprehensively and picked one up by a metal part sticking out of it.

"Brilliant," I muttered. They were difficult little things to clean, and I delicately moved the cloth in and out of the intricate patterns, being careful to avoid touching them with my bare hands.

Betty cleared her throat awkwardly from the other side of the shop and addressed my grandmother. "Joan? I wonder if it's possible for me to take this afternoon off?" There came no reply, and I peered over the dusty shelf as Betty fidgeted with her scarf. "I'm not feeling too well, you see…"

"The afternoon off?" Grandmother repeated loudly. "On a Saturday? Well, I don't know. Luna will have stay and cover—"

"I'll stay," I interrupted quickly, peering around the shelf. "I don't mind." I rather enjoyed keeping Grandmother company when it was just the two of us. I also had a sneaking suspicion that Betty's afternoon off would be spent in the presence of a certain blond-haired boy; George's father usually let him have one afternoon off at the weekends and one day in the week.

I disappeared again behind the dusty shelf and recommenced the polishing of the mechanical creatures. "Well, alright then," I heard Grandmother say slowly. "If you're under the weather, are you sure you're feeling well enough to stay this morning?" I conjured up an image of Grandmother scrutinising Betty through her multicoloured eyes and smiled faintly.

"Y-yes," Betty stammered, "I'm sure I'll be fine for the next couple of hours. Then I'll go and get some rest." I heard Grandmother instructing her to pick one of the glass orbs on the shelf for her next client.

"Mind it's a cloudy one though, those tend to yield better results." She sniffed. "I've got a strange feeling about today." I smiled again. Grandmother said she had a strange feeling at least once a week.

I started at a faint whirring and frowned down at one of the little detectors. I could have sworn I'd seen one of its arms move. It remained innocently still on the shelf I had placed it on. I was about to open my mouth and tell Grandmother what I'd thought I'd seen when a great crash from the street outside interrupted my opportunity.

THIRTY

The three of us rushed out of the shop as though escaping a fire. It sounded as though someone had dropped a very large object from a substantial height. We must have looked a comical trio: Grandmother struggling to extract the feather duster that had got caught in the door, Betty clutching one of the glass orbs as though her life depended on it and me, one glove on, one glove off, tripping up on the cobbles in my eagerness. We stared at the formerly empty building next door and at a broken table that lay askew in front of the display windows, the victim of someone's clumsy hands. "You were supposed to lower it slowly, Tristan!"

The angry voice echoed down the street. A man, dressed in a dark leather jacket, sporting brown stubble and thick, wavy hair, looked up in annoyance. The three of us simultaneously peered up to see a younger man leaning precariously out of the window one floor above. He looked down and shrugged, unaffected by the scolding, and turned back inside.

I gasped as I saw his profile from the side, suddenly recognising that caramel skin and those bright blue eyes. I dropped one of my gloves. It was the man from the forest. I vaguely heard Grandmother expressing annoyance that I should take better care of what was supposed to protect us from evil spirits and waited for him to reappear. He did not, and I instead watched the older man curiously as he ignored us and stared half-heartedly at the broken table in front of him, trying to muster the strength to lift it up again.

Grandmother cleared her throat and looked at me bemused. She pointed at the old jeweller's and picked up the fallen glove. On her way back up she grunted, "I see they've arrived already."

I followed her back into the shop and tried to keep my voice casual. "Who are they?"

"That man there, Isaac Brewer, he's in the medical profession. He's come to repurpose the jeweller's into an apothecary. He's brought his nephew, Tristan, with him to help run it. They weren't supposed to arrive until tomorrow." Grandmother's tone indicated that she clearly didn't approve of this situation. Her feather duster paused in mid-air as she lowered her voice. "Rumour has it, the boy's parents used to live in Blackthorn, but moved away after some kind of scandal."

I exchanged a bewildered look with Betty, surprised by my grandmother's sudden knowledge of village gossip. "How do you know all of this?"

She waved away my astonishment with a flamboyant sweep of feathers. "Ingrid told me at the haberdashery yesterday." I smiled. Of course; my grandmother's trusty circle of informants were always poking their noses about. "Anyway," she flapped both hands at us and Betty swerved the long pole to avoid having her eye taken out, "my next client will be here soon. Luna, you can finish polishing the detectors later and, Betty, can you go in the back, my dear, and get the stove on? You know how he likes his tea. Quickly now, girls. He's never been late, not once, bless his heart... I'll be needing that orb now, Betty, as well!" I grinned at her as she hurriedly placed the circular object on the little table in front of Grandmother's chair, and we disappeared into the back room.

Every Saturday at eleven o'clock, Grandmother's most reliable client shuffled slowly over the threshold and into the chair opposite her, to have his fortune told. Grandmother told us that she didn't like us hanging around in the shadows whenever she was with someone; it made for a better experience for them to have a one-on-one session. These sessions usually lasted around half an hour giving Betty and I plenty of chances to sit gossiping for a while in the back.

I was glad of this today, for it gave Betty no opportunity to avoid me, as I knew she had been trying to do ever since I had witnessed her exchange with George that morning. She set about the stove, taking an absurdly long amount of time to put the water on, and stood tapping her fingernails on the surface humming along to a tune I did not recognise. "It's okay, you know." I sat down at the table behind her and sighed heavily.

She turned around slowly, her wide eyes even larger than usual. "What is?"

I had to raise my voice slightly over the whistle of the kettle. "You and George." She stared at me for a few seconds and then gave a great exhalation, sat down opposite me and took my hands in hers.

"I'm so sorry, Luna. You're one of my best friends, and I should have told you sooner." She looked at me imploringly, her blonde hair wild, and I saw dark shadows underneath her eyes. "I've wanted to tell you for weeks, but... I just didn't know how! I didn't want to upset you or... George asked me not to... I know that—"

I squeezed her hand and interrupted her stammering flow that I feared may erupt into tears. "Don't be silly! Honestly, I'm happy for you, I really am," I said, surprising myself at the sincerity in my voice. "Please don't feel like you need to tiptoe around me. I'd hate to think that we couldn't be friends anymore." I stood up and took the kettle off the stove, as it was now emitting a great noise. Betty blinked up at me in the sudden silence, her eyes grateful.

"Are you sure?"

"One hundred per cent," I said gravely, and then smiled at her. "Now you'd best take in Ghostly's tea or he'll come and haunt you when he finally realises he's dead." She giggled and took the steaming mug out of my hand as she left the room.

"Thanks, Luna." I wasn't quite sure if she was thanking me for the tea or for my permission, but it didn't really matter.

She returned one minute later with her hands empty, hoisted herself up onto the kitchen side and sat with her legs swinging against the cupboards underneath. Grandmother hated it when she did that. "Two spoons of sugar?" I asked her as I sat back down again at the table. She grinned and nodded. "You know the drill." Ghostly was our nickname for Grandmother's current client.

The elderly man was so ancient he looked as though he had simply got up from his armchair one day and had not realised that he had passed over. Always dressed head to toe in fine fabrics with a white handkerchief poking out of his breast pocket, the only communication we ever had with him was when we set his cup of tea down in front of him and he asked if there were two spoons of sugar in it. We always nodded in the affirmative and that was that. He was a simple man. Grandmother had informed us once when she caught us using his nickname that his real name was Joseph if we ever felt inclined to address him as such.

A little while later, Grandmother retrieved us from the back room, interrupting our ponderings on the new apothecary, what Betty was going to do on her secret afternoon off and the violent storm last night. I had not told either of them about my strange encounter with the man I now knew to be called Tristan; there was no way on this earth Grandmother would approve of me venturing into the forest at night.

"Come on then, girls, there's work to be done. Luna, if you could finish polishing the detectors and, Betty, if you're feeling up to it, I've got stacks of cards that all need organising and arranging." The bell rang in the room beyond. "I'll see to this customer."

The three of us exited the back room, and I said quickly, "Oh, Grandmother, that reminds me—" She had not heard me, however, and was now conversing with a frightened-looking woman who was convinced her house was haunted. I was about to tell her how I had noticed one of the instruments move out of the corner of my eye, but it was driven out of my mind again.

THIRTY-ONE

Over the course of the next hour we watched as various people struggled across the cobbles. They hauled broken furniture and dusty glass cases out of the old jeweller's building. I spotted the man in the brown jacket standing with arms crossed, brows furrowed, and his mouth opening and closing in what I assumed were accusatory tones as the people moving the furniture looked disgruntled and hurried along. I was sure it would take a lot less time if he helped.

There came a few gentler crashes, and I imagined Tristan lowering structures out of the upper window, with a few shouts in return from unsuspecting bystanders. I felt a slight annoyance at the thought of him; he had left me on the forest floor without even checking if I was okay. His arrogance at his uncle had furthered my annoyance, although I couldn't really blame him for that, as his uncle's haughty demeanour was enough to irk anyone.

At midday, Betty made her excuses in a small voice and exited the shop, leaving Grandmother and myself alone. The next few hours passed in a flurry of customers all looking to obtain spiritual wares from Luna's Luck. A pleasant couple purchased a very expensive golden locket containing protective powers for their daughter's birthday gift, a worried-looking man set up a series of tarot readings with Grandmother, and finally at four o'clock, a surly teenager entered the shop. Grandmother finished dusting pastry flakes off herself (I had popped into the bakery over the road a couple of hours earlier to stock up on sweet delicacies) and eyed him warily.

He said he was after some sage to burn. "My things keep moving around, and at night-time, I hear things," he said very quickly.

"What kind of things?" Grandmother enquired as I went to check if we had any sage.

"Doesn't matter." He shrugged, and grumbled, "You got any or what?" He kept checking over his shoulder and out of the shop front, as though afraid someone might find out he was scared. Grandmother reprimanded him for his rude behaviour, and he apologised and handed over some money to me without asking how much it was. He hurried out of the shop as she shouted after him not to burn the house down.

Grandmother chuckled to herself quietly. "Honestly, people afraid of things that go bump in the night? Really now..." As I inserted the money into the till, the door crashed open, and a short, stout man with a handlebar moustache puffed his way into the shop, a gigantic cardboard box in his arms labelled 'This Way Up'.

"Sorry, ma'am, been chock-a-block today!" He set down the box in the middle of the shop floor with a sigh of relief and straightened up to look at us, clearly expecting some kind of gratitude for what had just happened.

When we stared at him blankly, he gestured out into the street. "Got five more of them boxes coming, where d'you want 'em?" Grandmother clapped her hands to her forehead and took the sleeves of her glittering shawl with them. The tassels draped dramatically down over her face.

"I forgot!" she wailed. She moved forward to look at the box and pointed at a place by the window. "Just over there, if you don't mind!"

"Grandmother, what—" I was interrupted by the wheezing man as he bent down again and moved the box into position.

He disappeared and reappeared with another bulky box. He enacted this awkward manoeuvre three more times until all five boxes were stacked haphazardly in the corner. One of the 'This Way Up' signs was upside down. The delivery man stood for a few minutes in the door of the shop, catching his breath, as I quickly righted the box on top.

The man tipped his hat at us as I smiled. Grandmother thanked him as he tumbled out onto the cobbles, still apologising profusely for the lateness of the delivery. I checked my watch. It was half past four and those boxes were not going to unload themselves. Grandmother sat down on her hard-backed chair with a great huff. "Uh... Grandmother," I reminded her of my presence. "What's in those boxes?" She looked me up and down as though faintly surprised I was still there.

"Oh... Luna... sorry, I was thinking about what I'm going to do with them. They're crystal orbs. I've got somebody coming into the shop tomorrow to purchase a large shipment, and they all need polishing and checking before they can be sold."

I walked over to the windowsill and peered down at the sealed boxes. "Well, what time is the buyer coming tomorrow?"

Grandmother wrung her hands. "First thing in the morning. They're very eager. I can't believe I forgot! And I've told Ingrid I'll do her tarot reading at her house at quarter past five tonight after the shop closes. She's not very mobile now with her hip..." Grandmother's eyes found mine. The sapphire and emerald, usually bright and sparkling, looked a little tired, and her brow furrowed into great lines across her forehead.

"I'll stay and polish the orbs for you. No, I don't mind." I interrupted her protestations. "That way they'll be ready for the morning, and you won't have to worry. You go ahead to Ingrid's."

"What would I do without you, my lovely Luna?" Grandmother's eyes twinkled again as she smiled across the room at me. "I do appreciate you being around to help me." I shrugged off her gratitude.

"It's nothing, honestly, I'm glad to help!" After a quick hug and demonstration of how she wanted me to check each orb, Grandmother grabbed her coat and scarf from her living quarters upstairs and gathered her tarot cards from the neat pile Betty had left on the front counter. She hesitated in the doorway of Luna's Luck as a sudden cold draught entered and extinguished one of the candles.

Grandmother eyed the wall opposite her, as though trying to see through into the new apothecary. "Are you sure you're going to be alright on your own? I'm probably going to be a couple of hours, as I think Ingrid's granddaughter wants a reading as well. She can talk the hind legs off a donkey." I smiled in appreciation of her concern.

"How many times have you left me here on my own, Grandmother? I'll be just fine."

She wrapped her scarf tighter around herself. "Of course you will. I forget how old you are, Luna." She gave me one last lingering look in which I felt she was thinking about times long past, and left the shop.

THIRTY-TWO

I pocketed the spare key and began to unload the boxes. I soon realised how much work I had signed up for; each box contained fifty tightly wrapped packages, which meant there were 250 orbs to check and polish. I sighed and reached for my polishing cloth. I was going to be there for hours.

I undid the wrappings on the first one and held the circular object in my hand. It was unnaturally cold, and the faint candyfloss clouds swirled around each other in a hazy whirlpool. I held it up to my eye; Grandmother had asked me to check for any cracks or signs of damage. It looked intact to me. I blinked a couple of times. It was easy to get absorbed in the patterns that reflected the light of the candle beside me.

Voices outside broke my reverie, and I looked up. The sunlight never seemed to last very long in Blackthorn this time of year, and I could tell that in a month or so we would be plunged into the long winter nights that seemed never to end. It became difficult to discern in the sudden gloom to whom the voices belonged. I placed the first orb in the empty box beside me as I listened curiously. It sounded as though people were leaving for the evening; a chain of goodbyes and see you tomorrows and a couple of disgruntled murmurs about ungrateful people echoed down the street and disappeared into alleyways as people hurried on their way.

The cobbles fell silent. I looked down at the box and realised I had only finished one orb. "Two hundred and forty nine to go," I muttered darkly, picking up the next lot of wrappings. I sat for an hour and finished one of the boxes, listening to the wind gusting outside as it picked up the crisp autumn leaves and tossed them about, thinking it was nothing compared to the night before. My mind wandered to George and Betty and how she had been so guilty about staying quiet. Yet he was the one who had asked her not to say anything. I frowned. Perhaps he was under the impression that I still thought of him that way. I must admit that I had been lonely at times over the past year. Still, I thought as I reached for the second box of orbs, was it better to spend time with someone simply because you were lonely or because you actually wanted to?

The chair I sat in was uncomfortable. There were no squashy armchairs or fluffy pillows in Grandmother's shop; her clients were to remain alert and focused upon whatever spiritual answer they were trying to ascertain. "There's no time for sitting back and relaxing, Luna! Do you think I'm running a tea shop?" she had said to me one day when I pointed out that she could have a waiting area for those clients who were early. I smiled and thought that if she had asked Betty this question, Betty, who always ensured that everyone had a strong cup of tea or coffee to help prepare themselves for what was about to come, may have had a different answer in mind.

I stood up and stretched my back out like a cat awakening from a long slumber. I thought guiltily of Luna; she would have to wait for her dinner as well as her breakfast. I gathered my hair up behind my head and secured the long chestnut wave in a ponytail. I caught sight of myself in the shop window, and my brown eyes blinked back at me. I looked like my mother. I was the spitting image of her, which accounted for those rare moments when Grandmother struggled to look at me, although neither of us would ever admit that we knew the reason why.

I ensured that the entrance door was locked before brewing up a strong coffee and emptying the remains of the sugar jar

141

into it. I set my mug down on the windowsill and resumed my position in front of the glass. I picked up the pace, thinking that I did not want to be there all night, and settled into a speedy routine of bending, checking, polishing, bending, checking, polishing...

I didn't know if it was the wisp of steam rising from my mug, a trick of the candlelight, or something else. As I rose from placing the final orb of the second box into the completed pile, I dropped the next one, and a dark shape loomed out of the shadows on the cobbles outside. I managed to catch the orb in mid-air before it smashed on the shop floor. It was just somebody passing by. I raised my coffee mug to my lips as I watched them walk from right to left in front of me. Blackthorn's cobbles were too poorly lit for me to see their face, but I thought I saw a tall figure with arms shoved into the pockets of a dark jacket.

As the bittersweet liquid trickled down my throat and I moved to replace the mug, the figure moved, and turned in my direction. I froze. They hesitated on the street outside, having made a double-take perhaps in surprise at seeing somebody positioned eerily in the candle-lit window. They paused for a few seconds. They could see me, but I could not see them. I narrowed my eyes, unnerved at their sudden change of direction, thinking that maybe it was someone I knew.

Should I wave in acknowledgment? Something told me not to. A pair of bright blue eyes hovered, and I knew in that moment who they belonged to. This time it was I who was trapped in the headlights. I felt as though a great spotlight had been placed over my head and I was being scrutinised, growing more vulnerable by the second. Before I could do anything else, Tristan moved on, and the blue spheres were swallowed up by the darkness.

THIRTY-THREE

I shifted uneasily in my seat and finished the rest of my coffee, thinking hard, my mind racing. The shock of recognising me from our previous encounter had obviously thrown him off. Another surge of annoyance washed over me. What right did he have to stand there and look at me as though I had done something wrong? He was the one who had left me during a raging storm, without even a look back, or the hint of a possible helping hand.

I moved the cloth irritably over the orbs back and forth in methodical sweeping circular motions cursing anyone who wanted to buy 250 of these things. The orbs in the third box were so shiny you could see your own reflection in them. As the hour approached seven and the shop was getting stuffy, my poor night's sleep was causing my eyelids to droop, and the silence furthered my drowsiness. I needed something to wake me up, and there was no sign of Grandmother. I reached for the brass key in my pocket and unlocked the shop, intending to step outside for a few moments and breathe in the fresh evening air.

I had no sooner inhaled my first breath than another figure swept over the cobbles. I held it as they passed.

Covered in a black cloak from head to toe, they slunk purposefully past me, my presence remaining hidden. I couldn't see through the night's veil if they were man or woman – just an anonymous villager. They reached the other side of the apothecary and turned to their right down the alleyway next to it. Subconsciously I took a few steps out into the street, and before I knew it, I was in the shadows of the apothecary building as I watched the cloaked figure in the alleyway.

They knocked thrice on a door I could not see. Ten seconds passed before a small wooden entrance swung open on its hinges. They stepped through the concealed doorway and entered the apothecary. The temperature dropped and I stood, shivering in my cardigan, key in hand, waiting with bated breath until they reappeared. The lack of any lights in the apothecary gave the intended wrong impression that no one was home.

After a couple of minutes, the tiny door opened once more and they stepped clumsily out, clutching something tight to their chest, looking furtively about them. Once they were convinced no one was looking, they retreated towards the bookshop, stumbling upon the cobbles in their impatience. I remained as still as a statue for fear of being discovered as they passed close by. They disappeared out of sight with their mysterious package.

I swallowed anxiously. The apothecary was still. I went back into the safety of the shop trying not to draw any attention. This was very odd behaviour from the villagers of Blackthorn; it was unusual to venture out in the evening apart from visiting friends or the local pub, as everything else remained closed. What would they be buying from the apothecary at this hour? And why would they enter via a hidden door? I had seen Tristan leave, so did that mean his uncle was still inside?

I sat down again in the hard-backed chair with my mind racing. The tinkle of the bell made me jump. "Goodness gracious, my dear girl, you look like you've seen a ghost!" Grandmother entered the shop and unbuttoned her long coat. She gestured back to the door. "Have you not locked the door the whole time you've been here?"

"No, I… I just stepped out for some fresh air… You didn't see anyone just now, did you?"

Grandmother looked bemused.

"Well, I've just come back from Ingrid's. That woman, honestly. Thinks she's going to be as dead as a doornail in two weeks' time, and nothing I can say will make her think otherwise. It's just a bad hip, I told her, for goodness' sake. If we all dropped dead from our minor ailments, we'd have very short lives indeed..." This was not what I had meant, but I let Grandmother carry on as she expressed her exasperation for Ingrid and her granddaughter's lack of spiritual auras. "How are you getting on anyway?" she asked, shaking a couple of leaves out of her scarf.

"I've got two boxes left," I said a little miserably.

Grandmother patted me on the head. "I'll put the kettle on the stove and sit with you until we've finished them."

"Don't be silly." I looked at her, taking in her faded crimson lipstick and bloodshot eyes. "You need rest. There's no point both of us sitting here in the cold. You go ahead upstairs and put your feet up." I took her hand kindly and bade her goodnight.

She looked unsure, but the thought of a comfy armchair and a warm fire beckoned too much to protest. "Alright then, Luna, if you're sure... I'll probably see you tomorrow at some point. Thank you for this." I nodded in reply. I heard her slowly walking up the stairs before pausing and shouting, "Don't forget to lock the door. You can bring the key back tomorrow!"

"Yes, Grandmother." I smiled. "Now get some rest." I heard her creaking around upstairs for a little while, and then all was silent. There was no point telling her that she wasn't as young as she used to be.

My eyelids drooped again as I breathed in the still-burning incense. Eight o'clock came and eight o'clock went. I forced myself to continue as the crystal balls felt heavier in my hands. I picked up the last orb at half past eight and stopped dead as I looked out of the window. It was now pitch black. But I had heard something. I was sure that Grandmother had long been snoozing. I couldn't hear the words exactly, but a pair of muffled voices entered my ears through the glass, and I sat up a little straighter.

There were people on the street outside. In my mind's eye I imagined another two cloaked figures hurrying past, their voices quick buzzes of unidentifiable musings. The voices grew quieter and then faded. I closed my eyes. I was waiting for them to return. I almost hoped that they didn't; that my suspicions would be incorrect and they were simply a husband and wife taking a stroll in the dark.

The silence filled my ears as I waited with bated breath. The rhythm of my own heartbeat signalled the passage of time. It wasn't more than five minutes later when their voices sounded again and they retraced their steps from whence they came. I exhaled slowly, my hands shaking slightly, knowing that I was not the only one working late tonight.

Somebody was sitting next door, mere metres away from me, selling something to the villagers of Blackthorn that they could not purchase in the light of day.

For some reason this thought unnerved me more than it should have done. If somebody (and I thought I knew who) was operating under the cloak of night, that meant they were hiding something. I had a bad feeling about this. All I wanted to do was lock up and hurry home before I was witness to anything else that I didn't fully understand. I resealed all the boxes and left a scribbled note to Grandmother letting her know that they were all ready for the next morning. I grabbed my coat from behind the front counter and wrapped myself up, walking around the shop blowing out candles and extinguishing incense sticks, casting the shop into darkness. I tugged my hair out from my ponytail, thinking that it would act as a scarf in the cold air, and exited the shop with a faint tinkle from the bell.

As the key clicked in the lock, securing Grandmother safely in her bed, a harsh wind flew past and I shivered. The apothecary was still dark as I passed by, and I couldn't help but feel vulnerable during the short walk home. I kept looking over my shoulder, fearing a dark figure following behind, and tapped hurriedly on the now deserted cobbles.

Luna mewed pitifully as soon as I stepped through the cottage door. "I'm sorry," I said, looking down at my ankles as she nipped hungrily at them. She set upon her food with great relish whilst I whipped up a quick supper of bread and meats, suddenly ravenous, and ate with great appreciation. There was no point in lighting a fire; I had dragged myself up to the bathroom and had a hot bath as soon as my food had gone down. Wrapping myself up in my favourite fluffy blanket, I sat by the window in my bedroom, looking out into the trees. All I could discern through the gloom were the spiky branches of the great wilderness that stretched beyond. I wondered how often I had sat and marvelled at what great mysteries Blackthorn Forest concealed.

But now there was a new mystery, I thought as I yawned heavily, incapable of comprehending all that had taken place that day.

A seemingly deserted apothecary in a sleepy little village. A tight-knit community of villagers who hid their secrets under the cover of night. A boy and his uncle returning from a family whose roots lay sleeping beneath the cobbles.

THIRTY-FOUR

A sudden illness took hold of Betty the next day resulting in her being absent from the shop. Grandmother greeted me with this news as I stepped through the door at mid-morning. "Honestly, that girl. She shouldn't even have come in yesterday! If you or I catch something now..." Grandmother trailed off, shaking her head. I untied my cloak from around my shoulders and shook off a few autumn leaves before hanging it on the hook next to the door.

"What's wrong with her?" I stepped into the warmth of the cosy room as Grandmother counted a significant sum of money into the till.

"Flu," she replied irritably.

I eyed her busy hands. "They bought all the orbs then?"

"Oh yes! They were so pleased, and it wouldn't have happened if it weren't for you. I do hope you weren't here too late?"

"I got home about nine, but it was fine." I gratefully accepted a steaming mug of tea.

"Bless you. You didn't have to come in today, but saying that, what with Betty ill... Oh!" She jumped up from her stool, and it clattered to the floor. I spilt boiling hot tea over my right hand and winced. When Grandmother operated at full speed, she really was reminiscent of a great steam train derailing in its haste.

"Shit!" I yelled, shaking the remaining tea off my already red hand. She made to walk away from behind the counter, but a tassel from her shawl had got caught in the till, and she bounced back like a puppet. The fact that she had not reprimanded me for my language told me that she really was distracted.

"I need to ask another favour, Luna."

I set down my tea, still smarting from the burn, and sighed. "Only if you do me a favour and calm down!"

Grandmother unhooked her tassel from the mouth of the till and sat back down again on her stool, a sheepish expression on her face. "I'm sorry. I'm just a little flustered. I've got a client coming in ten minutes, and Betty's mother has just left—"

"Why would anybody want 250 orbs anyway?" I asked distractedly, voicing aloud my thoughts from last night.

"Lord knows." Grandmother was baffled by the question. "Perhaps they're teaching a class, or it's for their own stock… but anyway, Luna, that favour?"

"Yes?" I gave in wearily. I thought that I had had a good night's sleep, but Grandmother was quickly proving that wrong.

"Betty's mother can't get time off work to go and get her anything for the flu. The bakery's always slammed on a Sunday. She only just managed to pop in here and let me know that Betty had been throwing up all morning." I frowned. "I promised her that we would get something from the apothecary that she can pick up after work." I had to refrain from telling Grandmother that Betty's mother needn't worry, as the apothecary was open after hours.

"Would you mind popping next door? I'm sure they'd have a tonic or something. Everyone's been raving about that place since it opened yesterday afternoon."

I drank the last of my tea with a gulp as a funny sensation twisted in my stomach. "I can go and get something. I might have to queue though. There was already one when I passed by just now."

Grandmother wasn't even listening and was setting up the cards on her table. I walked into the kitchen and emptied the dregs of my tea into the sink. I pressed a cold towel to the burn on my right wrist. The cold was soothing. I closed my eyes. The thought of going into the apothecary and facing Tristan and his uncle made my stomach squirm. I didn't trust the pair of them, and the only desire I had about the apothecary was to get as far away from it as possible.

When I couldn't put it off any longer, I deposited the towel in the sink with a great sigh and left the kitchen. Grandmother told me to take some money out of the till and Betty's mother would pay us back later. I left my cloak hanging on the hook with the thought of not being gone for very long, and as the next client (a windswept elderly lady) stepped into the shop, I stepped out onto the cobbles.

THIRTY-FIVE

Blackthorn was buzzing. A queue chattered outside the bakery. The bookshop windows opposite were steamed up from the number of browsers in there. I turned to my right, and sure enough, a couple of people stood in a line outside the great glass windows of the apothecary, waiting to get inside.

A cold breeze played about my hair and swept it behind me as I joined the queue and shivered. I shifted impatiently from foot to foot with my arms wrapped around myself, watching the hustle and bustle inside, contemplating how much warmer it would be from the heat of all those bodies. I cursed myself for not bringing the cloak.

The newly refurbished apothecary was a sight to behold. I had to admit that I was impressed at how quickly they had transformed the building into a viable business venture. The dust and grime had been eliminated from the vast windows, and they now sparkled in the sunshine, twinkling at potential customers passing by. I scanned over the various signs and banners out the front that had slogans like:

Got an ailment? We've got the remedy!

Come in for a chat – no problem is too great or small!

Curiosity taking over, I stood on tiptoe to try and peer through the glass, wishing the two people in front of me would move. Bottles had been lined up in the display window, their crystal cases surrounding different coloured liquids, all professing to have solutions for common ailments. Beyond the display, I spied women and children, husbands and wives, families all perusing the shelves chatting to each other and to Isaac, who stood with his hands on his hips, smirking faintly as though unsurprised by the sheer amount of people in his shop. Every now and then he would catch the eye of a passing lady and run his hands through his shoulder-length hair as they moved on, blushing, taking their wares to be purchased. With a sudden jolt I recognised Tristan standing behind the till. I looked away quickly for fear of being spotted.

Five minutes later, a few of Isaac's customers departed the apothecary, leaving room for the couple in front of me and myself to enter the shop. They collared Isaac and disappeared into a little side room that I assumed was being used for confidential discussions. I forced my way further into the shop and was pushed and shoved by the jostling crowd. I gazed up at the shelves and wondered if Betty's mother was after a book entitled *Herbal Remedies for the Soul*, or *How to Make the Most Out of Your Everyday Health*.

I looked around a little despairingly, not knowing what to get, or what it would look like. My gaze ended at the till. The crowd had thinned a little at the back of the shop, and Tristan stood counting money carefully in a spare moment. I hesitated, anxious to ask for his help when he had been so unwilling two nights ago. But I was given little choice when he met my eyes.

I dropped my gaze and walked slowly over to where he stood. I reached the counter and looked up, but before I could open my mouth he began to talk. "I wondered when I'd be seeing you again." A smile played around the corners of his lips as he smirked.

"I..." I frowned and narrowed my eyes. I had never seen him properly in the daylight before; our encounters had always been in the gloom.

His black hair curled thickly on his head, and the electric-blue eyes that had loomed out of the darkness last night were difficult to look into directly. He looked at me through dark lashes, and I swallowed all the words I had ever known. His smirk vanished when I didn't reply, and his jaw set firmly in the expression of mild annoyance I had seen before when leaning out of the upper window. I wasn't sure if it was the set-up of the counter or his height, but to speak to him properly, I had to look up significantly, which irritated me.

"Well, I suppose I could just run away?" I replied eventually, not being able to help the accusatory tone in my voice. There was a pause, and then a wide smile stretched across his golden features. He laughed out loud, laying both of his hands down on the counter so we stood facing each other properly.

"Yeah," he continued. "Sorry about that. I was trying not to scare you, but I realise I probably did the opposite. Can you forgive me?" He traced a line in the engravings on the woodwork and looked down at me.

"Do you have anything for the flu?" I blurted out, avoiding his question.

He looked mildly surprised. "Well, yes, but you don't look very ill, Luna."

"I'm not ill, it's for... How do you know my name?"

"Luna's Luck?" he replied quickly. "I figured you were Luna, right? Plus..." he bent down and moved a little closer before continuing, "I've only been around for a day, but people round here sure love to gossip." He inclined his head behind me with a small smile, and I followed his gaze. Among the crowd of people in the apothecary a bright blond-haired head whipped back around to peer at one of the shelves. George had been watching our exchange.

"Brilliant," I muttered, wondering what on earth that conversation had been about.

"So, do you have anything for the flu or not? Well, actually..." I continued before Tristan could reply, "I'm pretty sure it's a hangover my friend has, but for all intents and purposes, do

153

you have anything for the flu?" I repeated for the third time, sounding slightly ridiculous. He stepped out from behind the counter with a grand flourish.

"Follow me, my lady, for I can grant ye wishes." Slightly bemused, I shook my head and smiled, following him to a nearby shelf. "First," he said grabbing a bottle off the top row with ease, "we take this, and then…" I followed him to a bottom row shelf on the opposite side of the apothecary, "we take this, and…" He looked back at the till. There was no one standing there; everyone was still browsing the shelves. "Follow me."

THIRTY-SIX

He led me into a little side room and closed the door with a snap. The din quietened. I wondered briefly who would be minding the till. He placed both bottles down on the single table and gestured for me to take the seat opposite him. "What on earth are you doing?" I asked, perplexed.

He smiled apologetically. "Sorry, it's just... If my uncle looks in, it has to look like we're having a proper consultation."

"We are having a proper consultation," I insisted, sitting down. I leaned back in the chair and folded my arms, having no idea what was about to happen.

He stood up and rummaged around in his pocket, unearthing a larger bottle than the other two, and placed it before us. "This one," he tapped the first bottle of dark blue liquid, "is to aid symptoms of the flu... and this one," he tapped the second bottle of yellowish liquid with another sweep of his arms, "is to settle the stomach from alcohol-induced upsets... for want of a better phrase. So," he continued and furrowed his dark eyebrows, "together they will cure both what your friend has told their parents they have and what your friend actually has."

He uncorked both bottles and tipped them into the third empty bottle. They swirled together and settled into an emerald colour. I remembered the second amber liquid. "And you're sure one of them wasn't just Arthur's ale from the local pub?" I teased.

He placed his hand over his heart mockingly. "Are you saying you don't trust us?" Before I could reply, he sat back in his chair, and a serious expression passed over his features. "If they weren't safe, we wouldn't be allowed to sell them, I can tell you that much, Luna."

I smiled and nodded appreciatively. "Thank you."

I watched as he sealed the bottle and pushed it slowly across the table towards me. "You're welcome." The low rumble of noise from the room beyond seemed to grow quieter as we looked at each other. "I really am sorry about leaving you in the forest. It was pretty shitty of me in fact, but what were you—" Tristan's question was interrupted by the loud banging of the door behind him. His uncle stood framed in the doorway with a look of indignation on his sharp face. He pushed his greasy hair off his forehead as he glared at us.

"What do you think you're doing in here, boy?"

"I'm with a customer," Tristan replied in an obvious tone.

Isaac's nostrils flared. "You do not carry out private consultations. That is my job. And if this lady..." he eyed me up and down, and I felt a sudden hatred directed towards my seat, "wishes to discuss her medical problems, it is me she needs to talk to." Tristan turned his back on Isaac and rolled his eyes at me.

I stood up quickly. "I think I have everything I need, thank you."

Isaac's presence had brought a sudden chill into the room. I was thankful when he departed again, but not before making another jab at his nephew. "Then make yourself useful and accompany this lady to the till, won't you." He disappeared. Tristan said nothing but forced a smile and gestured for me to leave the room ahead of him. I returned his smile with what must have been something of a concerned stare and found myself surrounded by people again.

"Come on then." Tristan did not seem embarrassed by the encounter and resumed his position by the till. I pointed back vaguely in the direction of the consultation room. "I'm sorry if I—"

"Don't apologise, please. It's not your fault he's like that sometimes." I fiddled with my money as he gently deposited the bottle in my hand. As I accepted the emerald liquid in the palm of my hand I winced quickly as it touched the raw skin on my wrist from my scalding earlier. He stopped and knitted his brows together, suddenly concerned. "And you'll be needing something for that too."

I looked down. "It's nothing, honestly."

He looked at me with that look of annoyance again. "Don't be silly." His voice was muffled as he bent down behind the counter to retrieve something. He placed a tiny tube of ointment on the wooden surface. "Twice a day, and only a small amount... but if you need more then come and find me."

"Well, thank you. How much for everything?"

"On the house." He looked at me seriously. "It's the least I can do."

"Are you sure?" I paused, not wanting him to get into trouble for this too. He hesitated.

"Actually no, it's not the least I can do." He referred to my comment from a few minutes earlier. "Would you accept one of Arthur's ales as an apology for both leaving you in the forest and the behaviour of my uncle today?"

I opened my mouth to reply, not quite sure what I was about to say, when a short bark from his uncle interrupted our conversation. "There's a queue, Tristan!"

I pocketed both the bottle and the ointment and smiled at him. "I think that's my cue."

He sighed and looked over my shoulder. "I'll see you at eight then."

THIRTY-SEVEN

Luna sniffed my hand and bristled with distaste at the unpleasant scent as she settled herself down on the rug in front of me. The ointment Tristan had given me had worked wonders for my burn; the scarlet patch had calmed down, and I felt little to no irritation on the affected area. If Betty's concoction was just as powerful, she wouldn't know how lucky she was. There had been no sign of her all day, and I had endured Grandmother's grumbles until five o'clock when I had left her to continue quibbling about the girl from the comfort of her own armchair. I smiled faintly; Grandmother loved Betty and would be distraught if anything serious happened to her.

On dark evenings like this I couldn't help but think back to the previous hustle and bustle of the cottage, with us all cooking dinner and squabbling about who got the chair in front of the fire. Sighing wistfully, I raised my teacup to my lips, craving something stronger. I looked purposefully at the grandfather clock in the corner and watched as its great hands ticked away. I had one hour to decide if I was going to show my face in Arthur's Tavern.

Luna grew bored of the rug and pounced onto my lap, kneading my legs until she achieved a suitable level of comfort, and rolled over onto her belly to look at me. I scratched her fur absentmindedly until her claws signalled to me that enough was enough, and it was time for a nap. I sipped the rest of my tea wondering if it was a good idea to meet with Tristan or not.

On the one hand, he had been kind to me and had offered tonight as a simple apology for the way that both he and his uncle had behaved. If I didn't turn up it would seem as though I were declining his apology. On the other hand, did I really want to be mixed up with a family like Tristan's who had caused a scandal in Blackthorn before? I didn't trust Isaac, and seeing the way that he had treated his nephew earlier in front of a stranger did nothing but further my disdain towards him. My indecisiveness bothered me; I had always known exactly what I wanted and been confident with the decisions I made. But now I felt different. I didn't have anyone but myself to guide me. I sat for a few moments more until I decided the answer that I think I knew the moment I had been asked the question. After all, I thought as I disturbed Luna and looked about the empty cottage contemplating an evening full of loneliness, what could I possibly have to lose?

Two tired-looking eyes and a bedraggled mess of chestnut hair greeted me when I looked in the mirror upstairs. "Wow," I muttered, grabbing a hairbrush and attacking the haystack before briefly dabbing some concealer under my eyes and pale rouge powder on my cheeks. I rummaged in the top of the wardrobe and unearthed the only lipstick I owned, a crimson tube that I hoped would breathe life into my ghostly complexion. I picked out a navy outfit that I would usually wear for Luna's Luck; this was only a friendly drink after all. As I laced up my long black boots, Luna padded into the bedroom to glare at me from the window seat, as though questioning my decision.

I scratched behind her ear and peered out the dark window. I heard the whoosh of the wind at the panes and decided I'd better wrap up. I grabbed my cloak from off the hook downstairs – thankfully it had dried out from the downpour two nights ago – and knotted the strings tightly around my neck. I fidgeted with my half-moon amulet, rearranging it under my clothing, and decided that that was enough messing around. I collected my things and departed the cottage.

The wind lifted my hair up around my shoulders as I stepped out into the sudden darkness. My boots clicked on the ground as I made my way over to the gate and closed it behind me with a resounding snap. I started on the path to the village. The distant hoot of an owl perched atop a spiky branch of the forest soon faded away, and I entered the eerily quiet square. The only noise sounded from the heels of my boots tapping on the cobbles.

The tavern sat on the right of the village green, and as I approached, the low hum of voices entered my ears. I took a deep breath and pushed open the heavy wooden doors. The booming voice of the proprietor greeted me from behind the bar. Arthur manoeuvred his substantial belly, the result of copious ale and baked delights, and stood facing me with a widening grin upon his moustached features. "Luna! What a lovely surprise. We haven't seen you in a while!" Arthur had been my trusty companion on the dark days when I craved the burn of his famous harsh amber liquid to dull the senses. I looked around for Tristan, aware that I had just drawn attention to myself, but instead met the faces of several villagers who had been disturbed from their evening stupor.

"Hi, Arthur. Yes, I know, the shop's been manic lately! I've had no time to indulge in your ales, but I have the day off tomorrow," I replied with a mischievous smile and sat down on a stool. I rested my elbows on the bar, my feet dangling above the floor, and the elderly man to my right shot me a mistrustful stare.

"And how is the lovely Joan?" Arthur's eyes twinkled; he had a soft spot for my grandmother.

"Same as ever. Always rushing around and won't listen to me when I tell her to put her feet up... We'll have to both come for a drink soon. You're right, it has been a while."

Arthur feigned an expression of utmost disappointment with his wide hand across his heart. "Too long!" he exclaimed and then smiled. "The Redlocks are always welcome in my tavern, you know that."

I lifted my head off my hands and peered at the row of pumps situated in front of the elderly man. He was now eyeing them warily, trying to determine what his next poison was to be, or perhaps trying to remember how many he had consumed. "Ahem…" Arthur cleared his throat awkwardly as I opened my mouth having decided on an ale I hadn't seen before. "I don't mean to intervene, lovely Luna… but I think your drink's already been bought for you." He gave a short nod to his left. I swung my legs across the cushioned stool in the direction of the darkened corner of the tavern he had indicated. Tristan sat alone at a small table in the dingiest corner silently watching our exchange. Two sturdy flagons of ale sat waiting.

THIRTY-EIGHT

"Sweet Siren," Tristan greeted me with as I took the stool opposite. He wore his dark jacket despite the warmth of the fire next to us and leaned back casually against the wood panelling.

I paused, bemused. "Excuse me?"

"Arthur's new brew," he said quickly.

"And is it?" I replied, eyeing the copper liquid that swam in the great tankard before me.

Tristan smiled faintly. "More like Bitter Hag, I think."

I laughed and we raised the flagons simultaneously to our lips. The liquid was chilled, and a fruity, bittersweet flavour hit my taste buds as it trickled down the back of my throat. "Not bad," I considered.

Tristan set down his flagon with a thump and leaned across the table. "I meant what I said about apologising, Luna, I shouldn't have left you in the forest the way I did. And as for my uncle this morning—"

"It's okay," I interrupted, a little embarrassed. "You don't have to apologise for leaving me. It was dark and horrible. You were right to just get out of there. I did the same after you left. As for your uncle..." I trailed off and smiled awkwardly, playing with the handle of my flagon.

Tristan did not return my smile. He seemed to drift to a faraway place as he looked back at his own reflection in the great tankard before him. A dark look passed over his face as he muttered. "My uncle, yes, well, there's nothing that will fix that really…" I raised the pewter absentmindedly to my lips and waited for him to continue. He did not and seemed to be lost in his own blue whirlpools.

"I gather the two of you don't get on then?" I asked, encouraging him into answering me.

Tristan shook his head slightly and grinned. "Sorry, I'm not ignoring you, it's just difficult to know where to start." He took a long gulp of his ale and leaned back in his seat.

I fiddled with the strings of my cloak and, shrugging, said, "I have some time."

He returned my smile with warmth as he looked me up and down. "You look nice, by the way." Before I could reply he launched into conversation. "My parents used to live in Blackthorn when I was little, my uncle too," he added as he set down his half-empty flagon in between us. "Until something happened which made them move away from the village – and from my uncle. I was too young to remember, and whenever I ask Isaac about it he just mumbles and makes some pathetic excuse not to answer." He sighed and looked about the tavern angrily. "I think my dad had an affair or something, but Mum and Dad never talk about it. I guess they just tried to put it behind them."

I put down my ale with a great clunk, spilling some over the edge, surprised that he had divulged such personal information within minutes of our exchange. "That's awful, I'm so sorry." I looked down at the carvings in the table between us and thought about Tristan's suspicions. "Why do you think it was an affair?"

He shrugged and looked into the crackling fire. "What else could it be for them never to talk about it? My uncle is clearly embarrassed by whatever my father did. They always had a strange relationship. If my dad did something my uncle didn't agree with, he would have made it known. My uncle shows up years later saying he's planning on moving back to Blackthorn and asking if I want to learn the family business. Well, I jumped at the idea, thought I could make something of myself... but ever since we've been back, he's just treated me like shit." I gave Tristan a sympathetic look, and he shook his head. "Anyway, what about you? The fortune-telling shop belongs to your grandmother, right? And, Luna..." Tristan raised his dark eyebrows at me, "are you going to ask for my help or are you going to keep struggling with that all night?"

I blushed. For the past five minutes or so I had been silently working at the tightly knotted strings on my cloak. The heat from the fire and the finished tankard of ale had warmed me through considerably, and I had been having some difficulty untying myself. "I didn't want to interrupt you." I laughed quietly. "Would you mind?"

"Of course not." Tristan rose from the table and removed his own jacket with ease to reveal a tightly fitted navy top. I had a feeling he had chosen that shirt on purpose, and I looked away from the way it clung to his muscles as he approached. I reminded myself that this was nothing more than an apology drink.

Grandmother did not trust the Brewers, and I had no reason to doubt her. I looked down at my empty tankard. But I had drunk the apology drink, I thought, so what now? His head brushed the top of the low tavern as I stood up, and he gently span me around on the spot. I tried to ignore the tingle that ran down my spine as skin touched skin and he rearranged my hair to one side. He untied the knot with a little difficulty. "Jesus Christ, what have you done here?" I laughed and glanced towards the bar. It had filled up, and I couldn't see Arthur behind the crowd. Tristan handed me back my cloak and disappeared into the crowd. I shook my hair down my back and fidgeted with my amulet. I sat down again and tapped my fingernails impatiently on the table. We had so much to talk about.

THIRTY-NINE

Tristan arrived back at the table in record time with two more ales, and I looked towards the bar. I was sure there had been people before him in the queue. "I know," he said, seeing my expression. "You really are a favourite of Arthur's."

"I think it's more my grandmother," I replied, and then remembered his previous question. "You're right, the shop does belong to her, but how did you know that?"

Tristan looked away, a little humiliated, and brushed an invisible fleck of dirt off his shirt. "I may have done a little digging when I arrived." He looked in Arthur's direction. I could see his face bobbing up and down in between customers with his red cheeks puffed out as he poured a short drink of clear liquid into four goblets. I shook my head in amusement, and then my smile faded. I sighed and thought I'd better get the inevitable out of the way.

"I'm sorry if you're looking for a happier family history than yours, but you're not going to find it with me. Both of my parents died a year ago," I stated bluntly. "An accident in the woods."

I met Tristan's eye as he sat up straight and stuttered for words. "It's okay." I interrupted his stammers. "I still have Grandmother. She's been brilliant over the years." Suddenly, Tristan leaned over the table and put his hand on top of mine. It was warm, and a buzz of energy travelled up my arm as he looked at me seriously. "If there's anything I can do, Luna, just let me know, okay?" I was grateful for his sincerity, and for the first time since I had met Tristan, he appeared humble. He didn't probe further about their death.

I gently removed his hand, picked up the handle next to it, and drained half the tankard of ale. "Hmm," I said as the fizz travelled through me. "Sweet Siren's definitely growing on me."

"I can tell." Tristan grinned and copied me. "So do you live with your grandmother then?"

"Not anymore, no. She lives above the shop, I think she's quite happy there, and I have the cottage on the edge of the woods."

"By yourself?"

"Yes."

"Doesn't it get lonely?"

I hesitated and then shrugged off his question. "Sometimes, but I have Luna." Tristan blinked a couple of times, wondering if he'd misheard, and decided he hadn't.

"You have who now?"

"Luna," I repeated with a smile. "My tabby cat. She belonged to Grandmother, and now she's mine."

Tristan shuddered a little. "I've never really liked cats. Don't trust them..." I glared at him. He smiled. He raised his arms in a sweeping motion, reminiscent of when he had directed me to the bottles in the apothecary, and winked. "I'm sorry if I have offended you, my lady..." He paused and met my eye quickly. "I'm sure if I met her I'd love her." I leaned back in my chair, shaking my head with a small smile, before becoming distracted by the sound of a man's loud voice at the bar. Tristan looked toward the bar for a few seconds. His face fell. "Ah shit."

The sky outside the tiny windows had grown pitch black. The tavern was dimly lit with flickering candles. I squinted across the dingy room and identified the disturber of the peace. Tristan's uncle, Isaac, sat perched atop a stool. The crowd had thinned out around him, and a few couples had eagerly scooted across to the tables instead.

He took his hand out of one of the pockets of his brown jacket and swept his wavy hair from his face. "What do you mean there's none left?" He was sneering at Arthur's befuddled expression, who stood with a dirty glass in one hand and a crystal decanter in the other, midway in forgetting which job he was doing first.

"Begging your pardon, sir, but it's been drunk dry! Been the most popular tonight." Arthur swung his belly across to the pumps, narrowly avoiding smashing the decanter across Isaac's face as he jumped back on his stool and almost toppled over. He glanced around, as though suddenly angry that anyone had seen this, and caught my eye. I started and checked my watch to look away (was it really nine o'clock already?) but it was too late; Isaac had spied us both and did a double-take as he noticed me staring.

He raised his chin and made no effort to acknowledge his nephew. "I'm sure we've got something here you would prefer, eh?" Arthur distracted him, a pleading look in his eye, gesturing towards his other ales. "Old Pale Hen, or perhaps a Goblin's Hops?" It took Isaac a couple of seconds to realise that Arthur was not insulting him and was in fact offering him different ales.

"Must be little brother syndrome." Tristan shot me a wry smile as we both looked away from the bar at the same time.

"How much older is your father?" I enquired as I glanced down at the fizzing liquid before me, feeling a little guilty.

"Only a year," Tristan replied. "But I think it was always something that bugged Isaac. Dad was the first to do everything, and whenever his younger brother achieved something, it was never as big a deal. Do you have any brothers or sisters?" We bonded over the fact that both of us were only children. "Looks like they're more trouble than they're worth," Tristan noted dryly as he glanced towards the bar again.

Tristan was more of a talker and I more of a listener, but conversation flowed easily between us, as did Arthur's ales, and

I had consumed my third tankard along with a small goblet of amber liquid slipped slyly onto the table by Arthur's generous hand while we were engrossed in each other's words. The bar began to empty. We talked about what Tristan's parents had told him of Blackthorn and how much of it remained the same, how the night we met he had been gathering ingredients from the forest for his uncle's herbal remedies, and even a few memories of my mum and dad cropped up, which made me smile. He made it easy to talk about them, easier than George ever had, but I quickly pushed this thought out of my head and tried to focus on the words that were coming out of Tristan's mouth and not his candle-lit features. He stopped mid-sentence and leaned across the table. "Luna? Have I lost you?"

I blinked a couple of times and smiled. "Sorry, I haven't drunk this much in a while..." I admitted as I checked my watch. I saw two of them without registering the time. "And it's getting pretty late so—"

"Me neither," Tristan hiccupped and slumped in his seat as he ignored my last comment. He pushed his empty tankard away (perhaps his fourth?) and looked me in the eyes, his a little blurry. I struggled to focus on the electric blue, but perhaps for a different reason. He didn't say anything for a little while, expression serious, and then cleared his throat and looked away as though he had been caught doing something he shouldn't.

A cold draught snaked its way around the tavern every now and then as more and more people slunk away into the night and home to their warm beds. "Are you hungry?" Tristan asked suddenly, and this time I checked my watch properly.

"Tristan, it's almost eleven..." I looked quickly to the bar and refocused for a couple of seconds. "I'm pretty sure Arthur is closing up the bar."

He smiled as I said his name. "Must have lost track of time, sorry." He registered the pile of empty drinking vessels on the table. "Maybe another time, eh?"

I was saved the embarrassment of answering by Isaac's loud departure as he shouted over in our direction. "Eight o'clock tomorrow, Tristan, and don't be late!" Several heads turned as the heavy doors crashed shut behind him and I tried to make myself look as small as possible.

Tristan's face grew serious, his expression sobering. "What's wrong?" I asked in a quiet voice. "Apart from the fact that you have work tomorrow." He smiled his half-smile at me, the one where he tried to pretend he wasn't smiling at all.

"I don't trust him, you know, Isaac." I remained silent. He sat up straight with unexpected urgency. I had to lean in to hear his hushed voice. "He's been disappearing into the forest for the past couple of days and..." Tristan glanced over my shoulder, "he keeps a locked room upstairs in the apothecary. He's told me I'm forbidden from going in."

I gulped as a sudden vision of a cloaked figure clutching a hidden package shone like a bright light in my mind. Should I mention anything? Before I could consider, Tristan stood up and gestured for me to follow, picking up my cloak which lay abandoned on the bench next to him. "I don't want to keep you out too late, Luna, and that's enough serious talk for me." He handed me my cloak, and I knotted it again with a little difficulty as he watched me. "Thanks Arthur, you've been a fantastic host." Tristan turned to look over his shoulder as I waved back at an exhausted-looking face wiping the bar with a rather dirty rag. "He looks like he needs a good night's sleep," Tristan whispered in my ear as he opened the door out into the night.

169

FORTY

My giggle was stifled by the bone-chilling frost that had settled over Blackthorn like an uncomfortable blanket. "I miss that fire now," I moaned as I turned to Tristan outside the doors. I realised that I'd never actually asked him where he lived, and dithered on the spot. He noticed my awkwardness.

"My uncle's house is that way, and is unfortunately where I'm staying."

"My cottage is that way." I pointed in the opposite direction as he squinted through the darkness. "Just outside of the village and towards the forest."

"Come on then." Tristan didn't hesitate as he started walking. "I'll get you home."

"Oh there's no need really," I protested. "Get yourself home and get warm."

"That place is no home to me, but honestly, I'd prefer to walk you to your cottage. It's cold and dark. I'd only be worrying otherwise." I smiled to myself and neglected to mention that I was no stranger to walking Blackthorn at night, not to mention the deep expanse of the forest too.

We walked side by side, shivering at harsh gusts of wind, moving closer to each other so the fabric of my cloak brushed his jacket every so often. The path to the cottage was pitch black, and we had to pick up our feet to avoid dragging the leaves we couldn't see. The crunch of the frozen leaves filled the silence as

I struggled with my internal dilemma. I had to tell him; after all, I trusted Tristan a lot more than I trusted Isaac.

"Tristan, there's something I have to tell you," I said eventually, slowing my pace despite the chill.

"Oh yeah?" he replied, a tone of expectancy in his voice.

"I saw people going into the apothecary last night after you left. They used a side door in the alleyway and not the main entrance... I-I only noticed because I was working late for Grandmother, polishing about a million orbs for her." I rushed my words, not wanting him to think I was snooping, but he listened intently. "I saw someone leave, and they were clutching some kind of package. I didn't see who it was or what they were carrying, but it definitely came from the apothecary. All the lights were off so it didn't look like there was anyone inside."

Tristan did not reply but slowed to a snail's pace. "Look, I don't want to make things worse with your uncle or interfere in what you're doing... but I thought you ought to know – what with everything you've said about Isaac tonight." I hesitated, wondering if it was acceptable for me to say my next comment. Arthur's ale urged me on. "I think he's selling something secret to the villagers that he can't legitimately sell in the day. I don't trust him either."

There was a brief silence while Tristan contemplated my words. I grew fearful that I had said too much. I looked up at his face in the darkness wishing I could see it. "Thank you for telling me, Luna," he said in a low voice, and I breathed out. "He said he was going to rearrange some shelves around after closing, and as for the side door, well, I noticed it but he said it wasn't in use." Tristan put one foot in front of the other, and I followed. "I bet it's whatever's in that locked room," he whispered into the night, and I nodded, forgetting he couldn't see me.

The orange lights from my cottage approached, and we said no more on the subject. "Well, I can see why you like it here on the edge of the forest," Tristan remarked as his eyes took in the cottage from the lights in the windows.

"Yes." I smiled. "Thank you for tonight, Tristan," I said sincerely. "It's been… different."

He looked down at me and cocked his head. "And is different good?"

I shook my head, thinking I should have used a different word, and then nodded as he looked disappointed at my mixed signals. "Yes, it's good," I clarified, laughing. "It's been nice to talk to someone who doesn't look at me like a broken little girl."

"I don't think you're a broken little girl, far from it, in fact."

We stood in the moonlight in front of the little cottage as Tristan leaned across me slowly, the breeze ruffling his curls. My heart jumped a little before I realised that he was untying the strings on my cloak again. "Just in case," he whispered with a smile. He undid the latch on the cottage gate with a deft movement. "Goodnight, Luna." He turned away with a strange expression and disappeared into the darkness.

"Goodnight," I called out and stood for a few seconds in the pale white light. I shook out the leaves that had dragged underneath the bottom of my cloak, opened the gate and walked unsteadily up the path. Luna mewed for me as her furry body rippled in the sudden cold.

Despite the grandfather clock warning me that the hour grew late, I had the inclination to sit up for a while, so I lit a fire in the grate and searched for one of my father's books. I clumsily set a glass of water on the table above me, and some of it slopped over the edge. Sitting cross-legged on the rug behind Luna I opened the creaky spine of my favourite fairy tales. After a few moments I tossed the book aside with a sigh and stared absentmindedly into the blazing heat with a small smile. I no longer wanted to immerse myself in the grizzly tales of bloodshed and battle, or to fear the wolf's eyes as they lit up the trees, and especially did not want to pine with the princesses who lay waiting for their princes to rescue them.

I sat long into the night watching the red-hot flames leap and dance in the grate like playful children, their woes forgotten, their futures burning bright ahead of them.

FORTY-ONE

I awoke the next morning in a cold sweat and tried to extricate myself from the twisted bed sheets. Opening and closing my eyes a couple of times, I swallowed against sandpaper, my head drooping like a melon. I gazed blearily out of my bedroom window. The forest was being freshly doused in rainfall plummeting hard onto its treetops. The banging I had heard in my dreams sounded again.

Three booming knocks against the cottage door rattled the windows. I sat up straighter, wild thoughts of Tristan running through my head, standing outside in the downpour waiting for me. But no, I reasoned with myself as I pulled on my dressing gown, there was no reason for him to call. The unknown knocker struck again with increasing urgency. I had half a mind to shout downstairs that they ought to rein in their knocks and practise common courtesy.

Grabbing onto the wooden banister, I jumped the last three steps into the hallway, and there came a quick succession of five knocks in a row upon the front door. "Okay, okay, I'm coming!" I shouted hoarsely and fumbled with the latch. A figure in a navy-blue raincoat barged their way in before I could open the door fully. They shook their umbrella out all over the floor, and I grimaced. "Well, fancy leaving your own grandmother standing out in the rain like that!" Her exclamation was not a welcoming sound to my sore head. I tugged my dressing gown tighter about me in the draught that had entered with her.

She turned around to face me as she unbuttoned her long coat and hung it up. I saw her eyes rove over my bedraggled hair, bare feet and heavy eyes. "Goodness gracious, did I wake you?" she said with a trace of amusement and bustled her way into the kitchen. "Seeing as you haven't offered me a cup of tea, I shall put a pot on myself." She eyed me up and down disapprovingly. "Unless you'd like something stronger of course?"

I groaned and walked into the living room. "Good morning, Grandmother." No sooner had the words escaped my lips than the clock in the corner chimed midday. "Shit."

"What was that?" Grandmother poked her head around the corner.

"Nothing." I sat in a chair and tried to make out as though I hadn't just woken up and was now facing the consequences of too much ale and not enough sleep. Grandmother carried a tray heavily laden with cups, saucers and delicacies and set it down in front of me with an innocent smile. My stomach churned. She made herself at home in the armchair opposite me and fixed me with a hard stare.

"Late night?" I avoided the question by reaching for two cups on the tray. Her eyes scanned over my cloak tossed carelessly onto the rug, the spilt glass of water on the little table and my father's book that lay with its spine open on the floor. "Luna." She cleared her throat. Her irises danced sapphire and emerald, and I could have sworn that a slight hint of ruby fire flashed in their circles as she pursed her lips. "I don't want you hanging around with that Brewer boy. I don't trust them."

I dropped one of the teacups and chipped the handle. "Word travels fast," I replied dryly and stirred the pot with a great sigh.

"Luna!" Grandmother reproached me for my tone. I carried the other teacup over to her and placed it in her hands. She narrowed her eyes in clear distaste for my hungover condition. I sat back down opposite her.

175

"I'm sorry, but I don't think it's anyone else's business who I choose to spend time with." The words came out more severely than I had anticipated, and the ruby fire I had spied a few moments earlier erupted. The lava spat out of her in a long chain of protest.

"How dare you! I am your grandmother, Luna. I know you're not as young as you used to be but by God you're still a Redlock, and if your father were here…" She paused as she took an aggressive sip of tea and tried to tame the wildfire. "You shouldn't be mixed up in a family like that—"

"Like what?" I interrupted as my head pounded. "A family like what, Grandmother?"

"They were involved in a scandal!"

"A scandal where no one even knows what happened! Tristan doesn't even—"

"The Brewers are bad news! I have my reasons for not trusting them and so does half the village."

A stagnant silence fell in the cottage and the downpour outside eased. I sighed and looked at Grandmother, hoping that she would see reason. "You don't even know them."

"And neither do you," she snapped back. I looked down at the chipped teacup and fiddled with the handle, contemplating if it could be fixed, or if it was simply too broken and ought to be thrown away. I met Grandmother's eyes and swallowed. Her features softened as she set her cup down.

"You know that I only want the best for you, don't you?" When I didn't reply she took this as an opportunity to gather velocity. "I think that boy and his uncle are best left alone to their apothecary. Mark my words, if there's been a scandal in the past there will be another, and I'd sooner turn in my grave than see you involved in anything like that. There's a reason their family left Blackthorn, Luna, and whatever it was, it can't be good. You're better off away from them."

Grandmother finished her tea and stood up, indicating that her untimely visit was almost at an end. She fixed me square in the eyes and I blinked. "I need you to promise me that you'll stay away from them – that you won't allow yourself to be involved in that family. Will you do that for me?" Feeling like it was easier to appease her than fight with her, I nodded weakly, and she seemed satisfied.

"Very well."

All pretence left her, and she indicated the pastries and sandwiches she had not touched. "Eat, Luna. You look pale." She swept out of the living room, buttoned up her coat and reacquainted herself with the fog of Blackthorn.

FORTY-TWO

The door closed on our frosty exchange. I laid my head upon the table and took a few deep breaths. The smell of the food beside me made me both queasy and ravenous. I couldn't remember when I'd last eaten. I warily reached for a sandwich and took a bite. The beast of hunger reared its head, and I demolished most of what Grandmother had left. Feeling slightly more like a human being, I took myself upstairs and into the bathroom, feeling that now my cage had been rattled I may as well get washed and dressed.

I thought of Tristan with a pang of sympathy; he had consumed more of Arthur's ale than I and now had to endure working with Isaac all day. There was some truth in what Grandmother had said, and I felt suddenly regretful. How could I have let myself get carried away like that? I had spoken about Grandmother, about my parents; we had confided in each other and yet we barely knew each other. Except, I felt as though we did know each other; Tristan was so easy to get on with that I felt as though I had known him for years. The hot water trickling down my back, and the fresh scent of washed hair did me a world of good, and as I dressed into my day clothes, I contemplated Grandmother's warning.

Grandmother happened to be annoyingly correct about a lot of things. Yes, the Brewer family was surrounded with gossip and rumours, and yes, I was a Redlock and ought to know better than to go chasing trouble… but being a Redlock meant more to me than that. My parents had taught me to follow my instincts – to trust in myself. There was no denying that Isaac was a rotten apple in both demeanour and back-alley transactions. But the fact that Tristan had voiced aloud his mistrust of Isaac forced me to arrive at the conclusion that they could not be formed out of the same crooked mould. My half-hearted promise to Grandmother was one that I had little intention of keeping. I had been backed into a corner and felt that her personal prejudices were not enough of a reason for me to avoid the Brewers. I was not intent upon actively getting involved in their lives; their business was their own. But I felt as though I'd be a poor human being if I avoided someone based on events in their past, and most of all, events they had no control over. Tristan could not change his parents' past any more than I could change mine.

As I dragged the hairbrush through my curls, the effects of the Sweet Siren began to wear off, and I scratched behind Luna's ears as she sat on the bed watching me. I had made up my mind. I was going to try and find out more about the Brewers without having to talk to them. That way I could momentarily keep my promise to Grandmother and satisfy my own morbid curiosity.

Blackthorn's bookstore held records of every family that had come and gone in the village. If Tristan's family had once lived here there must be records of them. The only problem would be getting Delilah to divulge the records. This, however, was more of a problem for snoopers other than me; Delilah was George's mother and always had a soft spot where I was concerned. She also happened to be the owner of the bookstore and therefore the protector of potentially sensitive information. Delilah Fallow had written her own extensive history of Blackthorn. I could see in my mind's eye the thick book that adorned the misty windows of the bookshop.

The bell tinkled as I stepped across the threshold and picked up a copy of *An Extensive History of Blackthorn's Bloodlines*, by D. Fallow. The real D. Fallow smiled wholeheartedly at me and paused in stacking a shelf behind her with copies of *Herbal Remedies for the Soul*, by M. I. Hawthornthwaite, emblazoned across the front in glittering letters. I groaned. Blackthorn's newfound fad for everything apothecarial had charmed its way into the village bookshop too.

Delilah smiled at me before an expression of confusion spread across her familiar features as I slammed all 924 pages of her masterpiece down on the counter. She tucked her mousy brown bob behind her ears. "Luna," she said as she picked up her book, "in all the many years I have known you, you have not once expressed any interest in reading this hefty old thing. Why change the habit of a lifetime?"

"I'm looking to expand my knowledge," I replied with a small smile. Delilah almost dragged me over the counter as she pulled me into a bear hug.

"It's so good to see you!" she exclaimed as I smiled into the comforting folds of her soft jumpers that I had confided into many times before.

"How have you been?" I hesitated, thinking back to the last time I had seen George's mother, a couple of weeks ago in passing on the street. She had been with her son, and I had not wanted to linger despite the good nature between all of us.

"I'm doing well, thanks. I hope you are too." I pulled away from her hug and stepped back with a smile. I inclined my head in the direction of the shelf above her. "I see they're all after those kinds of books now?" Delilah widened her eyes and leaned closer.

"I've never seen anything like it. They're flying off the shelves. We're a village obsessed!" She laughed and then her look darkened. "Although Mr Brewer doesn't approve of my selling the same books as he does at a cheaper price..." She said Isaac's name with an air of distaste as though recounting a past unpleasant meeting with the man. I could certainly imagine how that had gone down.

Delilah put her book back down on the counter with a thud and eyed me suspiciously. "So what are you really doing with this thing?" I played with the loose strings of my cloak remembering how she was never one to beat about the bush. I resigned myself to the knowledge that I would not be able to hide my intentions from this woman even if I tried. I swallowed.

"I'm looking for some information about a family that have recently moved to Blackthorn."

Delilah glanced over my shoulder and smiled at a man who had just entered the bookshop. "Let me know if you need any help, Philip!"

"Oh, just browsing today." The man flashed her a charming smile and turned back to the shelves.

She focused her attention on me and darted her eyes down at the great book that lay before us. Her voice lowered. "You won't find any information on the Brewers in there, Luna."

"I-I-" I stood for a few seconds spewing forth gibberish until Delilah saved me from myself.

"You think you're the only one to come looking? An uncle and his nephew move back here after a mysterious scandal, manage to set up a brand spanking new apothecary in one day, and you think no one else in Blackthorn is intrigued to know why?"

I looked at her dumbfounded and felt a little sheepish that I had forgotten Blackthorn's obsession with gossip; of course I was not the only one who had come to Delilah for information she didn't have. Delilah resumed her stacking of the shelves. "I'd never even heard of the Brewers until they arrived a few days ago." She shrugged as she placed the last copy on the end of the shelf and turned back to me. "For some reason they were just… kept out of all the old records. I'm sorry, Luna, I can't help you."

FORTY-THREE

I looked down at *An Extensive History of Blackthorn's Bloodlines* with a disheartened sigh; if Delilah couldn't help me, it was unlikely that anybody else could. The little bell above the door sounded its pleasant tinkle, and she looked up. With one deft movement, she swept the book off the side, and tucked it out of sight beneath the counter. She gave me a look of warning.

"Mrs Fallow! What say you and I put our differences aside and for a significant sum of money you have this manuscript bound for me in your finest leather by this time tomorrow?" Isaac's voice boomed with invisible waves of self-importance that bounced off the spines of the books. I kept my back to him for fear of being recognised, although my crimson cloak probably gave me away, and continued to peruse the shelves with little interest as I eavesdropped on their conversation.

Delilah greeted him coldly and explained that she would struggle to have his manuscript bound to his level of perfection in so little time. "I wouldn't like to disappoint you, Mr Brewer."

I smirked at the books as he tried to persuade her with an even larger sum of money. As I listened to their bargaining, my attention was momentarily drawn to a large book bound in black leather directly in front of me. There was no lettering on the spine, which I thought odd. I ran my fingertip along the edge, expecting to feel the odd bump from where the old title had worn away perhaps, but found it to be smooth and unmarked. Lifting it off the shelf with a little difficulty, I turned it over in my hands. An elaborate golden padlock engraved with strange markings enclosed the pages within. I rotated the tiny key in the lock, dubious if it would work, and to my surprise it clicked open. I flipped through the pages. The book was blank. Each page was lined, expectant, as though waiting eagerly for someone to fill in the story. Why would Delilah be selling an empty book? I locked the curious book and placed it back up on the shelf, thinking that I would ask her about it later, and tuned in to their conversation, which seemed to be coming to an end.

"Very well," Delilah agreed as I heard the clink of coins hit the counter. "This time tomorrow." She looked at her wristwatch as if for clarification. "Half past two."

Isaac departed the bookshop in silence, and the tinkle of the bell seemed duller than normal as he stepped out onto the cobbles. I eyed the large handwritten copy on the front counter, and Delilah gave me a reproachful look as she read my mind. "Don't even think about it, Luna."

"Oh come on," I teased her. "Just one little look?" She looked at the manuscript intently for a few seconds as though trying to see through into its contents. She chuckled suddenly.

"I can easily bind this old thing in a couple of hours, but I was never going to tell him that."

I looked about the empty bookshop. The other man had left without buying anything, and in the sudden silence I was struck by a thought. A wild, dangerous thought, but one that could potentially reveal the answers I was seeking. I spoke slowly. "Then technically... you don't need that manuscript until tomorrow morning..."

Delilah furrowed her brows and then, "No way, Luna! What if anyone finds out?"

"Who's going to know?" Perhaps I was chancing my luck in thinking that Delilah would loan me the manuscript for the evening; Delilah was, after all, not a dishonest woman.

"I could lose my job." She fidgeted with her woolly jumper and toyed with the edges of the thick papers. I looked at her blankly.

"You own this bookshop. Who is going to fire you?" My smile faded as she looked at me, and I could see the internal struggle taking place inside her brain.

"What if someone finds out, Luna?" she whispered. I fixed her with a hard stare and raised my eyebrows.

"No one is going to find out."

Leaving the bookshop with a grin on my face, I readjusted my cloak to ensure that no one would notice the bulky package beneath, and made a beeline for the apothecary opposite. I had clocked Isaac turning towards the forest on his departure a couple of minutes earlier. He evidently had business to attend to elsewhere. I spied Tristan through the sparkling glass window conversing with a middle-aged man whom Isaac had employed part time. I had been informed of this man's ineptitude last night when Tristan suggested alternative uses for his lack of brains.

Tristan pointed at something, and the man looked perplexed. Tristan pointed again in earnest, and the man hurried over to a lady who stood dithering in the middle of the apothecary, clearly searching for an object she was having difficulty locating. Tristan ran his hands through his dishevelled hair, propped his head up as he leant his elbows on the tall counter and looked out through bleary eyes. His right elbow slipped off the side of the counter as I walked in. He fiddled with a loose curl that had slipped over his eye.

"You look awful." I smirked, looking up at him with a wry smile. He shot me a look of good-natured annoyance.

"And you look like you've actually had a good night's sleep."

"Far from it," I muttered and glanced over my shoulder. Tristan picked up on my unease and lowered his voice.

"I wasn't expecting to see you so soon. What's wrong?"

"Has your uncle told you anything about an old manuscript?" I was taking a huge risk here. If Tristan knew about Isaac's papers then I would look as though I was poking my nose in a great big vial of something better left alone. But something told me that Isaac wanted to keep this manuscript a secret.

Tristan blinked a couple of times through his bloodshot eyes. The rusty cogs whirred at a slower velocity than usual. "A what now?"

"A manuscript," I repeated impatiently, trying to avoid revealing what was underneath my cloak in the middle of the apothecary. I stood on tiptoes, and Tristan bent down, confused. I whispered into his ear, trying immensely hard to ignore the closeness of our exchange, and explained how Isaac had dropped off an ancient-looking manuscript and how I now had ownership of it for one evening. Tristan's eyes widened in sudden understanding.

"Well, I can't take it from you now. What if he comes back? I've got nowhere to hide it. I'll come over later and have a look. You're right, it might explain his secret trips into the forest and give us a clue as to what he's up to."

Before I could protest that Tristan had just invited himself over to my cottage for the evening, the disgruntled-looking lady approached the front counter, complaining that the man still hadn't pointed her in the right direction and that if she needed to go elsewhere to purchase her wart cream then she would most certainly do that. Tristan shot me a despairing look. I gave him a half-smile and turned on the spot, departing the apothecary as my cloak swept over the floorboards, still concealing the collection of yellowed papers out of sight.

FORTY-FOUR

I strode from one side of the living room to the other. Frequently glancing at the grandfather clock, I grew more impatient by the minute, and the flames from the fire danced shadows across the dimly lit walls. The pale sun had shrunk into its bed for the night, and the clock struck eight as the wind battered the cottage gate. I heard a faint creak as it swung open on its hinges and once again reminded myself that it needed fixing.

Tristan and I had not agreed a time, and the possibility of him appearing at any moment rendered me somewhat restless. The manuscript lay on the little table on which Grandmother had taken her tea that very morning. I grimaced as I imagined what she would say if she knew that I had invited one of the Brewers over. If we were focusing on technicalities, I thought as I eyed the manuscript uneasily, Tristan had invited himself over. What choice had I been given? I couldn't exactly open the collection in the middle of the apothecary.

I pulled at the sleeves of my thick navy dress as goose bumps erupted across the back of my neck. An unusual chill had settled over the cottage. This matter could usually be resolved by lighting a fire in the grate, however this time was different. I felt as though a strange sort of energy buzzed about the room, and as I snuck another suspicious glance at the manuscript, I couldn't help but suspect that it was the source of the glacial atmosphere.

My search for warmer garments became inconsequential as one short knock at the door sounded. Luna looked at me, as though suddenly affronted that I had not warned her of possible company, and padded over to the rug by the fire. I froze in the hallway for a few seconds contemplating the best way to greet him when I opened the door. Another knock ended my indecisiveness. I unlocked the door.

"You're as impatient as my grandmother, you know!" I exclaimed irritably to two electric-blue orbs that widened in the dark.

"She's not here, is she?" Tristan peered up at my front window. I laughed at his sudden fear.

"No, I just meant… Oh, never mind—"

"I was afraid you might not be in. I know that we didn't agree a time, and I'm sorry I sort of invited myself over… but I needed to see… what's in that manuscript…" Tristan struggled to formulate proper sentences. He dithered on the spot until I opened the door wider.

"Come in." He stepped inside.

Tristan retrieved a small bottle from his deep pockets and handed it over as he hung his coat up on the hook. I eyed the periwinkle liquid mistrustfully, unscrewed the cap and took a tentative sniff. Tristan laughed heartily and took the bottle back as he walked into the kitchen. "I promise it's safe." He looked around for some glasses. "It's only elderberry juice. I bought it from the lady who lives next door. She has a whole garden of them and makes her own." I watched him move about my kitchen, opening and closing cupboards, pouring out the liquid as a small smile played about my lips. He turned around and handed me one of the glasses. "In all honesty…" he looked me up and down a little sheepishly, "I think I overdid it last night."

"You think?" I mocked him as I raised the glass to my lips. The elderberry juice was sweet and refreshing – the perfect cure for a headache. "It's delicious, thank you."

"No problem. I'm sorry I'm here so late, Luna. If I'm honest with you, I, er…" he ran his hand through his hair before grinning at me, "I fell asleep. Isaac wasn't in the best of states this morning either, but I haven't seen him since you said he disappeared into the forest this afternoon."

"Well, you can stop apologising to me and come and look at this manuscript." I directed him into the living room. "I know it was wrong of me to take it, and I hope that you don't think less of me for doing it, but I thought it might give you some answers about your uncle."

Tristan set his glass down on the table and walked over to me. He bent down slightly to look directly into my eyes. Looking soberly at me he said, "I am very thankful that you are so good at snooping on my uncle." He cracked a smile as he reached the end of his sentence and almost got his drink spilt all over the floor. He gently grabbed the end of my sleeve and then down to my hand. My fingers tingled at the sudden contact, but his smile faded.

"Seriously, I do appreciate this. I have a right to know what secrets he's keeping." I nodded slowly and then looked down at our fingers that had interlaced with each other. Tristan looked down suddenly as well, but not at our hands, at his own feet. Luna sniffed his boots distastefully as she snaked her way around his ankles, arching her back every now and then as she looked up, her glowering eyes wide. Tristan let go of my hand to bend down and scratch her tabby fur. Before he could pet her, she leapt onto the armchair. She kneaded the fabric of the chair, eyeing Tristan all the while, and curled her bushy tail around herself as she settled down with a look of satisfaction. Tristan blinked and looked away from Luna as she maintained her hard stare in his direction. He exhaled slowly. I laughed and went over to stroke Luna's head as she pushed up against me and started to purr. "She's very protective of you," Tristan said.

"We sort of look after each other." I sighed and sat down on the rug in front of the fire.

Tristan picked up the old manuscript with care and joined me on the floor. We sat cross-legged facing each other. "Why would he want this old thing binding anyway? It looks ancient."

"I don't know," I murmured as I watched him thumb through the pages.

"It's cold," he remarked, pressing one of the pages in between his hands. "Feels like it's been left outside in the frost," he muttered as he continued to inspect the outside of it.

"I know," I agreed with him. "I thought it was just me at first, but it feels colder in here than usual."

Tristan looked up at me suddenly. "Have you opened it?"

"No," I replied instantly, and he looked apologetic.

"Not that it would matter if you did," he clarified. "I just wondered if you'd looked in it already."

"I didn't..." I was going to say steal, but that would not have been the correct word, "I didn't acquire it for me to look at."

"I know," he said softly, and bit his lip, looking down at the yellowing pages. He paused and stared at me intently. I fidgeted with the locket round my neck. As though coming to a sudden decision he placed the manuscript on the rug in between us and opened the first page.

I expected a contents page or something to that effect, but when I peered closer I had to blink a couple of times to fathom what I was looking at. A series of strange symbols scattered the old paper. Hand drawn in black ink, they were spiky and confusing, having no clear pattern across the page. I tilted my head to the side, trying to make sense of them, thinking perhaps that they were drawings. Circles, triangles and lines erratically interspersed with each other, and after a couple of minutes I sighed and shook my head. I may as well have been looking at ancient hieroglyphics.

I studied Tristan's face as he stared at the page and his eyes darted back and forth. His brows knitted together. I waited patiently for him to finish studying the symbols and say something. He looked up at me, as though surprised I had lost interest so soon. "Have you read it?" I stared at him in bewilderment, and after a minute or so he grew a little embarrassed. I cleared my throat and pointed down at the page.

"You can read this?" The wind whooshed by outside in the silence as Tristan blinked back at me in confusion.

"Can't you?"

"No!" I exclaimed, pulling the page towards me as he continued to look perplexed. "Are we looking at the same thing?" I pointed to three markings together and traced the shapes with my finger. "They're just weird symbols! They're not even words!"

Tristan shifted his position on the rug, leaning closer to look at the page, and swallowed uncomfortably. He raised his head and looked at me. "Most of them look just like normal words to me. Granted, they don't make much sense, but yes, I can read some of them."

"Tristan, if you're teasing me again—"

"I'm not, Luna, I swear it." I couldn't take my eyes off his blue whirlpools and felt as though I were drowning in a sea of tangled symbols.

"Well… what does it say?" I asked in a whisper.

Tristan gave a half-shrug and pulled the manuscript out of my hands. "Like I said, it doesn't make much sense at all. It looks like half of it is in English and half of it in Latin – which no, I can't read." He answered my next question before it had left my lips. He ran his finger across the page, mouth working silently, and I waited for him to explain. "If you keep staring at me this hard you're going to burn a hole in my head," he muttered. I ignored this comment and he continued, "The first part here mentions Isaac by name and says that his hard work has contributed to this manuscript. Apart from…" he went back to the line before and shook his head quickly, "they don't call it a manuscript. They call it a manual."

"A manual for what?" I questioned.

"I can't make it out." Tristan squinted so hard at the paper before him and brought it right up to his nose to inspect it. I had a wild desire to laugh out loud. "There's another word here but I think it's in a different language... Could be an 'm', an 'a' and a 'g'..."

I shook my head impatiently. "What else does it say?"

"It says that the writers cannot guarantee results, that it is down to... There's that word again that I can't decipher. Let's just say the reader. It's down to the reader what the results will be. It hints at some kind of darkness. I don't understand if it means a place or something else." Tristan paused and looked up.

"What is it?" I asked.

"The last part gives a sort of warning. It says to read with caution and under supervision..."

A log popped in the grate, and I jumped. Tristan noticed my unease and closed the manuscript. "You don't have to know what's in it if you don't want to."

"It all seems a bit vague," I said slowly. "But I can't help feeling like there's a darker element underneath all of this. I mean, it gives a warning, Tristan. What does it all mean?" Tristan stretched out his long legs in front of the fire and then returned to a sitting position across from me.

"I guess we'll never know if we don't go past the first page." He was right, but I think we both knew that it was too late to turn back now. I retrieved our glasses from the table and sat back down at Tristan's side so our shoulders touched. He laid the manuscript across both of our laps, and I tentatively turned the pages. Feeling as though even touching the corner of the pages was a criminal act, I could feel Tristan watching me, and I looked up into his eyes as I reached the second and third pages.

"Tell me what it says."

FORTY-FIVE

Tristan placed his hand on the second page, which happened to be on my right knee. Another shiver ran down my back, but this one was not out of fear. "This makes a little more sense." Tristan breathed quietly, completely oblivious to the effect he had on me. I looked down quickly at the pages before us. "It talks about barriers and how to get through them. Look here." Tristan pointed down to inky sketches that adorned the paper, and I found that I could make sense of some of them. I traced the drawings with my fingers, and Tristan shifted beside me to get a better look. He was right; the manual depicted various physical barriers. I listed them out loud as Tristan nodded at each one.

"Gates, archways, tunnels, mirrors..." I stopped at a faded drawing. "Is that supposed to be a portcullis or something?"

"Yeah, I think so... like old castle gates maybe... and look here, there's loads of drawings of padlocks."

"What the hell are those?" I pointed to the engravings that surrounded the drawings; more of the strange symbols that Tristan could decipher. He scanned the pages, and then looked into the fire for a few minutes as though thinking hard. He seemed to choose his words very carefully as though he were still trying to understand what they meant.

"It seems as though my uncle is obsessed with trying to get through something."

The cogs whirred in my brain. "Do you mean he's trying to get through something that's locked or out of reach?"

Tristan nodded slowly, his curls bouncing. "Maybe. It's as though he's trying to see what's on the other side. But the other side of what, I haven't figured out. You're right what you said before, Luna, it's all very vague."

I laughed, which seemed to take him by surprise. "Trust me, you're making a lot more sense out of it than I can." I became suddenly aware of our closeness as we looked at each other. I studied the firmly set jaw. The firelight bounced off his tan skin, and I watched as his mouth relaxed and he broke into a smile. He lifted his hand off my knee and reached for a strand of my chestnut hair, his fingers playing about my neck lightly.

"I do trust you, Luna, and I hope you trust me too." He leaned in closer as I licked my lips in anticipation and prepared to give him my answer, but Tristan yelped suddenly and cut short our exchange. Luna had sprung up from her armchair and launched an attack from behind enemy lines.

Once I had extracted her claws from his hair, I couldn't help but set about laughing, and the tension was broken. Tristan massaged his scalp with a grimace and then shook his head. "What did I say earlier about that cat being too protective?" Luna nuzzled around my ankles as I shrugged playfully. Tristan smirked at me as he brushed off Luna's fur. I stretched my legs and disappeared into the kitchen to put the kettle on the stove; it felt as though we could be here a while deciphering Isaac's scribblings. "Dear God, don't leave me alone with her!" Tristan shouted from the living room. I smiled as I rattled around with the cups and saucers in the kitchen; it had been a long time since the cottage had felt this homely.

Bending down gingerly I laid the tea tray on the floor and sat down opposite Tristan again. He eyed the little sandwiches ravenously. I nodded in the direction of the plate. "Help yourself."

"Sorry, I just haven't eaten since this morning, and I couldn't really face much." He reached for a nearby sandwich and managed to cram most of it into his mouth at once. "I'll have to repay the favour sometime," he said eagerly after swallowing the last bite.

"I know what you mean," I murmured, reminiscing about my lurching stomach that morning.

I carefully poured us two cups of tea as Tristan rifled through the manuscript. His lips formed silent words, and I could tell that he was attempting to make sense of the curious markings. I watched him in silence as he flicked through the pages, pausing every so often, and doing a double-take at certain drawings or crooked letters. I felt as though I were in the presence of a strange translator; how could he understand the manuscript and I couldn't? It was as though we were looking at different things and there was something in Tristan's brain that enabled him to understand the odd phrase or scribble that wasn't present in mine.

"Any luck?" I enquired after a couple of minutes of listening to the rain pour down outside. He tore his eyes away from the page.

"I'm sorry, there's just so much in here to go through."

"That's okay. Let me know if you find anything."

"This here," he answered immediately, gesturing for me to sit beside him as he pointed at something on the page. I peered at the old paper, and a strange scene met my eye. Someone had inked a large, swirling circle that ended in a blot of pitch black. Peculiar symbols decorated the spaces in between the swirls and adorned the edge of the shape.

"What am I looking at?" I asked Tristan, and looked up to see him studying me, anxiously biting one of his fingernails. His serious features looked into mine. "Honestly, Tristan, you're going to have to help me out here," I said with a smile.

He did not return it. "You're not going to believe me if I say it."

"I didn't believe a lot until tonight," I said bluntly, not quite sure what I was referring to. Perhaps that I could steal someone else's property in the blink of an eye. Perhaps that I had so willingly broken my promise to Grandmother. Or perhaps that a curious manuscript brimming with ancient symbols and an alluring darkness lay open on my living room floor.

He swallowed nervously. "It looks like it's instructions for some kind of spell work, but..." he eyed the symbols mistrustfully, "dark spell work."

The silence was broken only by the faint purrs of Luna who had settled in the armchair behind us. "What do you mean, like, magic?" The final word came out as a whisper.

"I told you you wouldn't believe me."

"It's not that," I rushed on in sudden fear that he would think I was mocking him. "But what kind of spell work?"

"It's all here." He pointed at the page impatiently. "It warns that performing these instructions will..." he flattened out the page on the floor in front of us and scrunched up his eyes in the dim light, "will transgress outside of normal boundaries. It warns that if performed incorrectly, it can lead to consequences... such as death."

"And what does it say the instructions are?" I tried to keep my tone matter-of-fact as I reached for my teacup and ignored my shaking hand.

"It's a series of words and actions, using an object to aid you... but I can't understand what that object is," Tristan continued uneasily. "What is Isaac up to?" He registered the chink of china as I set down my teacup. He closed the papers with a rustle and concealed the contents of the manuscript from sight. "I'm sorry, you don't have to be mixed up in all of this. I'll just take the manuscript home and figure it out there. I don't want to bring you into something dangerous."

"Don't be silly," I replied firmly. "I'm the one who meddled in Isaac's business. I'm the one who stole the manuscript. I can't be afraid of what's in it now. Besides," I reasoned, "I promised Delilah I'd return the manuscript first thing tomorrow morning, and that's not a promise I'm willing to break."

"Okay, okay." Tristan held up his arms in the air with a little smile. "I just didn't want to drag you into something before we realised what we were getting in to. Do you mind if I sit for a while then and see what else I can find?"

"Of course I don't mind," I said, swinging my legs beneath me and rising somewhat clumsily from the rug. I prodded the fire with a poker to ensure it was still burning. "I'll be back in a few minutes. I'm just going to feed Luna."

"Alright – and feed the cat too!" Tristan joked as I turned around and rolled my eyes. As soon as my back was turned my smile vanished. Transgressing boundaries? I couldn't pretend that none of this bothered me. Even if it was just the writings of a mad man, Isaac could be attempting something dangerous to both himself and Tristan, and how could I just stand by and let that happen? My hands shook slightly as I tipped out the cat food into Luna's bowl. Once she was happily crunching her food, I ventured back into the living room, ready to help Tristan with the next few pages.

I found him sitting in the armchair by the fire that Luna had just vacated. I was about to inform him that was a bad decision, as he would end up with cat hair all over his bum, but something about his expression made me stop short. He had grabbed a nearby candle and was holding it so close to the old papers that I was afraid they would catch alight.

A dark look passed across his features, and the shadow of the flames danced across his frightened face. His breath quickened as he leaned back in the armchair, staring at something invisible across the room, the manuscript held limply in one hand, candle still in the other. I moved across the room and took the candle gently from his hand. "What is it?" I whispered. It took a few seconds for him to come to his senses, and he inhaled slowly. When he did not reply I eased the manuscript out of his hands and turned to the page he held with his thumb.

TRUTH SERUM

- 2 dew drops, taken on a winter morning
- 4 berries of the ivy, whole
- 2 strips of pine bark
- The juice of 7 huckleberries
- 1 fragment of root from the willow

Incantation to follow

I could read no farther as the incantation was written in a different language. I stared at Tristan who nodded slowly. "Tristan? What is this?" I asked quietly.

"It's what he's been sending me into the forest for, and probably why he keeps disappearing too. I recognise that list. I thought they were just weird herbal ingredients for those people who believe in that sort of thing, so Isaac could market his remedies that way, you know." I shook my head, trying to understand, and Tristan continued, "He's been sending me to collect ingredients for whatever he's brewing up in that bloody locked room of his. I bet that's what he's selling in secret. How could I have been so stupid?"

"But what is he brewing in that locked room?"

"It says right there, Luna!" Tristan's voice rose as he threw his hands into the air and looked at me imploringly. "Truth Serum! And God knows what else!" I watched as Tristan ran his hands through his dishevelled hair, eyes wide, dark circles prevalent. Wild thoughts raced through my head as I watched him grow frantic.

"That's it," I said, running into the hallway and grabbing my cloak. "Grab your coat."

"What are you—" I reached for his hand and pulled him up from the armchair before he could protest.

"We're going to break into that locked room."

FORTY-SIX

"I've never met anyone like you, Luna." Tristan stumbled over an uneven cobblestone as he hurried to keep up with me.

"Thank you," I replied, catching him before he hit the ground. The recent rainfall had ceased, leaving the worn-away cobbles polished smooth. "What if Isaac's working late again?" I had a sudden horrible thought about bursting in on him in the shadows.

"He won't be," Tristan reassured me quickly. "He told me he was visiting a friend tonight."

"Yes, but he doesn't tell you a lot, does he?" I murmured, scanning the empty alleyways. A silence fell upon my ears, and I stopped short and waited for Tristan to catch up. His dark hair blended in with the night. "I'm sorry," I said. "Is this a crazy idea?"

He looked at me gravely and nodded. "Yes, it's a crazy idea. But you're right, I have to know what's in that room, and this is the only way that I'm going to find out. Isaac will never tell me what he's up to." We slunk in and out of the shadows as I prayed that we wouldn't meet another human soul.

As we approached the apothecary, the glass bottles in the window twinkled in the moonlight, and I reached up in my hair for a pin. "Don't bother," Tristan intervened. "I still have the spare key in my pocket. Save your pins for the one upstairs." He rummaged in the pockets of his coat and extracted the key. I stepped back for him to open the lock, and he glanced up and down the deserted street before doing so.

The apothecary was eerie in the dark. I dreaded to think what was suspended in those pale glass jars that hung from the low ceiling. Tristan took my hand and ushered me past the front counter through the hallway that lay beyond. "Come on." He turned to his left and peered at the wall.

"What are you—"

"This door," he whispered, running his hands along the wall. "This must be the door that you saw people coming in through."

"Hang on." I disappeared into the main part of the apothecary and re-emerged into the hallway with a couple of candles and holders that I had spied on our way in. No doubt they were aids to Isaac's late-night shifts.

I handed one to Tristan, who thanked me quietly as our fingers brushed against each other. I couldn't help but notice the slight lurch in my chest, and I turned to the strange door to try and distract myself. The inside was covered with an intricate locking mechanism. I watched as Tristan traced the interlocking spirals. After a couple of minutes, he shook his head in defeat and turned his wide eyes up to the ceiling. "Shall we go upstairs?" I nodded in reply, and in the candlelight I could have sworn he smirked slightly as we ascended the rickety staircase.

As each step creaked loudly, I prayed that no one occupied the locked room above us, and we reached the dusty landing. I coughed unexpectedly and Tristan cleared his throat. "We, er, never got around to dusting." I smiled at him and then looked expectantly at the only door that stood before us. We paused. I had been confident that our actions were necessary; discovering Isaac's manuscript had given me goose bumps, and Tristan had a right to know what sinister element it had hinted at. But as we stood in the darkened hallway and faced the room before us, a wild desire to hurry back down the staircase and out of the apothecary almost overcame me; the part of me that wished to enter the secret room had shrunk to a tiny sliver.

I felt something in my hair and shuddered, thinking of giant spiders and jelly-like creatures ascending from the ceiling below us, only to find that it was Tristan gently extracting a hairpin from my haystack of curls. "I should be the one to do it, that way you can't be blamed if we get into trouble," he explained with a nervous grin. I tried to muster some confidence and gave him a small smile.

"Let's just get this over with. I'm sure whatever's in there is nothing compared to what we're both imagining."

He worked the lock for what felt like a very long time as I paced back and forth on the landing. I sighed impatiently and was on the brink of suggesting that he simply kick the door down when a clunky noise sounded and the lock clicked open. Tristan clambered up off the floor from where he had been kneeling and tried the circular handle. It twisted to the right, and he opened the door a tiny fraction. He turned back to me. "After you," I managed in a small whisper. He swung open the door with an uncomfortable creak and gave a sharp intake of breath.

I inched past him slowly so that we could stand side by side. I blinked up at the light source. An iridescent orb hung as though suspended by an invisible string in the middle of the ceiling. It seemed to emit a pale light, a weak imitation of the moon that shone bright in the night sky outside. An immense mahogany table stretched from one end of the room to the window at the other. Behind the exquisitely carved apothecary table towered sturdy shelves that reached all the way up to the ceiling and spanned the length of the room. A myriad of shapes and colours lined up in perfection; bottled liquids that glimmered of their own accord, enticing you to lift them right off the shelf and unscrew their delicate encasings. We gazed upon a plethora of crystal bottles as thin as champagne flutes, translucent decanters as thick as brass chalices and engraved vials that hosted faintly swirling liquid that clouded the glass.

Tristan stood rooted to the spot beside me, but my cloak draped across the polished floor as I edged around the table eager to see more. The bottles twinkled at me, and I gazed up at the shelves, craning my neck to observe the strange elixirs on the top, and crouching down to peer at the odd concoctions on the bottom. Each bottle had its own individual label, and by reading the italic scrawls I slowly deduced that the array before me had not been organised according to shape, size or colour, but by what properties the liquid contained.

I stood back, tripping on my cloak, suddenly becoming aware of the magnitude of what I was looking at. I became vaguely aware that Tristan had joined me and waited for him to speak. When he did not, I turned sideways to gauge his reaction, and met a dumbfounded expression. He tore his eyes away from the shelves and looked at me, still seeing the sparkling bottles in his eyes, and closed his mouth that had fallen open into an 'o' of surprise.

"They're potions, aren't they?" He turned back to the shelves and began walking up and down the wooden rows, examining bottles here and there. "Every single one of them," he murmured. "Isaac's been brewing them up here. He must have started all this before we came to Blackthorn. There's no way he would have been able to make all of these in the past four days." He looked at me questioningly. I took another few steps behind me and stumbled into the table. I leaned both my palms on it so I could perch against it awkwardly and surveyed the scene before me.

"I think this has been going on for a very long time, Tristan."

FORTY-SEVEN

I watched as Tristan paced the shelves back and forth, his footsteps creaking on loose floorboards, his expression growing more disbelieving with every bottle he selected. He began to line them up on the mahogany table – the smallest bottle to the largest in all their different shapes and colours. After a couple of minutes he stood at the narrow end of the table with his hands in his pockets. He seemed to have completed his task. "As far as I can tell, this is a complete selection of all the different potions on these shelves." I got up off my perch and walked around to where he had carefully lined them up.

"Are you sure?" I picked up the smallest, most fragile-looking bottle and examined the thin glass encasing. Tristan watched me with interest.

"Yes, some of them are in different bottles, but if you look at the labels you can tell which ones are which. The colours give them away as well." He nodded his head sourly at the little bottle in my right hand. "And I'm sure you can recognise that handwriting." I held the bottle up to the peculiar orb on the ceiling and nodded; the light shone on the same inky scrawls that had been scratched onto the manuscript.

"The manuscript!" I remembered suddenly. "Did you bring it with you?" Tristan extracted a mass of papers from within his coat and nodded in the affirmative.

"Thanks," I said with relief. "I was going to leave it somewhere for Delilah to find in the morning so she knows I've kept my promise."

The vial I had been clutching on to was no bigger than my little finger, and its cylindrical crystal case surrounded a voluptuous cacophony of deep reds and purples that interspersed their tendrils of colour. The tiny silver label on the side professed it to be Truth Serum. I set down the vial gingerly on the edge of the row, fearful of chipping the thin glass, and examined the others in turn. Tristan had lined up twelve bottles in total, and as we surveyed them the moon itself seemed to shine through the window and aid our examination.

The largest decanter was home to a vibrant green liquid that Isaac's filing system declared to be Fertility Elixir. This liquid was still and lay flat just underneath the giant glass stopper in the top. My eye was drawn to a beautifully engraved crystal bottle a little further down the line. The lavender blue liquid it held was gloopy, and as I turned the bottle upside down, the liquid flowed thickly to the other side, sticking briefly to the sides of the crystal. My mouth began to water; I was sure that if I were to place a drop on the tip of my tongue it would taste like honey.

"What's that one?" Tristan interrupted my musings, and I righted the bottle and set it back in its place in the row. I peered at the label and cleared my throat.

"Love Potion."

We moved on. A rather strange oblong container enveloped a concoction that kept fogging up the glass and seemed to swirl as though desperately trying to escape its prison.

"That's the only one that doesn't have a label," Tristan declared. The metallic silver liquid flowed away from the sides of the glass as though an invisible person shook it continually.

"It looks like molten metal," I whispered.

Included in Isaac's repertoire of odd concoctions were labels such as Healing Remedy, Beauty Potion, Memory Restorative and Sleeping Draught. As we examined each of the potions in turn, I became aware that the minutes of the clock ticked by, and we had spent almost half an hour in Isaac's secret stores.

We were pushing our luck, and our chances of being discovered were increasing. But Tristan had a more important issue at hand.

"I wonder what he does to them after I've gathered all the ingredients for him." The moon passed over, and his face was cast into shadow. "He's been using me." His tone was bitter. "I bet it's all in this manuscript – if only I could read it properly." I walked over to him and gently extracted the papers out of his tight grip.

"Perhaps you're better off not knowing, Tristan. Maybe there's a reason he hasn't told you about all of this…"

Tristan shot me a confused look. "Please tell me you're not standing up for him, Luna?" I recoiled at his harshness and tried to steer him away from the topic of Isaac's betrayal.

"How do we know they even work? Do you really believe in all of this? He could just be playing around… trying to make some extra money…"

"Oh, open your eyes!" Tristan shouted as the top shelves rattled. "Look around! You're so much in denial that you can't see what's right in front of you! And the fact that people keep coming back in the dead of night to buy them means that yes, word has probably got around that they work, don't you think?" I shot him an angry look and turned my back on him, not interested in being scolded like a child.

The room was silent for a minute or so. The iridescent orb seemed to have dimmed. I heard Tristan take a few deep breaths as I scrutinised the bottles in front of me wondering why I had bothered to help and what on earth we were going to do now. The familiar musky scent of the forest entered my nostrils along with something else I didn't recognise, and I breathed in deeply. As his arms made contact with my waist I realised that Tristan had came up behind me.

"I'm sorry," he whispered, his lips hovering at my neck. "I shouldn't be blaming you. I should be thanking you." My breath caught in my throat. "How do I thank you, Luna?" Tristan whispered. His breath tickled my neck, and a fire kindled deep in my stomach.

I welcomed the closeness. I reached for one of his arms and pulled it tighter around my waist. He moved aside a lock of my hair with the other as his lips brushed delicately against my collarbone. He held me tight as I felt his hard body encase me.

A sudden crashing sound came from behind us and we jolted apart.

FORTY-EIGHT

"What the hell do you think you're doing in here?" Isaac stood framed in the doorway, bedraggled hair a mess, the redness in his cheeks a tell-tale sign of his having been drinking. His angry eyes scanned over his nephew, the line-up of bottles on the apothecary table, the narrow slits finally resting on me. He opened his mouth to say something, but Tristan beat him to it.

"I could ask you the same thing."

Isaac took a step forward with a snarl. "None of your bloody business, boy."

"It is my bloody business if you keep sending me into the forest... all for..." Tristan turned around to face the shelves, "for this! Is this what it's all been for – your prize collection that you've been selling secretly on the side? How long were you going to keep all of this from me? Do Mum and Dad know about this?" Tristan's eyes were burning, and his face grew a deep red.

Isaac picked up one of the bottles from the line-up. He shook it angrily in Tristan's face as I retreated around the other side of the table. "Of course your father knows. He was the one that started this whole pissing thing!"

"What the hell are you talking abou—"

"You're just the same as my dear brother, aren't you?" Isaac snarled. "He was always meddling in things that didn't concern him! Destroying things he didn't understand!"

"I moved here with you thinking that we could do this together! That we could actually make this business work! You sold Blackthorn to me as an opportunity, but that was a lie, wasn't it?" Tristan moved around the table so he and his uncle stood facing each other. "You didn't want me here to learn the family business. I was just an easy option for you, wasn't I? Someone you could fool in order to gain..." Tristan looked around him wildly, "I don't even know – money? Power?" The colour flushed Isaac's cheeks as he staggered against the table. His eyes strayed to me as I stood watching the exchange.

"It looks like you've found other... activities here in Blackthorn," he snarled nastily.

"Don't bring Luna into this." The warning tone of Tristan's voice tipped Isaac over the edge.

He stumbled against the sturdy table. "Just like your bloody father!" The bottle he was holding smashed against the other side of the room. Tristan ducked as the shards shattered overhead, and I ran over to him.

"Tristan!" I pulled out the pieces from his hair, and he took my hands in his. "You should go, Luna. I don't want you here right now."

"But—" I looked over at Isaac to find that he had regressed into a drunken slump at the other end of the apothecary table.

"I can deal with him. He'll only sit there all night, but I think it's better if you go. I don't want you getting into any more trouble. I'll be fine," Tristan reassured me as my expression made it clear I did not want to leave him alone.

"I can stay and help. I—"

"Luna, trust me, it's not the right time." His eyes found mine, and after a few seconds I nodded. I looked at Isaac's slumped frame with disdain and reluctantly left Tristan to deal with the drunken idiot.

The horrible combination of guilt and fear plagued me for the rest of the night. Falling into an uncomfortable sleep in the armchair, I would jerk awake seeing a mirage of awful images of Isaac punishing Tristan, only to then console myself with his solemn figure slumped in that chair beneath the window ledge. Frustration then coursed through my body. Tristan's idiot of an uncle had cut short whatever was about to happen between us. The disappointment was too much to bear. This cycle repeated until the early hours of the morning when I took myself off to have a hot shower.

I laced up my boots and donned my cloak; there was someone I must speak to urgently. I had betrayed my grandmother's trust, resulting in potential danger to both myself and Tristan. There was no telling what lengths Isaac would go to in order to protect his secret. Grandmother knew more than she was letting on. Knew enough to try and warn me about the Brewers. A warning that I had not heeded.

FORTY-NINE

The first chirrup of the rising birds sounded as I closed the cottage gate behind me and started down the narrow path to the village. The mist had not lifted, and I felt as though I were walking through a cold blanket. Luna's Luck would not be open yet, but Grandmother, forever the early riser, would be awake.

The hazy drizzle was not as thick on the open cobbles, and I was able to see the greengrocer dragging out his stalls for the morning. A friendly wave came in my direction, which I returned quickly and hurried on my way; I couldn't help but feel as though the hands of the clock were ticking down to something foreboding. I glanced at the bottom of the bookshop door where I had carefully posted the manuscript through for Delilah to find first thing this morning. It had disappeared. Hopefully into the right hands, I thought grimly, and looked away.

"Luna!" A shout came from a little way up the street, and I veered off my course from the fortune-telling shop. Betty stood with her bright blonde hair hovering in the morning mist outside the front of the blacksmith's. I frowned. What was she doing up so early? My frown turned into a smile as I approached; as much as I was eager to be on my way I welcomed the comfort of a familiar face.

"Have you got five minutes?" Betty asked, gesturing inside. "I'm sure your grandmother won't mind. It's still early!" I looked up into her shining face. A spark of energy seemed to light her up and emit an aura of pure happiness.

"Morning." I returned her greeting with a scratchy word, and her spark dimmed.

"Are you alright, Luna? You look—" Before she could finish her question a tall figure strode out of the blacksmith's.

"Morning, Luna," George said brazenly. "Don't take this the wrong way but you look bloody awful. In need of a coffee?" I deliberated on the cobbles for a few seconds, glancing back towards Grandmother, but at the risk of being impolite I didn't want to decline their friendly invitation.

"Go on then, I've got a couple of minutes."

It was always sweltering inside the blacksmith's due to the continual fire that blazed in the forge. I looked about me with a familiar tenderness. Heavy hammers and chisels lay scattered about the place; it was obvious that George was in charge today and not his father. Pieces of ironwork dotted the shop, all at different stages of workmanship, waiting to be finished or sold. George disappeared into a different room to make the much-needed coffee, and Betty and I stood next to the fire warming ourselves.

"Seriously, Luna, you do look tired." Betty played with a strand of her hair as she studied me, and I grew irritable.

"Yes, thank you, I just haven't been sleeping well lately."

"Is it the weather?" Betty nodded as though in the know about my bedtime disturbances. "All these storms lately…" I nodded distractedly, thinking that perhaps this had been a mistake and I ought to seek out Grandmother instead.

"Maybe." I craned my neck behind her to see if George was reappearing with our drinks yet. He seemed to be taking an unusually long time to put hot water into three cups.

"I'll be in the shop this afternoon," Betty continued, oblivious to my intended haste. "Perhaps we could meet for dinner after at Arthur's. It's been a while since we've had a proper catch-up." I stopped looking over her shoulder and stared into her wide eyes.

"Yes," I said with sincerity. "You're right, we don't really speak properly anymore. Dinner would be nice." She beamed at me and walked over to the entrance of the shop. She seemed to float rather than walk away.

I cleared my throat. "I'm just going to see if George is finished with our drinks." Betty kept her back to me. I watched her apprehensively; there was something not quite right. I wandered past all the tools and ironwork into the little cluttered room at the back. My footsteps were padded, and George took no notice of my entrance. He rattled the cups around and hummed a strange melody. Every so often he would run his fingers through his blond hair. Both he and Betty had an annoying habit of doing so.

"Having fun?" I smirked, watching him from the doorway. As George uttered a little gasp of surprise and span around, he knocked something to the floor, and it shattered. My smirk faded. Sharp crystal shards once belonging to a delicate glass bottle scattered the floor. "What is this?" I whispered. A droplet of bluish liquid hung off one of the shards, and George looked at me in horror.

"Luna, I—"

"Were you going to put that in my drink?" I asked him coldly. His mouth opened and closed with silent lies and I shook my head in indignation.

"Don't tell me you've been putting love potion in Betty's drinks?" My boots crunched on the broken glass, and George looked at me imploringly.

"Luna, please don't—"

"Please don't what? Tell her? Of course I'm going to tell her!" I shouted resentfully. "How could you do this?" Instead of answering me, he bent down and tried to sweep up the glass with his bare hands, wincing every now and then as a shard struck his bare skin. "What makes you think you can—"

"Luna." Betty entered the room breathlessly. "I just saw Tristan running into Luna's Luck. He looked frantic, like he was on a mission or something..." Her words trailed off as she caught her breath and eyed the scene before her. "What's going on? Did you break something, darling?"

"Betty, I need to talk to you—" I started in a hurry, but she cut me off.

"Can't it wait? I need to help George clear this up first—"

"It can wait," George said flatly as he looked up at me. "By the sounds of it you need to go and find that Brewer boy." I shook my head in a panic as they both stooped to clear up the glass.

"No, you don't understand, Betty—" Words failed me as I stood dithering in the doorway, torn between her and Tristan. I had to make the decision in a split second. "Meet me in Arthur's Tavern later, Betty, like we said, remember?" There was no point trying to convince her of George's treachery while they were in the same room. She nodded her head distractedly, and I turned away in exasperation.

I burst through the doors of Luna's Luck seconds later, only to be greeted with a chaotic scene much the same as the one I had just departed. Tristan stood, heavy eyes wild, dark curls a mess, face to face with Grandmother, the only calm person in the room. She sat at her table shuffling a deck of tarot cards with an expression of mild disturbance, as though she had wholly expected Tristan to crash through the doors of the shop seconds before. "Good morning, Luna," she said matter-of-factly.

"What's going on?" I swallowed, my throat aching from lack of sleep.

"Tristan here has just asked me to delve into his family history." Tristan turned to me as I looked at him in surprise. His expression softened. He pulled me into a hug, and I relaxed at the comfort of his scent. I looked at Grandmother over his shoulder as she cleared her throat and raised her eyebrows. I grimaced as I realised what we were showcasing. She shook her head and let loose a small smile of resignation. I breathed out. I was forgiven.

Tristan released me and sat down opposite Grandmother. Her multicoloured eyes surveyed his electric-blue ones carefully. He looked at her apologetically. "I'm sorry to burst in on you like this, Joan. I should have made an appointment." Grandmother nodded slowly. "But I need to find out the truth about my family. Fortune telling can look into the past as well, right? My parents aren't around to talk to, I can't trust Isaac and..." he lowered his eyes away from mine, "I think I could be in danger." Grandmother remained silent for a few moments, and then her striking eyes met mine.

"What do you think, Luna?"

Taken aback by her question, I stuttered, "I-I think Tristan's right. There's something in his past that he doesn't know, and I think learning about it may help to understand a lot."

"Very well." Grandmother placed both her palms on the table and rose slowly. "My granddaughter seems to trust you." She paused and gave me a knowing look. "And as she tends to be an excellent judge of character, that's good enough for me." She made her way over to the entrance door and slid the bolt across it. She shuffled back across the room, lighting candles and incense sticks as I grabbed a nearby chair and placed it next to Tristan. He put his hand on my knee and smiled nervously.

"Thanks, Luna."

Grandmother resumed her position in the hard-backed chair, rearranged her glittering shawls about herself and took a deep breath.

"Now we begin."

FIFTY

Grandmother explained to Tristan how the tarot reading would work, as she shuffled the deck in plain sight, her red lips opening and closing in quick succession. "Five cards. Two for the past, two for the present and one for the future." She paused and looked at Tristan unsmiling. "The cards can only tell us so much, but they are a good place to start." She glanced over to the window as the mist disappeared and the raindrops began their rhythmic beat upon the windows, lashing the now deserted cobbles outside.

She deliberated, fiddling with the cards, as though deep in thought, and gave a great sigh as she laid the entire pack face down in the middle of the table. "I can't pretend that I haven't already delved into your past." Tristan was shocked but didn't say anything. "The moment a Brewer stepped foot into Blackthorn again I knew there'd be trouble. On the first night you and your uncle stayed here, I felt something pulling me into the darkness, like something malevolent had arrived." Tristan shifted uncomfortably in his seat, and I squeezed his hand in my lap. Grandmother licked her lips and laid out the top five cards in the deck across the table in a strange pyramid. "You're right not to trust your uncle." Her words hovered in the air like a pungent smell.

Her crimson fingernails upturned the first rectangle, and she closed her eyes as she inhaled and exhaled deeply. I moved closer as the sky outside grew dark and the candles flickered. I spied a circular building, tall and imposing surrounded by vines

214

on all sides. "The Tower," she declared. Opening her eyes, she continued, "A sudden upheaval haunts the past. A change that impacted you greatly..." she met Tristan's eyes and narrowed her own, "and still does."

Tristan looked up at me slowly, and I guessed that the sudden upheaval the card referred to was his family's move away from Blackthorn. Grandmother lowered her disturbing eyes back to the cards on the table and revealed the second one. She took a sharp intake of breath as her eyes misted over and she observed something we could not see. This card detailed a man lying face down, his identity hidden, jagged swords plunged gorily into his back. A foreboding feeling began to bubble up in my stomach.

"The Ten of Swords." She opened her eyes and gazed at Tristan. "A betrayal," she whispered, looking suddenly fearful. "An unforgiveable betrayal." She trembled and shook jerkily from side to side as though having a sudden fit. Afraid she would fall off her chair, I moved forward, but she had stopped as soon as she had begun and remained still. She was muttering underneath her breath, and I could barely distinguish the words through the sound of the pouring rain – "...the girl... the boy... united only by lies..." She proceeded to turn over the third card.

"Wait!" Tristan leaned across the table. "What betrayal? What are you talking about?" She tilted back slowly in her chair and fixed him with a calm stare.

"Alas, I did say the cards will only tell us so much." With this vague response, Tristan's shoulders sagged and he furrowed his brows, awaiting the third card in slight annoyance.

The first card for the present featured a robed figure, holding up a strange instrument, standing before a table full of objects I did not recognise. "The magician... is up to his old tricks." Grandmother rearranged her shawls about her small frame and craned her neck to one side, focusing on Tristan's eyes, reading them with great care. "Sorcery is a dangerous game that belongs only to the Devil." Thinking that this seemed like more of a warning than a prediction, I shifted on my feet and wondered if this card related to Tristan's uncle instead.

The fourth card was revealed with urgency, and Grandmother raised her thin eyebrows. "The Lovers." Tristan and I avoided each other's eyes awkwardly as I blushed and Grandmother played with the edges of the fifth card. She turned over the fifth card for the future, suddenly grim, and the sense of foreboding I had felt minutes before imploded inside me.

The door crashed open as the lock flew off and Grandmother rushed to her feet, knocking back her chair as she did so, pure horror erupting on her face. A great gust of wind rushed about the room. It extinguished every candle and blew the five cards off the table. They were catapulted into the air, but not before we had all seen what the final card had in store for Tristan: a sinister figure, skeletal in its appearance, and armed on either side with its instruments of death.

Grandmother rushed about the room, fumbling with an object I couldn't discern, as Tristan and I stood paralysed with fear. The sky had turned so black outside we had been cast into darkness; a storm was brewing. One by one, the matches were struck and the candles were relit as she muttered under her breath and seemed to have forgotten we were there.

She revolved slowly on the spot and turned to face us as Tristan grabbed for my hand and I clasped onto it. The candlelight flickered on her suddenly harsh features as she opened her mouth and whispered, "You will bring death and destruction to the village." I released Tristan's hand, feeling my heart thump in my chest, and gingerly put one foot in front of the other as I walked towards Grandmother. I had never seen her like this before. Tristan stood rooted to the spot.

"Grandmother?" I said softly. "Are you alright?" A sharp intake of breath, a slight shake of her head, and her features softened to those I recognised once more. She gave me a small smile of reassurance and ambled over to Tristan. She took his hand, and he looked at her expectantly. Her movements were slow, and when she spoke her voice sounded wearisome.

"Sit down, Tristan. I need to tell you the story of your past. On the night you arrived all of my crystal orbs clouded over." Grandmother gestured over to the windowsill where their glass shone innocently still. "I sat up with the stars and tried to interpret what it meant. They were trying to tell me something. I saw the face of a boy and a story of woe. It was only when I saw you the next day that I recognised the boy to be you, only you weren't a boy anymore, you were a man." Tristan fiddled with the buttons on his jacket and swallowed uneasily. "Are you sure you're ready to know the truth?" Grandmother asked. "I warn you, it's short but it's not a pleasant tale."

Tristan played with one of the tarot cards he had picked up from underfoot for a few moments and glanced outside at the building gale before delivering his reply. "I'm ready." His face was stern, and his features were set. Grandmother glanced over to me once and then back across to Tristan.

"Very well. I just hope it gives you the answers you are seeking." He nodded, and she began to unveil the truth. "Over twenty years ago, your parents fled Blackthorn never to return again. This departure was due to a terrible betrayal between your father and your uncle. Your mother was very much in love. But not with your father." Tristan leaned forward in his chair, as though to rebuke her ridiculous suggestion, but Grandmother held up her hand, and he was subdued. "Before you arrived in this world, your mother fell in love. The man she set her heart on was kind, caring and entirely devoted to her in turn. They were happy... until the man introduced her to his brother."

Tristan's breathing seemed to have ceased beside me. He didn't take his eyes off Grandmother as she sighed heavily and continued, "The man was your Uncle Isaac, Tristan. Your father stole your mother away from his own brother." A hard lump arose in my throat as Tristan remained in silence.

"But how did he steal her away if she was in love with Isaac?" I asked in a small voice. When Grandmother revealed the answer a heavy stone dropped in the pit of my stomach, as though I had known the answer all along.

"He administered a potent Love Potion, thereby convincing her that her feelings were true, and this continued for a number of years until they moved away." Tristan put his head in his hands, and his shoulders drooped as he leaned all of his weight on the rickety table.

"All this time." A muffled voice sounded from in between his fingers. He raised his head again slowly and looked at Grandmother suddenly horrified. "Do you mean to say that my father is still giving my mother this potion; that she's actually still in love with my uncle?"

Grandmother gave a sort of awkward half shrug and clasped her hands together. Her voice was gentle. "They say that if you use a Love Potion for long enough, its effect will eventually wear off, and the victim in question may develop their own natural feelings for the person."

"But not always?"

Grandmother looked at him. "No, not always."

A poignant silence fell in the fortune-telling shop as someone splashed their way across the cobbles outside. As the wind picked up in motion, Tristan kicked back his chair and towered over us both, a disbelieving expression displayed across his prominent features. "So you're saying that my father is an evil man? That he's been tricking my mother this whole time, and I'm just a result of lies and betrayal?" Before Grandmother or I had a chance to reply he had buttoned up his coat again and strode across the room. "How do I know you're not lying to me – making me out to look bad so Luna wants nothing to do with me?"

"I'm too old and too wise to play games with you, young man." Grandmother's voice was stern. "You asked to know the truth, and I gave it to you. Don't shoot the messenger just because you disagree with her." There was a pause as Tristan stood with his hand on the locked door, breathing heavily, and Grandmother arose from the chair. "You are not your father, Tristan." He slid the bolt across with one deft movement, swung the door wide open, and stepped outside into the storm without a second look back. As I kicked back my own chair and it tumbled to the floor behind me, Grandmother grabbed my hand and I looked down in shock. She restlessly fidgeted with her shawls, and then our eyes met. The whirlpools spun recklessly. "Luna, there's something else."

"What is it?" I whispered fearfully.

"I feel it in my bones. There's a darkness coming, my child. A darkness that hovers above Isaac. Tristan needs to exercise caution. I fear..." She whispered her final words before dropping my hands, and I departed the shop, running against the heavy droplets that plunged down from the turbulent sky. "I fear he is in grave danger."

FIFTY-ONE

As I stumbled outside onto the slippery cobbles I spotted Tristan's dark jacket headed down the alleyway next to the apothecary. I shouted as he ran in the opposite direction and yelled, "Tristan!" He didn't turn as I ran after him. I followed him past shop fronts and market awnings that pulled away from the ground in the strong winds. I didn't know if he couldn't hear me or if I was being ignored. He stopped eventually and bent over against a wall to catch his breath. His sopping-wet hair stuck to his forehead, and his lashes blinked away droplets as I caught up to him.

"Luna!" he exclaimed in surprise. "Why did you follow me?" I could barely hear him over the howl of the elements as he looked at me in anguish.

"I'm worried about you!" I shouted and swallowed a sudden deluge of rainwater from above. He shook his head and pointed distractedly over to a nearby telephone box. We clambered inside its tiny walls for shelter, and the downpour outside was muffled. We stood awkwardly crammed together as he looked down at me, raindrops falling off his face. "My grandmother wouldn't lie to you," I began in earnest before he could say anything. He ran his hands distractedly through his hair.

"I know, Luna. I'm sorry, it's just a lot to take in… to think that my father could do something so awful. No wonder they were always at each other's throats – that I always thought Isaac was jealous of him."

"I'm so sorry, Tristan." I began to shiver in the cold. He wrapped his arms around me. "It's not your fault. Are you okay? You're shaking!"

"I just… What if the last card was right?" I exclaimed into his shoulder. Tristan leaned back and cupped my chin with his hand to look at me properly.

"Well, I don't intend on dying today, Luna. I'm sure I'll be fine." He managed a small smile.

"I'm worried about you," I repeated in a whisper, unable to return his smile. "Grandmother thinks you're in danger."

"I respect your grandmother a lot. I shouldn't have blamed her for the truth."

"But what if she's—"

"I don't feel like I'm in danger now," Tristan said quietly and removed my wet hair from across my face. "Do you feel like you're in danger, Luna?" As I tried to take my eyes off his electric orbs he bent down gently and our lips met. Warmth flowed through me despite the sodden nature of our embrace, and my shivering ceased. He distracted me for a few seconds as the kiss deepened with an urgency neither of us was expecting. My body reacted, and I ran my fingers through his curls before I could help myself. My wet clothes were a thin layer, and I could feel every taut muscle in his body as he pulled my hips closer to his own. He pulled away breathlessly, and the pleasant glow inside me dimmed.

A dark shape streaked across the cobbles, and Tristan turned his head. "It's Isaac," he said darkly, and the mood instantly dampened. He made to open the door. I put my arm across as a barricade and looked at him beseechingly.

"Think about this, Tristan. He's up to something dark, and I don't think it's a good idea for you to get involved!"

"No offence, Luna, but you couldn't keep me in this telephone box even if you tried." He removed my arm gently. "He's heading into the forest, and I need to know why. I need to talk to him, to let him know that I know the truth. Perhaps I can stop him doing whatever he's up to."

I shook my head. "You can't stop him, Tristan. Whatever he's doing, he's more powerful than you!"

"I have to at least try." And with these words he ripped open the door and braved the storm once more.

I knew the forest better than Isaac. I could track him easily. His curly black hair bobbed up and down briefly, and then became obscured by the spiky branches reaching out onto the path, and he disappeared. Tracking Isaac was no difficult feat; his lack of expertise and knowledge of the trees meant that he left a disastrous trail of crashing and banging as he went. The rain had become a thin drizzle, and the footprints of his heavy boots sank with a squelch into the mud as he delved further into the depths of the forest.

After fifteen minutes or so of following his tracks I began to wonder where on earth he was leading us; even I rarely ventured this far into the trees. At the centre of the forest the paths begin to slide away into the stealthy arms of the waiting trees. I didn't know this part of Blackthorn Forest, and I watched uneasily as Isaac arrived at a fork in the path and took the left trail. Assuring myself that Isaac's cacophony of noise was still enough to shield our footsteps, we too took the left path, thinking after a couple of minutes that we must be close to his destination now. The weak morning sunlight did not possess enough strength to permeate through the dense thicket we now found ourselves in. Isaac had slowed down, hindered by the obscurity of the shaded paths, struggling to find a way through.

I took Tristan's hand, and we crouched hidden in the undergrowth and watched as Isaac hunted for a gap to pass through. He shifted his backpack and bent over. I blinked and he disappeared. I stood up quickly, not wanting to risk losing him, and tentatively crouched down and peered through the gap he had created in the thorny brambles. Isaac had emerged out of the tangled jungle and into a small clearing. Only a few trees scattered the green grass of his secret location deep in the heart of Blackthorn Forest.

A bramble scratched my cheek, and I felt a stinging sensation as I shifted my awkward position. We watched with wide eyes as he set his backpack down on the ground next to him. "What on earth is he up to?" Tristan muttered beside me. Isaac looked about the clearing as though readying himself for a great task ahead and unearthed various objects from his bag. The gentleness with which he placed these objects upon the forest floor left me with little doubt that they were glass bottles of his own creation. Isaac stood with his back to us, arms slightly lifted level with his shoulders, and recited a string of words that sounded like a different language. I waited with bated breath. Nothing happened. He reached down next to him and picked up one of the glass bottles. Unscrewing its cap, he turned back around, and his arms shook jerkily as he did something in front of him we struggled to see. A strange metallic trail lingered, suspended in mid-air, and I realised with a gasp it was the contents of the unlabelled bottle. When he replaced the bottle on the mossy floor it was empty. I swallowed, my throat suddenly dry, unable to take my eyes off Tristan's uncle.

FIFTY-TWO

Raising his arms up once more, Isaac recited the same strange incantation, and the clearing erupted with light and colour. A haze of deep purple streaked across the sky with a deafening crack that disturbed several roosting birds nearby. A magnificent burst of sunflower yellow followed in its wake, and Isaac raised his head upwards to the sky, revelling in his success. Strobes of bright white light struck and disappeared like lightning bolts that were interspersed with violent flashes of colour. Kaleidoscopic mirages of ruby red, emerald green and sapphire blue were reflected in my captive eyes as I watched the magnificent display before me.

Isaac reached down for another bottle and poured the liquid into the midst of all the colours. As the sorcerer chanted his bewitchment, the potion swirled in the air, crackling and fizzing. The liquid exploded with a boom that echoed around the clearing and formed an iridescent circle of shimmering light on the ground. I became paralysed with fear as the realisation dawned upon me. Isaac Brewer elevated his arms gleefully, turning about the clearing as the light vanished, revelling in the power of his success.

He span around at the sharp crack of a twig as the colour faded, and brambles tore at me as I forced myself through the undergrowth after Tristan. My cloak became trapped for a few seconds, and I ripped myself out of it, having not a second to spare, leaving it there. It trailed in the wind, reminiscent of the girl who had strayed from the path and been swallowed up by the trees. "Tristan!" I yelled through the gale as I heard crashing in front of me and watched as a leg passed through the gap in the undergrowth. "Tristan, wait!" I scrambled ahead and dived through the gap, trying to stop him, to warn him that he was in danger.

I was too late. He had already confronted his uncle, and they stood facing each other across the shimmering circle. It emitted a strange noise as it undulated, flowing in and out, gradually increasing and decreasing in size. Tristan was shouting at Isaac, shaking the raindrops out of his face, clearly distressed. "What have you been doing in the forest? Disappearing every day. I want to know what you're up to!" Tristan stood, teetering on the edge, staring into the glistening depths. Isaac raised both hands in alarm.

"Don't come any closer, Tristan! Stay where you are!"

"Are you going to answer me or not?"

"I'll tell you… I promise… just don't move—" Isaac caught sight of me emerging into the clearing, and Tristan followed his gaze. I ran forwards towards the circle and took up a third place around its border so we were standing in a strange triangle.

"No!" Isaac bellowed. "I've told you don't come any closer! It's dangerous!" He pointed a shaking finger at me. "Why did you bring the girl?"

"I know the truth about the past!" Tristan cried out desperately, ignoring his question. "We need to talk!" His screams were lost to the elements as the force of the wind snapped a tree branch that crashed down, narrowly avoiding us.

Tristan dodged out of the way and eyed the circle distractedly. "What is it?" he asked his uncle. Isaac looked around the clearing in panic and realised there was no escape.

"It's a portal! That's what I've been working on, boy – a portal to another world! And I've finally succeeded in creating one!" He looked gleefully at Tristan, expecting praise. We stared dumbstruck into its abyss; the light only extended so far. Darkness lay waiting in its depths.

"You can't control it!" I said confronting Isaac as I suddenly understood. "You don't know how it works, or how to get rid of it, do you? Isaac?" The ground shook, and all three of us staggered on the spot.

"I know how to control it!" he hissed at me. I squinted through the raindrops, imploring him to see reason.

"Then get rid of it! Get rid of it and we can all talk!" He paused and looked from me to Tristan, panic rising in his chest as he realised the portal was out of control. He nodded, raising his arms, and the ground gave an almighty tremor as though the earth were splitting in two. Isaac fell backwards onto the ground and struggled in the mud desperately trying to destroy what he had created.

I watched in horror as Tristan lurched into the portal and toppled over the edge. "NO!" I lunged forward in his direction, trying to catch him, to reel him back in. His hand slipped through my grasp, and he was enveloped by the swirling blackness. He vanished along with the shining entryway as my back collided violently with the forest floor and the wind was thumped out of my chest.

As I lay half in a faint with my eyes upturned to the stormy sky, Grandmother's words echoed in the recesses of my mind. As she had revealed the magician in Tristan's tarot reading and thought it to be him, she had uttered a prophecy that also belonged to Isaac: "You will bring death and destruction to the village."

The portal lay waiting underneath the earth, reverberating through the soil, pulsing its strange, continual beat.

PART FIVE

ISAAC AND JOANNA

FIFTY-THREE

ISAAC

I cursed my fingers for not working as they used to as I fumbled with the crystal decanter. The sorrowful reflection in the glass stared glumly back at me. It was a face both familiar and strange. I would not have called it my own had it not been for the indisputable proof the polished surface provided. I brought the decanter closer and peered mistrustfully at the bedraggled mop of brown curls that sat atop my head, the dark rings beneath my wild eyes and the bushy beard that adorned my face in the most alarming of manners. One hundred and forty years later and not one wrinkle. An entire century had passed and here I sat, still alive, still with the same face I knew from before. Yet another peculiarity of this cursed, godforsaken place.

My shepherd's hut shook in the persisting storm. I didn't flinch; the tiny structure had withstood gales stronger than tonight's. I looked around the room with resigned fondness. There were no creature comforts, for I did not deserve them. A little table, an uncomfortable bed and a small fire were all I needed to survive. I allowed myself the luxury of a small sigh and contemplated how much of a life it was anymore. One spent in complete solitude, banished from all civilisations, nestled in this crook in the hillside with only my guilt for company.

Bottles had been lined up in an untidy row before me as a result of my own trembling handiwork. The tremors had started perhaps forty years after I passed through. My body was, after all, simply a vessel hiding an ancient soul inside. If my calculations were correct, I was 183 years of age, yet my outward appearance was that of an unkempt forty-three-year-old. Hearing another great gust over the grassy mounds outside, I thought about all the poor creatures that wouldn't be able to take refuge. Whiling away my hours in the wilderness had caused me to become one with nature.

A squawk outside the hut startled me, and I upended the contents of the jar I was clutching onto the wooden table. The bone-chilling call resulted in heart palpitations whenever I either heard or caught sight of one of those awful birds. "They're getting closer again," I muttered, praying the ravens wouldn't find me in this hideaway I had cowered in for years. Shooting fearful glances at the windows and door, I mopped up the purple liquid and righted the bottle. I rested my weary head in my hands and questioned what the point was anymore. I was incapable of brewing a forgetfulness potion potent enough to provide me with blissful relief for the rest of my time in this place. I may as well give up trying to forget. That would be my ultimate punishment: to live out my years in the full knowledge that this had all been my doing and only I was to blame for the ruin of so many lives. Lord knows I had grown used to the inexplicable guilt that wracked me constantly. It was my only companion.

His innocent face still haunts me. The girl's too; her accusing eyes plague my nightmares. I suppose the chestnut curls would have faded to grey and withered into dust many years ago. This image made me shudder, and I hugged my heavy furs tighter about myself, longing for some form of protection against things long past. They were both so young, so keen, and I had taken all of that away in an instant. I owed them so much, but one was dead and the other, well... My sigh was audible as I watched a thin wisp of candle smoke trail away into the air. The best that I could hope for my nephew now was that he was still alive. I had so many questions and yet no way of seeking the answers.

My magic had faded with age; I seemed barely capable of brewing the simplest of potions nowadays. It had all been spent in futile attempts that had never amounted to anything. He had so many questions too. The day we travelled through, Tristan asked me so many questions I could not answer. I regret recklessly throwing myself into that swirling pit on the forest floor, but I had to. I promised my brother I would look after him, even if it was never for his sake. I wonder how they had felt when we never returned from Blackthorn. How did the girl explain it? I wonder how long she had mourned me for, or if Tristan's father had suppressed those feelings too.

The candle burnt out next to me, and the room grew darker. I closed my eyes and imagined that fateful day. Gasping for air, clutching at our chests, we emerged on what felt like the other side of the world. I had never planned on going through the portal. I just wanted the knowledge that I was good enough to create an entire realm of my own. I wanted a place that I could control, that I would be the master of, which I could destroy with the snap of a finger. But it was too late; there was no question of undoing something that we now inhabited. I didn't even – and still to this day do not – know how. I leant back in the chair and allowed myself to sink deeper into the memory.

*

"Where the hell have you taken us?" Tristan stared wildly at the spot in which the portal had disappeared.

"Where the hell have *I* taken us? I think you mean you, boy! I told you not to come any closer. Now look what you've done!" I snarled back at my nephew, trying to land the blame on anyone but myself. He ran his hands through his hair and looked about him, panicking. I mirrored his actions and took in the deserted landscape. There were no buildings or roads so far as the eye could see. There was simply a stretch of barren farmland and the faraway mooing of cattle. *This is wrong*, I couldn't help but think, *it was supposed to look more spectacular than this.* We trudged about the same patch for five minutes until Tristan turned to me.

"Take us back!" he demanded with a steely glint in his eye. "You have to take us back!" I shrugged apathetically.

"First of all the portal's disappeared, and I don't have any of my potions or spell work with me. What do you expect me to do right now? Besides," I interrupted Tristan's stammers, "don't you want to explore for a bit?" Tristan's nostrils flared.

"Take us back, Isaac," he managed through gritted teeth. I took a couple of steps away fearing he might suddenly swing for me.

"Stop your whining. Let's have a look around." I couldn't admit to him that I hadn't the least idea of how to 'take us back'.

I turned away from my nephew and began crossing the field towards a wooden signpost. Tristan followed me, muttering to himself and shaking his head, as we proceeded across the muddy ground. The dilapidated signpost had been crudely etched with the words:

TO THE MANOR

A roughly carved arrow pointed over a hill in the distance. "To the manor." I whispered the words, a sense of excitement building. This was more like it; a luxurious manor house awaited, all from my own creation.

"I have zero desire to go exploring in this little world you've created for yourself. God only knows what goes on in that warped mind of yours." Tristan roughly kicked the signpost, and I was thankful that he was aiming his annoyance at inanimate objects.

"Come on, boy, where's your sense of adventure?" I felt a tug on my arm and turned to see him hanging off my coat sleeve. He appealed to me, his tone softening.

"Isaac, please… Luna will be worried." I deliberated as I considered his request and couldn't help a small smile flit across my face; the power belonged to me.

"The girl will still be there in a couple of hours."

FIFTY-FOUR

Revelling in the glory of my new world I bounded over the hilltop. Tristan trudged miserably behind me. His lack of curiosity only fuelled mine; if he could see for a few hours what I had achieved he would surely be in awe of my magic. It's only when I cast my mind back now that I realise how foolish I had acted. If I hadn't been so drunk with power I may have noticed a few things on the way to the manor. I may have noticed the barren landscape was not the one I had envisioned. That this run-down muddy stretch of land did not excite any hope for displays of wealth or power. I may have noticed that the free-roaming cows were skinnier than usual – their great flanks not as powerful as the ones in our world. That their dead, hungry eyes watched us pass by with apathy. I may have noticed the bloodstains smeared across the horrible stakes that lined the path. I may have noticed the first signs of poverty, chaos and distress that were the result of a tyrannous rule. But I was blind to all of this and to Tristan's protestations.

The sign had not indicated the physical distance to the manor. I followed the arrow in blind faith, without knowing how much further to our destination, and without really caring. I began to take naive joy in the mundane landscape. I found glee at the freshly ploughed fields we passed; a smile formed at the ugliest of insects, even a raucous laugh at a perfectly formed cow pat. Had I taken more notice of my companion, I would have seen Tristan stare at me as you would at a madman. Perhaps, in that moment, I was mad.

We descended the hill and happened upon another signpost

battered in the wind. The words were impossible to read until we stood directly in front of it.

NO TRESPASSING

The etchings on the wood were not properly formed and gave the impression that somebody illiterate had tried their best to write the words. I frowned. The path began to widen as though in anticipation of larger transport. Tristan's glare bounced off the back of my head as I hurried along the track that was opening out. The mud turned into gravel, and the neat border of the hedgerows signified that someone had paid them some attention as we advanced.

"Didn't you see the sign?" Tristan's voice was an octave higher than usual, and I smirked.

"This is my land! Whoever put that sign up obviously doesn't know I've arrived."

"You're mad, Isaac!" Tristan was now panting to keep up with me, shooting furtive glances at the dirt track, as though afraid some great monster was going to attack from behind. "I don't want to be here! I think we should go back." I rolled my eyes and began walking backwards.

"I thought you were made of stronger stuff than this! We owe it to my creation to at least find out what's here." I tripped up on a rock and stumbled, twisting my ankle. I ignored the pain to listen to Tristan's reply. His raven curls danced lightly in the breeze, and for a moment I envied his youth. His long strides were an easy match for two of mine. He could have been the hero in a fairy tale. I pushed my jealously aside and caught the end of Tristan's sentence.

"…but that's just it, Isaac. What exactly is your creation? It looks just like wasteland to me."

"That's because you have no imagination in that thick head of yours!" I grinned at him.

"Don't call me thick! Just because you've got this stupid idea that you can be the master of—" Tristan stopped mid-sentence as his brow furrowed at something behind me.

My back prickled and, suddenly fearful, I whipped around to see what Tristan's eyes had locked on. I thought of monstrous beasts and horrendous beings as something loomed ahead in the landscape. A set of gigantic gates challenged us from going any further. The two stone pillars that stood proudly on either side seemed to stretch all the way up to the sky. My initial thoughts of monstrous beasts had not been far from the mark: two great dragons' heads stood atop each pillar and flanked the gate. Their gargantuan heads surveyed the surrounding area with ease. Their sharp teeth were set in jagged spikes, and if one of them had broken loose or fallen from that height, we would surely have been impaled. I could have sworn that a few of the teeth were missing and wondered if that was a defence mechanism. I shuddered and looked instead at the forked tongue that hissed and flicked at an invisible enemy in the sky. Its two prongs were ready for attack. If I had the misfortune to see those stone beasts again now, my faint heart wouldn't be able to take it.

Tristan, a braver man than I, although I would never admit it back then, strode over to the wooden slats and began examining them by hand. As he ran his fingers over the sturdy entranceway I could tell he was thinking of my manuscript. The scribbled gates and barriers that I had crafted with pencil had been brought to life. This gate took those small mechanisms to a whole new level. Intricate patterns in the wood had been hand carved and locked together with spikes and metal crosses. I was sure that it would take three people at least to open the gates. There were no handles or moving parts for us to grab and attempt this feat ourselves; it had to open from the inside. This gate was a manifestation from ideas taken deep within the recesses of my mind and blown up to a scale even I could not have imagined. If I could create this without intending to, what else was I capable of?

My feet wobbled. I became suddenly aware of the magnitude of our situation. Somebody had thought the manor important enough to erect two stone dragons and an impenetrable gate in front of it. Five minutes ago, the lure of a luxury manor house filled me with possibility, but that joyous feeling was fast being overtaken by something altogether different. Dread. During the creation of this world, I had envisioned a place in which I could rule and would have dominion over others, somewhere for once in my life I would be in control. I was the one who was supposed to be inside the manor, not locked on the outside. That meant that there was already somebody else here.

An almighty scraping sound was emitted, and instinctively both Tristan and I put our hands over our ears to block out the awful noise. He jumped back from the gate and withdrew his hand. He looked at me with wide eyes as though saying, 'It wasn't me.' I looked up to the sky. As the gates slowly opened, the immovable dragons remained atop the pillars. I had half expected the dull stab of one of their teeth to strike me down, but alas I was left standing. A solitary figure stood in the middle of the gates. They took a single step forward. They sported a shining suit of armour from head to toe, complete with a tail feather atop the helmet. A small sword hung from their waist. I gulped. A dreadful thought entered my mind. A striking, awful thought. I pushed it aside.

"State your purpose." The male voice was gravelly, as though he had not cleared his throat in many years. I caught Tristan's eye. His skin was pallid. I cleared my own throat and straightened my jacket. My voice did not ring as true as I had hoped, and the quiver in my throat was laughable. "The lord of the manor is here." I felt Tristan grimace beside me. The wind blew fiercely in our eardrums as a short silence followed my child-like announcement. From behind the metal plate the man's eyes narrowed into slits, and he gave a muffled chuckle. It was not the sort of good-natured chuckle that one might emit if enjoying a good joke; it was the sort of menacing chuckle that insinuated we had dug our own graves, and he fully intended on burying us in them. "The lord of the manor, eh?" He took another step forward. A good punch wouldn't have dented his attire. It clinked as he advanced. I had the sudden inclination to turn and run over the hills, past the signposts, locate the portal and get the hell out of there. But I stood my ground. I could not back down in front of my nephew.

The suit of armour halted a couple of paces ahead of us. I could feel my heart thump around in my chest, and I was sure that if I had been the one wearing the metal suit, you would have heard it hammering around, looking for an escape. The unidentifiable man looked us up and down. "And who might this be?" he asked gruffly, pointing his gauntlet at Tristan.

"M-my nephew," I stammered. Another brief pause before the man threw his helmet back and gave a raucous laugh as though now enjoying a joke with the dragons.

"The lord and his nephew have arrived! Well I never…" After he'd finished having his joke he snapped his head forward and his voice grew quiet. "You'd better come with me." He manoeuvred himself awkwardly and began to march away, a methodical left, right, left, right, in his clunky attire. The screeching of the gates started up again. I realised they were closing in on us as we stood in the middle of the pillars. It was a sudden choice of either move or be squashed. I grabbed Tristan by the arm and pulled him with me towards the manor.

"What are we doing, Isaac?" he hissed at me. "Why is he wearing a suit of armour?"

"Just trust me, boy, I know what I'm doing." A greater lie had never been told, but he had the decency, or perhaps the naivety, in that moment not to question me.

God knows I wish he had.

FIFTY-FIVE

My chair creaked as I leaned forward to relight the candle. It was not very often that I travelled back to these memories in such detail, and I felt as though light was required in order to remember properly. My bones felt weary. The storm had moved on across the hills, but the sky outside my little hut had grown dark. Dusk was approaching. I'd need to barricade the doors soon; the days when I could stay awake to keep watch at night had long faded. I heaved myself out of the uncomfortable chair, my heavy furs weighing me down, and locked and reinforced the weak door. It wouldn't hold long if the baron came looking, but it was necessary for my own peace of mind. I don't remember the last time that I felt truly safe. I thought back to that manor house and how its walls were a fortress compared to my hut. After avoiding death by dragons, Tristan and I found ourselves in a walled garden.

"What is this place?" Tristan whispered. If it were not for that pesky niggling feeling in my stomach, I would have been able to appreciate the sheer beauty of the glorious garden we walked in. I looked up warily at the stone walls looming above us, the ivy that twined up and up, the dragons' heads growing smaller but still following us. Nowhere on that smooth surface would provide a foothold strong enough for a grown man to scale the wall if needs be. We were trapped.

We traipsed behind our lacking host until my ankle began to pulse uncomfortably. I struggled to keep up with his slow pace on the gravelled path. Tristan shot me a disdainful look.

"What's wrong with you?"

I checked the suit of armour was not looking and rubbed my ankle, which was already starting to swell. "I think I twisted my ankle on a rock back there." Tristan snorted derisively.

"Some lord you are." I put my foot back on the ground. I wasn't going to get any sympathy from him. But, I thought as I winced at every other step, I couldn't really blame him. I was the one who was leading us into the lion's den, dragon's pit, whatever it was. I had to be the one who controlled it. And the master was coming home.

Thankfully the house came into view and the dull pain in my ankle disappeared. It stood proud at the end of the gravel drive – multiple stone buildings interconnected that could house hundreds of occupants. Now this I could be the master of. I pictured myself sitting at the head of a grand table as I ate and drank my fill, servants at my beck and call, a roaring fire to warm me through. I smiled smugly. After all these years of being second best, of losing the woman I loved to my own brother, surely this was the least that I deserved. Family meant nothing. Whereas wealth and power – now those you could rely on. Tristan pinched my arm. I shook out of my reverie and realised that the suit of armour had been talking to me. We halted under a low arch in front of a set of double doors.

"Well then, master of the house, make yourself at home," the gap in the metal plate sneered. As soon as my quivering finger touched the wooden doors, they swung open and we stepped gingerly inside. The feeling in my stomach imploded. I was on the brink of admitting the truth of what I had done, but allowed the grandeur of the hall to become a distraction instead. My fire roared in the grate behind a large table laden with silver plates and chunky drinking vessels. I enjoyed the mental image of me sitting at this table surrounded by servants. The suits of armour adorning the hall clinked. They were all occupied. The image faded.

We were invited by a nearby gauntlet (I didn't know if it was our original host or not) to take a seat upon a wooden bench to our left. This we did, and my gaze was drawn up high. The ceiling I marvelled at must have taken years to complete. It reminded me of the gates outside – the sharp twists and spikes knotted together intricately. My next thought was of Blackthorn Forest. The ceiling looked as though it was made with the same dark wood that their tree boughs were. I immediately ignored this resemblance; I could not entertain the idea that they could be one and the same. I locked this thought in the same vault the others had been banished to.

As Tristan shuffled uneasily in his seat he managed to scrape the bench along the polished floor. The noise bounced off the cavernous ceiling. The guards turned their anonymous heads towards us, and I suddenly wished I could transform us into mice. I followed Tristan's gaze as I swallowed uncomfortably, my throat dry. He looked at the torches that lined the walls, and their flames flickered with the electric blue in his eyes. The ruby-red blazes soon became unnerving as we waited for something to happen. A pretty serving girl could offer us a drink. Or even some food would be welcome.

I had little time to contemplate what our next actions should be before the set of double doors at the other end of the hall crashed open, and three figures emerged. The heavy oak bashed against the walls and made a great screeching noise as they closed again. Some of the suits of armour winced. Someone advanced briskly towards us flanked by two further suits of armour that stood prouder than the ones lining the hall. He came more clearly into view, and I could start to distinguish his features. My sandpaper throat closed for a few seconds, and Tristan let out an exhalation of shock.

"This had better be good enough to interrupt my afternoon prayers." The man enunciated each word with a perfect set of sparkling teeth. A sudden waft of alcohol entered my nostrils, and I wondered if he had been praying inside a brewery. I was unable to speak. This male's skin was clearer than mine without a wrinkle or fine line. His eyes were brighter, his teeth whiter, his hair a rich chestnut compared with my own thinning brown. He even seemed a couple of inches taller. His forest-green breeches were embossed with golden buttons, and the shirt tucked into them was as white as the purest snow. He sported a short coat over the top of this get-up that was embroidered with golden thread. A shining belt around his muscular middle completed the ridiculous ensemble.

I exchanged a look with Tristan. Mine was loaded with disbelief and his full of horror. I shifted on the bench to ensure that I hadn't been looking into a mirror.

The man standing proudly before us, put simply, was me.

FIFTY-SIX

"What the hell is going on?" Tristan hissed at my side.

My mirror image rested his hands on his hips in an authoritative stance. "I ask the questions around here, boy." I flinched at the familiarity of the phrase.

"Leave him out of it." I found the ability to speak again as the man turned his attention to me. "My name is Isaac Brewer." I threw caution to the wind. "I am the one who created the portal, and in turn, this world. My nephew here, Tristan, travelled through the portal with me from a village called Blackthorn. I am the lord and creator of this manor by right. Everything you see around you is all my own invention." The hall fell silent. I waited for his reply with bated breath, thinking that he would have more questions, but that I would be willing to educate him about the situation in hand. Tristan hung his head in his hands beside me in embarrassment.

The man did no more than indicate to his guards to follow with a simple flick of the wrist, turned on his heel and disappeared back through the doors they had all come from with a great cacophony of noise. The suits of armour slumped back down from the attentive stance they had withheld during the exchange. I looked at Tristan who was now resting his elbow on the edge of the bench as his hand propped up his head. "You've really gone and done it now, Isaac," he muttered. "Did you see their swords? Why does he look like you?" I ignored Tristan's questions. I still couldn't bring myself to admit what I had done.

I looked about the hall uneasily. What if the man was secretly giving his guards the order and we were about to be impaled gruesomely on the end of a sword?

A couple of minutes passed in stagnant silence. I noticed that three guards now flanked the entrance doors behind us. One of their swords glinted in the light emanating from the brackets as they turned to look at me. I looked away quickly. Footsteps echoed around the hall. I glanced over my shoulder. They grew louder and faster until a small figure emerged from a hidden side door. It was a girl. She passed the guards silently and made a beeline for the hard bench we sat on. We awaited her greeting with a little less unease than before. When she was a few paces away from us, she tossed her waist-length hair behind her back, and the bright blonde shimmered about her.

She stood before us and cocked her head on one side, her gaze travelling over Tristan and lingering there for a few moments, before finally resting on me. The guards righted their posture. I took in the regal blood red of her gown. She was obviously of high rank in the manor. I gave her my full attention; this could be important. "I am Letha Villinor," she announced in a cold voice. I looked at Tristan who raised his eyebrows. Clearly I would have to do the charming here.

"Well hello, Letha, what an unusual but beautiful name you ha—" I faltered as she exposed her small white teeth. It may have been the shadows that danced across her face, but the pearly whites looked pointy. She fixed me with her cool, blue eyes, and my blood ran cold. If ice queens existed, then one stood before us playing with a strand of her long locks. Her face set, and I noticed for the first time the jaggedness of her jaw.

"Don't bother with niceties." She carried herself with the air of one who was no stranger to issuing commands. We obeyed this one and remained in silence. "My father sent me." She returned our blank stares with impatience.

"Etimus? The man who left you just now?" It seemed as though the better version of me had a family too. She didn't wait for a reply but carried on brazenly.

"Anyway, he seems to think that you're an old fool." I recoiled at her words. "And you," she carried on, addressing Tristan, "are playing along with your uncle's lunacy hoping that someone will take pity on you and offer you a warm meal and a bed for the night. What fool let you into the manor anyway?" My gaze travelled to the edges of the hall. "Well, whoever let you through the gates needs punishing. Complete lack of security." She revolved on the spot, and her gown trailed behind her. The guards remained motionless.

Letha turned back to face us expectantly. "Well? What have you got to say for yourselves? I haven't got all day."

Tristan started, "My apologies, my lady, my uncle here is clearly ma—"

"Don't listen to him, he doesn't know what he's talking about, poor boy," I cut across him. Tristan scowled at me while Letha narrowed her eyes. I began to explain all about my magic, the potions and how it had taken years in the making to learn how to create a portal. I told her how Tristan and I had fallen through, how I created this world, and how I now had arrived at the manor ready to rule. She stood with arms folded across her chest and waited for me to finish, like a child who had grown bored of the game.

She eventually held up a small hand and pursed her lips. "Enough." The word rang in time with the chime of a distant bell tower. "I've heard enough. Both of you stay here." She took the skirts of her gown with her as she walked swiftly away. Two guards immediately marched behind her in unison, and her blonde hair rippled in waves down her back as she left through the double doors.

"Are you going to tell me why he looks like you?" Tristan blurted out as soon as we sat alone again. He turned to face me. "Isaac, what have you done? Did you create him too? And that... awful girl?" I shivered despite the warmth of the hall and instead fixed my gaze on a stag's head protruding from above the table laden for supper. I was spared from answering by the man who had been identified as Etimus re-entering the hall. I sat up straighter without thinking about it. These people seemed to have that effect on you. He approached our bench, and this time his daughter stood at his side with an unimpressed expression across her face. Etimus turned his youthful features towards us and cleared his throat. The deep noise produced an echo.

"Well, Isaac Brewer..." he formed my name with his mouth in disgust as though talking about some horrific ailment, "I have never heard of you and neither has my daughter. You speak of a portal." I looked up at him eagerly. "None of my guards has reported the sudden appearance of a portal, and I have never heard of anyone travelling through a gateway of this kind before." I looked away as my heart sank. "Therefore, I must arrive at the conclusion that you are mad."

I arose from the bench, and a silver arm immediately pushed me back down. "I'm not mad!" I countered. "I can show you!" Etimus held up a gloved hand in the same way his daughter had done mere moments before. His voice became a snarl.

"I'm not interested in games, Mr Brewer. You claim to be the ruler of this world, the..." he struggled for words and blinked his bleary eyes a few times, "the creator of everything here? You think you are... entitled to own my property simply by turning up at my gates?" The question hung in the air like a bad smell as I played with my hands in my lap.

Etimus took a few steps forward. My boots almost touched the end of his strange pointy shoes. He bent down so his face was level with mine, and I recoiled as though looking in a cruel mirror. I felt Tristan stir beside me, but laid a hand on the bench between us. No. I met Etimus's eyes and tried to avoid the stench of alcohol that seeped out of his pores. The man was clearly intoxicated. "And as for this place named Blackthorn you mention..." his lip curled, "you're in it." He righted himself and took a few steps back as he looked me in the eye.

"I am Etimus Villinor, the Baron of Blackthorn and owner of EVERYTHING you see." I felt the guard lay both hands on my shoulders and started as Etimus turned his back on us. His final words struck me like lightning before I was lifted roughly off the bench, one last blow to my ego, all dreams of luxury shattered. "Throw these peasants out of my manor."

FIFTY-SEVEN

"So let's get this straight." Tristan winced as his feet dragged over the gravel. "The world that you thought you created doesn't actually exist. And…" he batted away a feather from his face as a guard tried to headbutt him into silence, "instead, all you've done is take us back in time?" I groaned, mainly in pain, but also from having to admit the truth to my nephew. "But not only that," Tristan grimaced as the end of a sword poked into his back, courtesy of a third guard that gripped us tightly, "you've also created your own…" Tristan's arms flapped wildly, "alter ego in the form of a baron of Blackthorn – get off me – some mad tyrant who doesn't believe what's actually happened?" Tristan gave up the fight and allowed the guard to drag him unceremoniously from the manor. I kicked out at my own guard as I heard the awful screech of the gates start up again and flinched as a sharp smack from a gauntlet left me seeing stars.

"Well, when you put it like that," I panted as we were thrown through the gates and onto the hard ground. "That's about the long and short of it, yes." I massaged my rear and scowled at the guards as they retreated into the manor. I eyed the dragons above; would now be the time for their defence mechanism to kick in? Tristan bitterly spat out a mouthful of gravel.

"Isaac, you're an absolute idiot!" He rolled over onto his back, staring up at the sky, panting heavily. I sat cross-legged on the ground next to him and hung my pulsing temples in my hands…

Little flecks swirled in my irises as I opened my eyes again. The bottles before me were just distinguishable in the candlelight. I turned my head over my shoulder. My little fire had almost burnt out. The recollection surprised me; even now I managed to remember the look on my nephew's face once he realised the truth of what I had done. I think a part of me had known it. From the moment I had seen the suit of armour, I had concealed the truth from Tristan, barely able to admit to my own defeat, and had blundered along in the hope that I was wrong. But I hadn't been.

I thought back to that grand ceiling. The reason I had thought the dark wood reminded me of Blackthorn Forest was because the materials had been taken from those very trees. The same trees were now interspersed with fields for crops and cattle. I shook my head at the memory. Instead of transporting us to a new world brimming with opportunity, all my portal had done was take us back. Take us back in time to medieval Blackthorn, but not to how it had been in history, to a horrific version of my own creation. In doing so, I had also fabricated a doppelganger of myself, to be its ruler. I laughed derisively at my own incompetence. It had been too much to hope for that I had succeeded at something. No wonder Tristan hated me.

In the days that followed we bickered like two stubborn children. Unable to locate the portal entrance, we slept rough that night beneath a gorse bush, ferreting around for berries and fresh water from a nearby stream. I shuddered. The water had not been fresh; the cattle had frequented the water source too. We awoke the following morning, stiff and aching from sleeping on the hard ground and the blossoming bruises the guards had kindly left on us. We searched that field, and then the next, but still couldn't find the portal. It had disappeared without a trace, as though, having satisfactorily done its job, sunk beneath the soil again.

None of my bottled potions or spell work had accompanied us through. I didn't always need my potions to perform magic, but they were an invaluable aid. With nothing to source any energy from, it was as though a temporary block had been put on my powers. Tristan greeted this news with a sour face. He threw constant accusations at me, blaming me for everything (which was of course true), and demanding that I create another portal or magical item capable of transporting him back to present day and to his Luna.

On the second day of sleeping rough in the wilderness I grew angry with Tristan's surly mood swings. There was something else that fuelled my magic: emotion. Craving some peace and quiet from his constant complaints, I mustered all the energy I could from my irritation, and managed to conjure a small spark on the tip of my finger. I directed the spark at Tristan thinking I'd better make the most of it while I still had it. I wanted to teach him a lesson just for an hour or so. My intention was to turn him into a raven so I would no longer have to listen to his bitter words. As soon as the energy was transferred over to him he grew silent, and I closed my eyes, briefly revelling in the quiet.

I opened my eyes, and a sudden jolt passed through me, as though a fire had been lit in the gorse. I scrambled to my feet off the low wall I had been perching on. "Holy shit!"

A panicked squawk sounded from what used to be Tristan's mouth as I yelped. Acting on emotion alone meant that my magic had not quite done what I intended. I looked my nephew up and down. I had half transformed him into a raven: he was part man, part bird. He had grown in height and towered above me. He was at least seven foot tall. His clothing had ripped where black feathers protruded out of his skin. The feathers flapped loosely in the breeze. The great talons on his feet had torn through his shoes, and their sharp ends dug into the soil. His face was the most alarming part. His mouth and nose had been replaced with a small beak, his eyes were now two red circles (ravens don't have red eyes, do they?), and an impressive crop of feathers adorned the top of his head instead of his usual curls. They stuck out at odd angles and looked like a funny sort of hat. Despite this, his features remained oddly human, and I could tell that a man was disguised beneath the exterior. I struggled to look into those glowing eyes as I backed away.

"Oh God, Tristan... now look here... Ow!" He had started towards me, extending enormous wings that flapped behind him, and I tried to shield myself from them. "I only meant to—" Tristan took a swing at me. "Argh, geroff me!" I managed a muffled shout from beneath the feathers and winced as a sharp peck from his beak ended his attack. The red eyes narrowed as a guttural noise sounded from deep within him.

"What the hell have you done to me?" His words were rasping and deep, half human, half grotesque bird.

"Oh good." I clambered up off the dirt. "You can still speak. Sorry, my boy, I-I only meant to turn you into a little bird so I could have some peace and quiet. It obviously, er..." I eyed him up and down warily, "didn't quite work. Hang on, I'll turn you back, stay still!" He shifted impatiently from talon to talon as I delved deep and attempted to tap into something which I knew full well was no longer there. As it transpired, I couldn't turn him back, and he remained in this form for quite some time.

FIFTY-EIGHT

In the days that followed our exit from the manor, we had not been alone. Etimus had sent his guards to spy on us. I couldn't entertain the idea that he thought we were a threat to him – a failing magician and a surly teenager? It could have been morbid curiosity; there may have been a part of him not soaked in alcohol that wondered if we were telling the truth. Or maybe he too recognised the resemblance between us and, madman or not, that was something worth keeping an eye on. Whatever the reason for their spying, the guards had witnessed my failed attempt at transfiguring Tristan into a raven. We soon learnt that this information had been fed back into the manor.

They ambushed us. I am somewhat proud to say that it took three guards to take me down. They chased me over hillsides and through thorny brambles as I evaded capture the best I could. But they eventually took me down with a knee to the groin (cheap shot), and I crashed into the dirt at their feet. Tristan meanwhile had learnt that he could change shape. He was able to take on the form of a normal-sized raven, and I think managed to have a bit of fun for a while as he flew across the treetops and explored our surroundings. Of course, he would never admit to me how exhilarating this was and instead constantly demanded that I take us back as soon as he alighted again. He soon got the hang of it and could change from one form into another at will. He attempted to fly off when the guards appeared, but they had come prepared. They clumsily trapped him in a tiny cage, and I prayed he wouldn't try and break out of the sturdy metal contraption by taking on his larger form; he could do some serious damage to himself. Thankfully he gritted his beak and remained in his smaller guise as we were both escorted back through those awful gates.

Tristan was held at sword point and forced to transform repeatedly. It became apparent that this was more than a bit of light entertainment for the baron. He had a more nefarious reason for our being held captive. After poor Tristan had been chased about the hall for three hours, hiding away on a wooden beam up high, the little bird grew exhausted and fell from his perch. Etimus's guards caught him in the cage. The great Baron of Blackthorn could not even perform that feat himself. Tristan flapped weakly against the crude bars, but it was no use; he was a prisoner. I too was to be a prisoner for a few days but in a different sort of cage. They took me to the dungeons. That dank, festering pit beneath the earth that made you retch with every breath you took in the damp air. I felt sorry for whoever ended up inside those bars whatever they had done to deserve it. The dungeon cells were not fit for the rodents.

My living quarters soon became the least of my worries. The baron's guards would take turns lining the walls of the cell, intimidating me with their glinting swords, and occasionally letting me feel the harsh slash of one. Some of the scars from those two days never faded. The sadistic baron had taken somewhat of a liking to what I had accidentally transformed Tristan into. He saw them as an army of beasts he could have as his own. Faced with continuous threats to both mine and Tristan's lives, I was forced to continually tap into what little magic I could squeeze from my exhausted self, and perform this grotesque transformation over and over again. Some victims came willingly, those already under the baron's command keen to gain some credit or whatever he promised them in return for sacrificing their human form. It was the ones that didn't come willingly that I have never forgiven myself for.

They were brought from the nearby town in their rags kicking and screaming. Failure to comply resulted in the murder of their families. Young boys not fully grown, men who had been dragged from ploughing the fields trying to make a living for their wives and children at home, the elderly, the homeless, vagrants and beggars alike… No matter what form they arrived at the dungeons in, they would leave as seven-foot-tall monsters with glowing eyes. I contemplated getting hold of one of the guards' swords and cutting my own hands off. But they weren't having any of that. So I had to carry on, my hands trembling with the thought of keeping myself and Tristan alive, hating myself for every decision I had made that had brought me to that moment. After the hundredth person left the cell, I became an empty shell of myself, weakly doing Etimus's bidding, letting the darkness close in upon me.

FIFTY-NINE

I leaned back in my creaky chair. The darkness had never truly left me. The weight of what I had done pressed down upon me, suffocating me on the bad nights, the faces of screaming children whose lives I had ruined forever etched into my memory. Once the baron had taken his fill and there was nothing left of me, I was released from my cell. I was dragged up a dark corridor still feeling like I was in a cave, and dumped into that grand hall again, blinking away the sudden harsh light along with my tears. They allowed me to see Tristan one last time. The capability of speech had been beaten out of him. He was unresponsive in his great hulking form. I called out to him desperately as I was thrown from Etimus's domain. I tried to explain through choked sobs that I had done it all for him; that all the people he had seen arrive and leave in monstrous form was only because I had been trying to keep him alive. I tried to communicate to him how deeply sorry and ashamed I was… but I'm not sure the message ever got through those ruffled feathers.

I attempted to scale the walls many times but was met with constant attacks from the ravens. They came in great swarms with their awful crowing in my ears and their hooked talons ripping at my clothes. I could withstand it up until they drew blood, and then I would crash into the dirt beneath the dragons that looked scathingly down at me. Eventually they chased me from the manor grounds. Etimus's army had taken to doing his bidding like second nature. Or perhaps it had been threats to their families that had enforced their willing. They drove me to the hills. I always wondered if Tristan had been one of the hundreds that swooped down on me.

Stinging from cuts and bruises I wandered for days and finally stumbled upon an abandoned cottage deep in the forest. The cottage showed signs of a forgotten life: a little cot and blankets in the corner, a rusting kettle on the stove and a table laid for dinner with food that had grown mouldy. It was with gut-wrenching emotion that I tidied away these things and made the cottage my home. I knew it was my fault that the family that lived in it before had to uproot suddenly, the father and son flying sorrowfully above the manor grounds now. I became a coward. Or perhaps I always was one, I don't know. My shame and fear caused me to become a hermit, barely leaving the cottage, not able to cope with the consequences of what my magic had done. From the creation of the portal, refusing to find a way of taking us back, to transforming Tristan and countless others into monstrous beasts, I could no longer face myself in the cracked mirror on the wall.

I realised that the only thing that would grant me peace was to forget. I made it my mission over the next few years to try and erase from my memory everything that had happened. I ferreted around in the forest on the lookout for potion ingredients. I collected anything I thought might help me. I even forced myself to skin a few dead foxes and fashion warmer garments. With the days stretching out before me, each one slower than the last, I soon became an expert at hunting small animals and cooking them to keep me alive. Even when I lost the will and starved myself, my body kept on going. It operated as a shell of me. I realised that I could not die. It seemed a fitting punishment.

I ventured to the nearest taverns to try and hear the latest news of the baron. I encountered tales of woe and hardship, of families that had been ripped apart, of children starving in the streets, of the militant actions of the ravens in forcing continuous labour in the fields. They were in great contrast with the tales of the manor house. I learnt about how they lived in luxury with stores of grain and wine aplenty, whole herds of well-fed cattle, drinking and eating to their heart's content while people starved outside their gates.

At one point there had been a sort of rebellion. But it had not lasted long and neither had the rebels. The baron was too powerful and too protected to be overthrown. His boots were firmly under the table, and his guards and ravens, whether acting out of fear or loyalty, were too numerous. The worsening situation only strengthened my desire to live in blissful ignorance. I emptied the cottage's cupboards and drawers and collected all the pans, bottles, jars and utensils I could find. Great clouds of coloured smoke billowed out of the chimney at all hours. The little cottage puffed out a deep violet fog as I brewed with all the energy and magic I could muster.

The potions made me violently sick. Shortening or lengthening the brewing time did not make a difference. Switching the quantity or berry didn't work. Changing the components to different mixtures and volumes had no effect. My potions no longer worked. This did not deter me for long, and I changed tack. If I could not brew a potion that would make me forget, I would have to focus my energy on a physical object instead. I cast my mind back to when Tristan was a small boy and I would read to him his favourite fairy tales. Of course, magic in those stories was entirely different to real life, but it wouldn't hurt to draw inspiration. I thought of the enchanted spinning wheel and its cursed spindle. But that wouldn't work; I wanted to still be able to go about my life, and this wouldn't be possible if I put myself into a deep slumber. What about an amulet? A stone that contained magic powers that when worn would enable me to momentarily forget my troubles? I pictured it, the amber stone swinging methodically from a long chain, its sparkling gem a wondrous marvel.

Then I thought of the Pied Piper. I conjured an image of him, magic pipe in hand, gaining control over people through the power of music. Yes, that could work. It was an object I could use as a talisman for magic. I could use a forgetfulness spell that was only activated when the instrument was played. That way I could choose when to use it, and I would be prepared. I embarked on this task with renewed vigour, keen to put my plan into action, refreshed with the knowledge that my woes would soon be forgotten. I used resources from the wilderness as the building blocks for my project. I wasn't sure of the exact pipe that the piper played, but the idea in my head was a simple woodwind instrument that could be constructed quickly.

After a few days I realised it wasn't going to be as simple as I had thought. I was unable to construct the holes in a way that ensured the instrument could actually be played. Whenever I thought I had done it correctly, I would put it to my lips, and it would emit a pathetic noise that fizzled out into nothing. When there was a pile of castaway models of the same thing, I started to construct something else entirely. The instrument did not necessarily have to be woodwind; I was sure that a stringed one would be able to harbour the magic in the same way. I disturbed a few innocent-looking ravens from the branches of a giant beech tree. The tree would provide me with the materials I needed to make a simple structure for the instrument. I hesitantly made the journey across the bleak forest to pay a visit to the blacksmith.

"What do you mean you need iron strings for a harp?" He looked me up and down, stored his tools inside his filthy apron and wiped the soot from his befuddled features. "What in the blazes do you think you're doing, making a musical instrument in times like these? And you got no money to pay me? What do you take me for, eh?"

"Wait!" I implored as the blacksmith turned back to his forge. "I'm desperate, please! I-I'll work for you in return."

A bead of sweat dripped down his grubby forehead, and he rubbed the bags under his eyes. "Look, I'm not saying it's summat I can't do, I'm just bogged down with weapons and armour at the mo'. Townsfolk want to protect 'emselves from..." here he paused and looked out of the smoky entrance to his shop uneasily, "from the baron and those foul things that do his bidding. Well, the ones that can afford it anyway. From them seven-foot-tall folk, you know." He aimed his hammer at the door, and I ducked to avoid a blow to the head. "We had one of 'em patrolling the streets the other night, scared Meredith 'alf to death..." He narrowed his eyes. "We heard tell of some kind of magician round these parts. Folk say he's to blame for what's gone on, some magic gone wrong or summat. You wouldn't know anything about that, would you?"

I feigned interest in a nearby dagger dangling on a hook to avoid answering the question. "And what is this fine specimen here?"

"Aye," the blacksmith nodded, distracted. "Some of me finest work that is. Look at how the stones fit neatly into the handle, a right fine one. It's just small enough to slip under yer pillow, in case them black-cladded figures come knockin', or peckin', or..." I cleared my throat. If this man was to talk any more of the ravens I feared I might lose heart and retreat cowering back into my hidden abode.

"Well, like I said," I mustered a great smile, "I'm willing to work in return for the items I have requested." I looked at the breastplates, hammers and nails scattered haphazardly about the shop. "It looks like you could use some help for a couple of days, even if it's just to tidy up the place—"

"Alright, alright!" the blacksmith thundered and then sighed deeply. "A few days should do it." He lifted the dagger off the hook and inspected it thoroughly before pointing it roughly in my direction. "Only as long as you do what I say."

I bowed graciously with a great sweep of my furs. "I am at your disposal."

The blacksmith grunted. "You're not from round these parts, are ye?"

SIXTY

A man of my age, regardless of how immortal he might be, was not cut out for hard labour. The weight of the metalwork combined with the sweltering heat from the forge made for an unbearable work environment. But then again, I thought as I lugged about varying pieces of iron into a pile ready for welding, this was not exactly an ideal situation. I was relying on a man I barely knew for my harp strings, who had accepted an extra pair of hands on the premise that it couldn't do any harm in these desperate times, even if the person in question knew next to nothing about his craft. Between us, however, it seemed to work. The blacksmith was easy to get along with, and I his willing student, knowing I had no alternative. At the end of the two days he was satisfied I had worked enough for the iron strings. "Not a bad job you've done, eh?" He stood with his hands on his hips as his sooty apron protruded from his prominent belly. He surveyed his kingdom contentedly.

He handed the strings over to me, and I received them delicately. I held them in the palm of my hands with glee, the orange blaze from the fire reflecting in my wide eyes as my heart quickened. They were the finishing touch to my instrument, the final part that would encase the spell, the key element to my oblivion. "You alright?" the blacksmith asked. He looked at me curiously. I quickly bundled the strings into my pockets. "Could 'ave given you a bar of solid gold and you would have looked at it the same way ye looked at them strings jus' now…"

He chuckled. "Can I tempt you with an ale? Think you've earnt it. Best be going quick though, I don't like staying out past dark nowadays…"

I respectfully declined, under the guise that I must be getting back to my pretend daughter who I was fashioning the harp for, and scurried away into the forest. "Well, if ever ye need owt—" His kind gesture was lost to the trees. I had no intention of ever returning. I worked long into the night. The weak pearly light of the moon shone across the final stages of my creation, and it was not until my last candle had burnt down to the stump that I gave in to a restless sleep in my chair. I awoke early the next morning and rubbed my bleary eyes. The usual sound of birdsong chirped from the leafy trees that hid my cottage from the rest of the world. Pieces of bark stripped from the purple beech lay abandoned. Makeshift potion bottles lay upended on the kitchen side, multicoloured traces snaking their way down the bare cupboards, ending in a disappointing pool on the kitchen floor that had been collecting there for days. Despite all these familiar sights and sounds there was something that had changed.

My masterpiece stood proudly inches away from where I had rested my head upon my shoulders all night. I carefully lifted it onto the kitchen floor. It was smaller than your average harp. It was also featherweight, another charm that I had attached to the structure along with the memory spell encased in the strings. Avoiding the puddle of old potions, I placed it gingerly next to my chair, fearful that at any moment the strings would snap or the pedals would disintegrate at the lightest touch. I looked at it in wonder. It was me that was changed. This morning was the first morning I had experienced optimism for the future. Was the instrument standing here the answer to my woes?

I took the promise of my new life out into the cottage grounds and set it down in the hollow of an oak where I had carved out a little seat for myself. It was a cold spring morning. The sun had just risen, and the leaves crunched underfoot. I balanced the instrument upon my fur cloak and took a deep breath of morning air. This was it; the moment of my sweet oblivion was upon me. I had never learnt to play a musical instrument and so was pleasantly surprised to hear the sweet melody I could pluck from the strings. With every note I played, I felt as though I sank deeper into a hot bath, the music washing over me until I gave in to the sensation wholly and became dragged beneath the water into a murky world of memories.

Faces plagued me for a few moments. My nephew Tristan was the first to surface, his youthful face becoming ever distorted in the ripples of the music, until it faded away into the branches of the oak above where I lay. I saw the face of my brother, but this one passed quickly. I saw her. Her dark bronze skin sparkled in the sunshine as she smiled at me with those sweet lips. Her perfect ebony hair, so much like her son's, was gently tousled in the morning breeze. My Mirabel. My lovely Mirabel. I had done all of this for her, my true love, stolen from me in a barbarous act of betrayal at the hand of my own kin.

My brother's treachery had ultimately led me into despair. I wanted to prove that I was worthy of her, that I was better than my brother, that he would never be able to steal anything from me again. But in doing so, I had become him. Instead of trying to find beauty in the world I had sought to manipulate and control others. The greedy power lust of a distraught lover had led me to this base in the hollow of the oak tree, reliving my past regrets and decisions, in a different world, in another time.

Her face faded. Instead I was drowning in a misty pool where I could no longer identify faces or names. Who was she I desired? Who was the boy with the caramel complexion that resembled her so much? The panic of confusion lasted only a few seconds before I slipped into the unconscious oblivion of my mind...

The last log in the fire popped and fizzled out. The hills

outside my hut were silent in the pitch black. I checked my weak barricade and hobbled to the small bed, stretching out my back, aware of the weight of all these memories. The initial memory loss had lasted only a few minutes. All of my reasons for forgetting would come flooding back to me, and I would have to relive them all over again. This I did in a continuous loop for days. The melody from the harp became my drug. I grew desperate for those ten minutes when I was incapable of remembering my own name. In the parts where I was conscious, I managed to extend the magic for a few hours, having little strength to try and prolong the charm further. I passed blissful hours in the forest, living my life unawares of my worries or my past self, going through the motions in an accepted confusion.

The pain of re-entering the real world became too much for me, and I allowed as little time in it as possible. Every time Mirabel's face appeared it was more unbearable. I knew that I would never be able to truly forget. Time and time again I returned to my drug, the notes from the enchanted strings entering my veins, never giving myself enough time or sanity to finish the magic so it could last more than a few short hours.

I perched on the edge of the low bed with my head in my hands, stroking my ragged beard, deep in thought at my foolishness all those years ago. My state of incomprehension meant that I never saw them coming. They arrived in great swarms. Their wings beat waves across the spring air. Their red eyes were narrow and beady as they honed in on their prey. Their hooked talons almost destroyed the strings in their haste. The embellished wood was tugged out of my grip as I tried to protect my eyesight from the baron's army. Once I had realised what was happening, I begged for death, knowing I wouldn't be able to cope without it. They did not indulge me but left me pecked to shreds where they had found me, in the hollow of the oak tree squinting above, as they carried away my enchanted creation into the sky.

Weeks passed, and I found my will to live again. I forced myself to move on from that cottage; I couldn't risk them finding me again. Once the baron had worked out how the harp worked, I was sure that he would use it to his advantage and pay me an unexpected visit demanding more. I wandered away from the forest and sought solitude elsewhere. As I travelled I heard tales of the baron, and my suspicions were correct. Townsfolk talked of how he possessed a magical weapon that enabled complete strangers to serve him. Old wives' tales of magic and sorcery wormed their way out of the darkness. If only they knew who the sorcery belonged to they might not be as afraid.

I heard tell of a terrible little minstrel who patrolled the manor grounds and took delight in cursing all those who had the misfortune of living there with the music of the harp. From what I had gathered, only the baron, his daughter, the minstrel in question and those few who escaped into the towns were immune from the magic. My heart sank. Whoever fell through my portal next would have no chance. The confusion of landing in a different realm coupled with the memory loss would cause them to become his slaves. The whole of Blackthorn would soon be under his control.

My wandering path led me deep into the hills. Into the extreme conditions where the bitter winds blew and only steadfast animals survived. A tiny structure built into the hillside itself, abandoned for many years, the shepherd's hut seemed the perfect hideaway. Here I had dwelt ever since, learning the ways of the wild, the meeting of another human soul only occurring when someone had got lost in the hills and sought shelter for the night. But this had been long ago. I was better off away from the rest of humankind. Better not only for me but also for them.

As I shifted myself onto the bed and prepared for another unsettled night in this interminable life, something occurred which had not happened for 140 years.

There was a knock upon the door.

SIXTY-ONE

JOANNA

The only problem with hopping from canvas to canvas was that no matter where I went or how long I stayed, I would always have to return to the dingy corridors of Blackthorn House to dwell among the malignant souls that had taken root there. I only discovered my ability to travel among the paintings ten years after the witches bound me to that godforsaken house deep in the forest. Perhaps it was a desperate attempt at escaping my horrific reality: a slave to those awful women. They saw me as no more than an inconvenience and, at best, a mediocre washerwoman and cook. Their spell had also trapped me in the body of my former self: a sixteen-year-old girl not yet blossomed into womanhood. Freckles adorned my cheeks and nose, and my blonde hair fell in loose, girlish waves that bounced with the freedom of youth.

But I was not free. I was trapped. And I had been trapped for the past century.

In fact, more than a century had passed. I lost count when the year surpassed one hundred. I resigned myself to the solitary existence I deserved for bringing something so cruel to life. Remembering the way they clawed themselves out of the frame still makes me shudder now. The moment I freed them from their prison inside the canvas, the witches cast a darkened veil over the house, resulting in it becoming invisible to the human eye. When my aunt and uncle had departed the front steps to greet my parents they had never been able to return. Imagine their sheer bewilderment when the house disappeared in front of their eyes. I never got to see any of them again. I like to think they searched for the house, searched for me... This gave me comfort on the days when I still had hope.

I witnessed with horror the human sacrifices they offered to their devil, but soon the horror turned to indifference, and the indifference to apathy. I recognised that I was losing all trace of humanity and was becoming akin to the witches. I found the escape I craved among the canvases in the very frames I meticulously polished for my aunt all those years ago.

I could not surpass the property line. It was physically impossible. It was as though they had erected an iron barrier surrounding the gardens. I couldn't even clamber down those rickety steps. I debated many times what else I could bring to life from the paintings of Blackthorn House. What I would have given for a companion to share in all these long years. But it wasn't right. To bring somebody else into this mess, to force them to endure this cruel jail, it would be unforgivable. I resigned myself to loneliness.

There was, however, a small mercy on my travels through the canvases. The ones that depicted human portraits could talk to me. They would tell me stories of their families and the happier times in the house. They would convince me that there was a purpose to all of this. That one day I would be the one to destroy the witches and bring light to Blackthorn House once more. I tucked into my stale bread. Who were they kidding? As I dipped the crust half-heartedly into the watery stew, I heard a commotion outside the pantry door and decided it was time to scarper. I didn't fancy an encounter with any of those awful women right now. I jumped off my rickety chair and disappeared into a small seaside cove. The sensation of travelling into a canvas was more uncomfortable than painful. I always experienced a brief feeling of compression upon my body, and everything became muffled. I walked along the sandy beach as the tightening eased, and sat in the sand. No other humans were present in this canvas.

Thankfully it was one that had not been destroyed by the fire twenty years ago. Those poor girls. I don't think they made it out alive. I tried to contact them during their brief visit to the house, had heard their footsteps upon the stairs and had tried to warn them of the danger. But I had been held hostage and had to watch the house burn. Eventually some of the witches came to their senses and used their magic to stop the flames. It had not been soon enough, however. The fire destroyed the entire upper floor, and half of the second floor was still in disrepair. I had been trying ever since to bring the house to a liveable condition. No matter how much I scrubbed, or mended, or washed, it wasn't the same. It would never be the same again.

As I sat and watched the cathartic waves wash over the shore, I heard the muffled voices of a discussion taking place in the pantry, and sighed. They were raiding the stores again. The witches were insatiable beings. No matter how much they ate, drank or consumed, they were never full, their appetites never appeased. "Stop banging on about that bloody portal," one of them exclaimed in a high-pitched noise reminiscent of fingernails scratching down a blackboard. The voice belonged to Helena. "I ain't never heard of one of them. Wilhelmina just fell to her death, poor sod..." I hung my head in my hands and tried to focus on the calming noise of the ocean. Their protestations made this near impossible.

"Then what about all them rumours, eh?" Another aggressive voice sounded. "What if it is possible to travel to a different land?"

"Oh shut up, Wilkie," a third voice chimed in, this one clearly with a mouthful of food. "What's she cooking tonight?"

I kicked off my raggedy shoes and buried my toes in the sand.

She was me. They didn't allow me a sense of identity, not even using my proper name, or acknowledging my existence past back-handed smacks when my housekeeping was not up to their standards. As long as there was food on the table they left me alone most of the time. I put my shoes back on and stood up. God, I had to get away from this place. I was sick of listening to their stupid conversations. I sought peace. I walked into the darkness of the cove and didn't stop until I collided with a fragile boundary that I slipped easily through. There was that feeling of sudden compression again before it stopped.

It was a different time of day here. This was one of my favourite portraits and one that I frequented often. I wandered a moonlit glade on a clear summer night. The chirping of crickets sounded far away, and the gentle breeze that ruffled the blossom trees gave me a familiar sense of comfort. I knew that this portrait hung on the second floor of the house in a wing that was often avoided by the witches. They had no reason to come up here. I kicked off my shoes again to feel the luscious glades in between my toes and lay down flat on the grassy slope. The sky was just beginning to turn purple, and the stars twinkled down at me. Even though I knew deep down that someone had painted them in, their light still gave hope of a different place, a different galaxy other than the one I occupied.

I watched them as they watched me. My breathing eased. Then that silly question popped into my head again. The one that plagued me often, no matter how many times it was discussed or which portrait member it was discussed with, always resulted in more questions than answers. Was it a gift I had, or a curse? Most of the time I arrived at the conclusion that I was cursed. After all, nothing good had come out of my ability to bring paintings to life, had it? I tried to push the big question aside and enjoy the peace before I was summoned to cook another hot meal for wicked mouths.

There were so many of them. So many unique shapes and sizes of stars that it was a wonder how the artist had dreamt them all up. What a magnificent thing it must be – to be able to paint something so beautiful. I became aware of how lucky I was, and the thought jarred me a little. I was able to experience someone else's world in a way that they would never be able to. I could live in the vision of their creation, walk along their pathways and feel the bark of their trees upon my fingertips…

I sat up in the long grass. I looked about me as the idea formed, first slowly, and then like a whirlwind it manifested itself, and I could contain myself no longer. I exited the portrait into reality and went in search of a pencil and paper.

SIXTY-TWO

INSIDE THE SHEPHERD'S HUT

The knock startled him. He leaned forward on the edge of his rickety bed, ear turned towards the door, waiting to hear if it would sound again or if it had been his imagination. A minute passed. It came again, louder this time, and he jumped. Three concise knocks upon the wooden door.

Isaac launched himself, somewhat impressively, across the bed towards his threadbare pillow. His head raced with thoughts of the ravens, and he instinctively found the long knife he stowed there. He slowed, and took a deep breath, eyeing the now silent door. Hang on. The ravens wouldn't knock, they would just swarm the hut and peck it to shreds around him. He hid the knife away inside his furs and tentatively approached his front door.

"Hello?" Isaac's hand froze atop one of the barricades.

"Hello?" The voice sounded again. "Is there anybody in there? It's absolutely freezing out here!"

"Uh, hello?" Isaac called out gruffly. His words came forth as a low rasp, and he cleared his throat. "Who's out there?"

"I'm Joanna," the disembodied voice continued. "I know I've turned up unannounced but you see, I don't really know where I've ended up, and I could do with finding out." She had to shout as her words became muffled. Isaac flattened his ear against the door. "I've travelled from a different realm, from a village called

271

Blackthorn, where I've been trapped for quite some time. Would you mind letting me ins—"

Isaac tore off the barricades, flung them into a pile on the floor and crashed open the battered door before Joanna had finished her sentence. The man looked at the girl in bewilderment. The girl looked at the man inquisitively. They stood completely still on the dark, windy hillside as their two worlds collided. Isaac peered at her through the gloom. He looked first left, and then right, and then over her shoulder as if his eyesight were good enough to identify any spies lurking in the darkness. His voice was a low whisper as his flabbergasted mouth formed words. "Where did you say you've come from?"

"B-Blackthorn," Joanna stuttered. Her eyes roamed over his unkempt bushy beard and mop of faded brown curls that poked up at odd angles on top of his head.

"Excuse the mess," Isaac grunted as he kicked aside the pile of wooden beams in the doorway. "I wasn't exactly expecting visitors." He gestured for Joanna to take a seat upon the only chair in the hut as he perched awkwardly on the edge of the table. She played with the frilly apron in her lap, then with a lock of hair, and he looked at her pale face and freckles. He cleared his throat awkwardly. "Don't take this the wrong way... Joanna... but you look very young to be wandering about on a hillside all by yourself." She gratefully accepted the cup of warming liquid he handed her. She laughed to herself, but the amusement did not spread to her features. She looked up at him soberly.

"Would you believe me if I said I only looked sixteen but am in fact significantly older?" Isaac smiled then, for the first time.

"Would you believe me if I told you I am approximately 180 years old?"

Joanna sighed and took a sip from her cup. Isaac raised his flyaway eyebrows, sure he was about to be branded a madman. She set down the cup carefully on the little table among his potion bottles and fixed him with a steady gaze. "Honestly,

I don't think anything surprises me anymore. I've witnessed things that I didn't think were possible in this world. Now," she picked up the cup again and blew the hot steam away, "do tell me what you know of Blackthorn."

Isaac draped one of his better furs around Joanna's thin shoulders as they sat on the floor of the hut in front of the rekindled fire. He rummaged around the kitchen cupboard to find some meagre remains of his supper to share and there they sat, chipped teacups in their hands, a pitiful portion of food between them as they shared their stories. Isaac told her the very tale he had just been reliving that evening, and Joanna in turn divulged everything to him about the witches and her entrapment within the house in the woods. At this, Isaac furrowed his brows and stroked his beard. "I never heard of Blackthorn House, in the middle of the forest, you say? I can't believe I never stumbled across it. I spent a fair share of time scurrying about that place trying to find suitable places for my spell work."

Joanna nodded sorrowfully. "It's a beautiful place really, very well hidden. You wouldn't know it was there unless you were looking for it." She paused all of a sudden. "Well, it was a beautiful place. Until I brought the witches to life, and then the fire…" She trailed off and looked into the flames.

Isaac gave a great sigh as he shook his head and digested Joanna's tale. "All this time," he whispered in disbelief. Joanna looked at him. "We've both come from the same village." He spoke slowly. "From around the same time, and here we find ourselves over a hundred years later, in this godforsaken shed I call a home." He bitterly huffed out a breath of air. "Well, I have to say, Miss Woodgate," he looked at her sympathetically, "I'm bloody sorry that you've travelled here. This world isn't much better than the one you've left."

Joanna gave a firm shake of her head. "It might not be much better from what you've told me, you're right there… but at least here I can be free."

Isaac snorted before he could stop himself. "Free? Nobody's free here. Your choice is to be Etimus's slave or to die of starvation in the streets!" She recoiled at his outburst, and he swallowed uncomfortably. "I'm sorry," he said quietly. "I just don't want you to get the wrong impression of this place. This is not somewhere that you want to build a new life, Joanna."

Silence fell for the first time in hours. Isaac gently took Joanna's teacup out of her hands. "Do you want anything else to eat?" He was not quite sure why he'd asked this, as there wasn't anything else.

"No thank you," she mercifully replied, not taking her eyes off the fire. She looked weary. Isaac cast about awkwardly for something else to say or do. After all they had shared tonight, he was not quite sure where they would go from here.

"Can I see it?"

Joanna turned her back on the fire, distracted. "See what?"

"The picture you drew, of the portal?"

"Oh right." Joanna fished about in the pockets of her long black dress. "I'm definitely not an artist, however ironic that is... There you are." Isaac took the crumpled piece of paper into his hands as gently as if it were a newborn baby.

Joanna had not been sure if it was going to work. She had the idea that if she could travel through other people's creations then why not her own? Thankfully it hadn't been some unwritten rule of her curse (she had finally decided that it was a curse) that she could only pass through other people's artwork. After hearing the witches talk about the portal again, she was struck with the idea that she could leave the witches for another world entirely. She had put pencil to paper and done the best she could to draw that swirling pit on the forest floor. And now here she was; it had taken her right to the creator himself. Joanna had to admit the disappointment she felt that it wasn't a nice world full of wonderful people, but instead one of sadistic tyrants and terrifying ravens with glowing red eyes. She shuddered as the embers of the fire burnt out.

Joanna pulled the thin blanket over herself and settled down on the hard bed. She knew that she took a huge risk in travelling to this world. In leaving Blackthorn House she could also be leaving behind her immortality. She placed her hand over her heart and checked herself. She was still alive. No, she had a feeling she was still bound to the witches and that if she were to return to the house it would be like returning to the prison once more. The witches wouldn't even have noticed that she'd gone.

She glanced over to the floor where Isaac lay, graciously having given up the one sleeping place in the hut, insisting he would be fine on the floor. Isaac shifted on the hard ground to face the door that Joanna had helped him barricade again. Despite the uncomfortable positions they were in, both Joanna and Isaac couldn't help but feel a tiny wave of something warm wash over them. Whether it was relief, the joy at having a companion to finally talk to, or some small glimmer of hope it didn't matter. They had someone. Each understood the other, and it was proof that Blackthorn existed; that even after all these long years filled with pain and regret, there were two people on the earth that knew something of what the other had been through. Two people who possessed magical powers.

As the two unlikely companions fell into an uncomfortable slumber, the Baron of Blackthorn let out a great snore and rolled over in his drunken stupor, unaware that something in the earth had shifted.

SIXTY-THREE

It was a cold December afternoon. Joanna and Isaac shivered on the cobblestones and watched as a small boy shuffled past them in shoes with soles that were long worn and a filthy jumper that was so thin it was surprising he hadn't succumbed to frostbite. The boy ambled away into a side street. Joanna eyed the dilapidated buildings, the battered signs of old shops that were no longer in business and the shattered windows of houses. "Jesus," she whispered, staring at the place in which the boy had disappeared. Isaac habitually went to stroke his beard before remembering that it was no longer there. Joanna had made him shave it off that morning. He grumbled throughout the entire process, but upon looking in his cracked mirror had to admit that he looked at least fifty years younger. "It will make you more approachable," she had argued. "Less, you know... suspicious."

"Is that right?" He had sighed.

Isaac pulled his furs tighter and hoisted an old bag over his shoulder. A cold wind whipped by. "Are you sure this is a good idea?"

"I've told you," Joanna said in a low voice as she scanned the area, "I have to see for myself."

Isaac gestured around. "Well, here you are. Not much of a town is it?" Joanna had insisted this was something they must do together. She had argued that it was impossible for Isaac to know what things were truly like for the people of Blackthorn if he hadn't stepped out of his front door in a century. He'd had to agree that she'd made an excellent point. Isaac wasn't exactly sure why the girl, who was not actually a girl, had agreed to help him. Perhaps she too was lonely; it could be that he was not the only one who had spent countless years in his own company longing for another form of human contact. It could be that she was biding her time until she would draw herself another pretty picture and travel back through to the house.

Isaac marvelled at Joanna's gift. His admiration bordered on jealousy before he remembered that particular emotion was exactly what had condemned him to all these years of misery. It didn't matter what her reason was, he was glad of the company. After they had shared their stories last night, she had offered to get inside the manor for him, saying that she would likely be immune to the harps due to possessing her own magic. Isaac would be able to communicate with his nephew at long last.

Joanna had one condition to her offer: before doing so she must see this world for herself and decide if it was really worth the risk. "I don't do anything without good reason," she had stated confidently. Isaac thought these were the ironic words of a person who had been cooped up inside a big old house for too long. He did not voice this aloud. He castigated himself for being such an ungrateful bastard in the next train of thought. Here was a person willing to help him because – and although Isaac had only known Joanna for two days he knew this to be true – she was simply just a good person. She had nothing to gain and he had nothing to lose.

Nodding his head down an alleyway, Isaac indicated that Joanna should follow, and they slunk away from the main street. He wended his way around the cobblestones and back alleys with ease. "How do you know this place so well?" Joanna whispered as a hush descended upon the place.

"How do you think I spent my time in the early days?" Isaac said over his shoulder. His furs splayed out behind him in the wind as he confidently proceeded across the cobblestones, and

Joanna thought if it wasn't for his dire situation he could have been the hero in a grim fairy tale. "I had to get word of what the baron was up to, and the taverns around here were the best places to do so. People will spill anything when they're pissed." Isaac's face was flushed. He had taken somewhat kindly to being outside of his little hut and Joanna noted the spring in his step. "Mind you, looks like most of them have closed down."

"Or been forced to close down," Joanna muttered darkly as she followed after him.

Isaac halted abruptly. "Here we are."

Joanna gazed upwards and then, "Oh..." It was a tiny little tavern. One that a passerby wouldn't even have noticed. It seemed, over the years, as though the alley had slunk in on itself and the tavern had become part of the furniture. Joanna eyed the crooked sign. A faded female figure perched atop a rock next to the bough of a ship. Her long tail meandered down toward the bottom of the sign, and Joanna had to squint to read the peeling words on it.

THE SWEET SIREN

For Isaac, the name had jogged something deep within his memory, and perhaps that was why he had taken a liking to this particular watering hole. Joanna followed him through the crumbling front doors and surveyed the interior of the tavern. A fusty smell hit her nostrils, and her eyes watered. The bar was directly to their right, and seating lined the left wall and back windows. Joanna eyed the upholstery. It was impossible to tell what colour the furnishings had been. The seats were now grey and moth-eaten. The wooden tables were all coated with a thick layer of dust. Their shoes stuck to the floor, and it was clear that no one had mopped up spillages for many years. The fire on the other side of the room was unlit, and it didn't look as though the owner had the materials to do so anymore. Had it not been for the two other people inside, Joanna would have thought the place to be abandoned.

The landlord leaned against the other side of the bar. He looked stooped, as though the weight of running the place had worn him down. He was extremely thin, long limbs protruding at odd angles like a spider, and his white hair exposed his significant age. Another younger male was in the process of being served. His legs dangled precariously from the old stool upon which he sat. It creaked as he wobbled forward in his tipsy state and looked as though he may topple over at any moment. The odd piece of hay had attached itself to his grass-stained trousers, and Isaac thought that he was probably a labourer in the fields having given up for the day already. There wasn't anything to harvest, after all.

The pumps were all in disrepair. The top of one had broken off altogether, and it lay discarded gathering cobwebs. The remaining two looked as though they had not been cleaned properly in the last fifty years. The landlord offered up a dirty glass and pulled the pump handle down as it groaned in complaint. Isaac turned up his nose as he watched the glass fill up painstakingly slowly, as though it were dredging up what remained at the bottom of the barrel. The pale liquid looked like stale piss. Joanna's stomach turned.

The landlord of the tavern surveyed them through his watery eyes, instantly suspicious of anyone he did not recognise, and threw down his filthy rag. He looked at them unblinking as Isaac cleared his throat. "Good afternoon." Joanna winced. The afternoon was clearly not a good one. The landlord narrowed his eyes.

"Do you have two rooms available for a couple of nights?" The owner of the Sweet Siren's eyes lit up momentarily.

"You can pay?" he asked them expectantly. On their way into the town Isaac had sold some scraps of leftover iron from the blacksmith. He had stored them in the back of a cupboard in the shepherd's hut all these years. They hadn't got a lot for them, as nobody had a lot to pay, but it would be enough for a couple of nights and for another set of clothes for Joanna.

"Yes, we can pay," Joanna replied as the landlord turned to her. "This is my father," Isaac quickly hid his surprise, "and we are just passing through on our way to somewhere else, looking for two nights' rest. Can you accommodate us?"

The man resumed his polishing of the glasses. Or to be more precise, his shifting of dirt from one place to another, and Isaac eyed the glassware mistrustfully. He nodded slowly and Joanna let out a breath. "Aye, I can accommodate you folks." He lifted his arm up and placed the dirty glass back on its top shelf. He looked over his shoulder and gave them a hard stare. "I don't want any trouble, mind! First whiff of it and..." he pointed a bony arm to the door, "that's where you'll be going."

Isaac nodded curtly. "There won't be any trouble from us." The man looked them over again and eventually gave Joanna a small smile, which she returned. Seeming satisfied, he shuffled into a dark corner of the bar and rummaged about for a few minutes, returning with two large keys, which he set down between them. Room One and Room Two.

No other lodgers, Isaac noted, before reaching for the keys. But the man, with surprisingly quick instincts, slammed his hand down on them before Isaac could pick them up. He bared them a toothy grin. "Apologies, sir, but I require payment up front nowadays. You know how it is... had a lot of people taking advantage and not paying. I don't blame 'em, mind, you gotta take what you can in these times, but I still gotta run my business the best I can..." He trailed off, wrinkled hand still atop the keys. Isaac deftly paid the man almost everything they had got for the iron. "Alright then." He lifted his hand up. "Make yerselves at home. Up the stairs at the end of the bar and first two rooms on yer left. The name's Bill, pleased to meet yer." They nodded their thanks and departed the bar with their possessions.

SIXTY-FOUR

The interior of the rooms was one step up from the shepherd's hut. They were basic, shabby, and the foul musty odour they had encountered in the bar had originated from the furnishings inside them. Joanna and Isaac locked up their belongings and made their way back downstairs. Bill's only other customer was now sitting in the corner by the window, holding his almost finished pint, muttering something into the watery remains. It was apparent that this was a normal level of business for the Sweet Siren.

Bill saw them looking around and gestured for them to take seats upon the crooked bar stools in front of him. He sighed and nodded to the empty tables. "This is as good as it gets nowadays." He nodded to them. "What can I get for ye?" Isaac rested his head upon his hands and surveyed the unmarked pumps. He'd have to blow the spiders off the broken one, the next was the one that the watery pint had been served out of, and Isaac was suspicious if the one remaining had anything in it.

"What have you got?" The man nodded blithely as if to say yes that's about right. He disappeared for a moment as he bent down and reappeared with a dusty bottle of amber liquid.

"Judging by the look on yer face this should do the trick." He busied himself setting up a glass and poured a small amount of the liquid into it. Among all the dust, dirt and staining, the liquid looked like gold.

Isaac reached into his pockets, but Bill waved him away. "You've already paid for that in yer room money." At least he was an honest man, Isaac thought as he nodded appreciatively. "And what can I get for the lady?"

Joanna smiled. "I'll have an al—" She paused. She had been about to ask for an ale, and then remembered that she only looked sixteen, and wondered what the landlord would think. He chuckled again, with more feeling this time, and disappeared under the bar once more.

"We don't stand on ceremony. If the lady wants an ale, she can have an ale, as long as her father don't mind…"

Isaac paused in sniffing the amber liquid as he remembered he was supposed to be Joanna's father. He inclined his head. "Give the girl an ale." Bill smiled, displaying a significant lack of teeth, and handed Joanna a small bottle labelled Old Pale Hen.

"It's not meant as an insult, like," he clarified quickly, winking at her. "It's just all we've got left." She smiled with relief that her beverage had not come from those awful-looking taps.

There came a great cough and splutter next to her. The golden liquid had almost sprayed out of Isaac's mouth. He hadn't tasted alcohol like that in years. The strength and burn of it almost knocked him out as he could feel it lighting his insides on fire. It travelled through his body as though a hot poker had been shoved down his throat. Bill deftly slid another bottle of Old Pale Hen across the bar. "Perhaps something a bit more palatable, lad?" The old man seemed to have taken a liking to them and did not bother to hide his amusement. Isaac coughed a few times.

"Perhaps one for yourself as well if I've paid enough?"

"Don't mind if I do, thanking you kindly, sir." Bill reached for another glass. He tipped the liquid down smoothly and smiled, raising it to Isaac. He was obviously no stranger to the fire pit it created in one's throat.

"So what do I call you both?"

"I'm Lara and this is Theodore," Joanna answered a little too quickly. The last thing they needed was anyone knowing that a sorcerer and a curious girl with magic of her own were wandering about. They did not want the ravens to get wind of Isaac's existence in Blackthorn. Luckily, the last time that Isaac had been out and about in the real world was over a hundred years ago, so the chances of anybody recognising him were slim to none. Bill was not buying it.

"Alright, I get it, you want no trouble and by the looks of it no questions either. Can I at least ask where you're headed?"

A silence met his reply before Isaac muttered, "Trust me, you're better off not knowing."

Joanna decided to change the subject. "How long have you owned the Sweet Siren, Bill? It's a very pretty name for a tavern."

Bill's look drifted to somewhere far away as he said fondly, "It was my wife that chose it. She always had the better ideas out of the two of us."

"And is your wife around?" Joanna asked without thinking, raising herself up slightly off her stool, as if expecting Bill's wife to emerge out of the gloom. Bill broke out of his reverie and said, not unkindly, "No, no, she's not about, love. She's departed this world."

"Oh—" Joanna started. "I'm very sorry to hear that." Isaac grunted his agreement.

"Aye." Bill nodded his head and blinked a couple of times. "It's not yer fault, small mercy she didn't get to see the place like this! You should have seen it in its heyday! Talk o' the town, we were. Got folk from all over the country wanting to sample our ale." Bill scratched his head absentmindedly, lost in the good old days, and Joanna wondered if his mind was quite as intact as they had first thought.

Isaac took his first sip of Old Pale Hen and swallowed more appreciatively than before. "Why don't you tell us about it?" he asked Bill. "Tell us what it was like in those days?"

"There ain't no use talking about that now," Bill snapped. "What's done is done and I can't go pretending that this ship ain't sinking like the rest of 'em. Surprised we're still afloat." He poured himself another dash of the molten gold and lowered his voice. "The baron's a bastard."

Isaac and Joanna looked at each other uncomfortably. "What makes you say that?" Isaac asked lightly.

"Personal experience," came the gruff response, and Isaac thought it best not to push the subject. He was glad of Joanna's company, as conversation skills had never come naturally to him, and if they were going to probe further about what life was like in Blackthorn now he would need her.

She took his cue and asked, "Do you get much help in running the place now, Bill?"

"No, it's just me. There ain't nothing much to run anymore. The ravens have cleared me out."

"What do you mean, they've cleared you out?" Joanna invited him to explain.

"Well, they keep bloody knocking, don't they?" Bill gestured wildly to the door. "Always demanding more. Seems like every penny I own is taxed and it's never enough. Lord knows how they expect a decent man to earn a living anymore! Anyway," he turned away from the door, "I shouldn't complain. It could be a lot worse for me, and I know that a lotta people got it bad—"

As Bill was finishing his sentence the doors to the tavern crashed open. Joanna spilt her ale all over the bar. "Oh bloody hell, Mary," Bill started. "I told ye not to come back, I've got nothing left for ye!" A black-haired woman came rushing to the bar, her tight curls spilling all over her desperate face, clutching a bundle tight to her chest.

"Please, William," she whispered hoarsely. "I'm begging you, if not for me, then for his sake." She nodded her head to the bundle. A quiet little moan emitted from the swaddle of clothes, and Joanna realised that the bundle contained a baby.

"Mary…" Bill started again. "I've barely got enough to feed myself let alone people off the streets." But his tone softened, and it became apparent that this woman was more than just a person off the street to him.

"Please," she whispered again. "I promise this will be the last time."

"Aye, you said that last time, an' all," Bill said darkly. He let out a great sigh as her son wriggled in her arms. The woman stared at him, taking no notice of Isaac and Joanna, and then: "Oh alright, gimme a minute, let me see if I got any scraps."

Bill shuffled away into another room, and the woman looked at Joanna. "I'm sorry for the intrusion but I'm in somewhat of a desperate situation. My husband's just died and left me with no money and a son to bring up. Kind old William helps me out sometimes." She nodded with wide eyes. "You know, when he can." Joanna was about to open her mouth and say some kind words to her when Bill returned with a small hunk of bread and the remains of what looked like a stew. The woman's eyes slunk away from Joanna towards the food.

"That's all I can spare today." Bill offered her what was left.

"Oh bless you, Bill, bless you." She took it with thanks and was still giving words of appreciation as she backed out into the bitter cold.

Bill read the look on Joanna's face. "No, Lara, I can't give her a bed for the night. At one point I had folks crammed in here, all staying free of charge just to get off the streets, away from those ravens. I couldn't keep doing it. I had to say to meself enough's enough, Bill, you can't save everyone and not everyone deserves savin.'"

"I-I wasn't going to judge," Joanna began.

"Good, because you don't know what it was like. The people of Blackthorn were desperate, they still are!" Bill thundered. Isaac stood up. He wasn't sure where the landlord's sudden temper had come from. Perhaps the amber liquid had been too much for him.

"I thank you for your hospitality, but we'd best leave you to it, for it's been a long day." Bill quietened and reached for their bottles, a begrudging expression on his face.

"Alright then, nice to meet you, Theodore an'… ah blast it, they ain't your proper names anyway. I'll bring you up some supper if you want it… yes? Can't promise it'll be much though, and Mary's just nicked mine…" They left him to grumble and retreated to the musty rooms.

SIXTY-FIVE

"How can you be such a bloody coward, Isaac? It's your fault you've ended up here. You've got a hundred years of people's lives to make up for! I'm not taking you back and that's that." Joanna's face was flushed as she let her anger get the better of her. Isaac held up his hands, leaned back against the furnishings and picked up his glass of watery luminescent liquid that Bill had tried to convince him was orange juice.

"Alright, alright!" he roared. "I would never actually do it, I just wondered if it was possible that's all." Joanna scowled at him as he looked toward the bar where Bill had been eavesdropping, a smirk on his wrinkled face, as though amused he was getting a telling off. Bill quickly attended to one of the leaking pumps and feigned concentration elsewhere.

As soon as he asked Joanna the question that had been plaguing him ever since he'd seen her drawing of the portal, she'd shot him down immediately. He knew that Joanna's magic could take both of them back to Blackthorn. All she had to do was paint a picture of the forest and he could be back there in a heartbeat, away from the baron, away from the ravens, a hot meal and soft bed awaiting him in a proper house, with a proper roof. But his heart wrenched. He couldn't leave Tristan. He owed it to the people of Blackthorn to undo what he had done and bring peace to their lives. He and Joanna had been sitting at a table in the Sweet Siren all morning trying to figure out how they were going to achieve just that.

Despite Bill's attempts to overhear them, Isaac, with a lot of strained effort and about ten failed attempts, had managed to cast a small spell over the table that muffled their conversation. The landlord was therefore oblivious to the murder plot that was currently taking place inside his tavern. After hours of discussion, they arrived at the conclusion that the only way was to go right to the centre of the magic source and destroy it.

"The Baron of Blackthorn is the key to everything," Isaac explained to Joanna as she tried to wrap her head around the plan. "Destroying the portal itself is out of the question. There are too many innocents living inside it." Joanna nodded in agreement as Isaac leaned across the table with an odd glint in his eye. "Our end goal is to obliterate the baron. His very existence stems from dark magic, and he is the reason this world has spiralled into poverty and violence. I'm convinced that eliminating him will destroy all the subsequent magic since his creation. The ravens will go back to their human forms. There will be no minions of his to play the harps, so the memory magic will also fade and people will have their freedom back."

Joanna didn't look convinced. "And by obliterate, you mean..."

Isaac bowed his head grimly. "Yes, the baron must die."

"You know there is a definite possibility that the people of Blackthorn will kill you for ruining their lives once they realise you've been cowering in a hut for centuries?" Isaac swallowed some more of the weak orange juice, and it left a bitter taste in his mouth along with Joanna's truth. They were also going to have to decide what to do with the baron's daughter, Letha. But he didn't want to think about that right now or answer her very justified question.

A sudden thought struck the sorcerer. He found himself wondering what had become of Mrs Villinor. As far as he was aware the baron did not have a wife. But yet he had a daughter – a monstrous creature capable of turning blood to ice. But then, Isaac considered miserably as he toyed with the frayed edges of one of the maps he had drawn up earlier, if the baron was supposed to be his doppelganger, perhaps he mirrored his exceedingly bad luck with romance. Isaac was neither married nor had anyone remotely special in his life to fulfil the position of partner, and a man of his age certainly could not foresee that in the future.

"I've never murdered anyone before," Joanna said absentmindedly. "I mean, I've seen the witches do it countless times but…" Isaac spluttered orange juice onto the papers spread between them. Joanna gave him a disgusted look before delicately dabbing the spots away with a handkerchief. "Be careful! I'm going to need these!"

"Sorry, I just didn't expect you to say it so…" He trailed off.

"So what?" Joanna countered. She put down the map she had been studying. "Look, you're either on board, or you're not, because it's going to take two of us to—"

"I'm very much on board, and I appreciate your help, more than you know." A hush descended between them. Joanna nodded and picked up a piece of old parchment from the pile they had managed to scrape together. She resumed her study of Isaac's diagrams.

Casting his mind back a hundred years had not been an easy feat to accomplish. It had taken Isaac all morning, but with Joanna's help, he had sketched out a map of Blackthorn Manor and the surrounding area. He had never got to see much of the house for himself, other than the grand hall and putrid dungeons, which he skipped over briefly. He was able to give Joanna a map of the gates and the gardens. "The intricacies are the most important," Joanna explained. "This is what I'm going to use to get into the manor – only we need to draw it from the other side, otherwise I'm going to be trapped on the wrong side of the gates."

Isaac easily described the gates in great detail: how the wooden slats had fitted together, the two stone pillars that framed them on either side, the great dragons' heads with their pronged forks that whipped at the air above. He used a pencil to shade in the stone of the walled gardens. He leaned back in his chair, and a feeling of dread crept upon him. Nothing made this seem more real than seeing those gates again.

The weight of a hundred years pressed down upon him. His shoulders sagged, and his throat constricted. His hands shook, and his heart grew heavy. Joanna was right. This girl who had arrived on his hillside, who had pledged her help out of the goodness of her own heart, had forced him to start making the right decisions. The path to redemption lay before him, and Isaac knew it was going to be rocky. The baron must be destroyed. He would have to risk his life in order to save others, and this was the first time that Isaac truly understood what this meant. It was time to undo his wrongs from over a century ago. He swallowed and leaned over the scattered papers. "Let's go through the plan again."

"I'm going to get into the manor and find your nephew. You've told me what he looked like." Joanna paused. "And I'm sure if I ask a few questions on the sly I'll be able to find him." She narrowed her eyes. "I'll be careful not to draw too much attention to myself. Once I've found him," Isaac liked her confidence, "I'll tell him that you're looking for him and that we are hatching a plot to destroy the baron and hopefully he can help." Bill shuffled past the table and topped up their glasses of orange juice. He eyed the maps and drawings warily. To his eyes they would be blurry.

"When Tristan's on board, I'll come back for the potion, and together we can end this once and for all." Isaac swirled the orange liquid round and round in his glass, a little queasy. They had hit a potential snag in the plan. Joanna had tasked Isaac with brewing up an odourless, colourless potion that would ultimately be administered to the baron and cause his death. He had not been capable of such a task in years.

"What if I can't brew it? And how will I know it works before I give it to you?"

"Give it to me?" Joanna raised her pale eyebrows. "Oh no." She gave a sort of half-chuckle. "Don't think you're getting away with it that easily, Mr Brewer. When it comes to that part of the plan, you'll be the one slipping it into the baron's drink, thank you very much. This is your doing and therefore must be your undoing."

Isaac nodded quickly. "Yes, point taken, but what if I can't brew it in the first place? Then what are we going to do? Cut his head off with one of the swords hanging in the hall?" Joanna's face remained sincere, and he hoped she wasn't considering this as a viable alternative. She stretched back in her chair against the musty cushioning and surveyed him through her pale blue eyes.

"Your power has been growing stronger every day, Isaac. I can feel it. It's like… a buzz of energy." Isaac's eyes darted away from her, not letting himself believe. Joanna gestured between them at the table. "Even this spell, whatever it is, you wouldn't have been able to cast it two days ago." Isaac considered her words as she ended with, "Perhaps it's because you've finally started using your powers for the right reasons. You have a new purpose now, something you actually have faith in."

His heart lifted, and he smiled slowly. A new purpose. Yes, he liked the sound of that. Joanna began collecting the papers into a neat pile. "I think we need a break. I'm going to store these away safely up in the room and try and get some rest. All this plotting has tired me out."

Isaac wrinkled his nose at the thought of those awful-smelling rooms and knew he wouldn't be able to relax in there. "I'm going out for a walk."

"Alright." Joanna rose from the table. "Be careful."

SIXTY-SIX

Isaac paced the cobblestones for two hours. He encountered three homeless people, four starving children and countless shards of glass from shattered windows that crunched underfoot. A woman sat in an alley with her hood up and head bowed. He deposited some coins into her outstretched palm, and she looked up in shock as though this were an uncommon occurrence. He eyed the swaddle of clothes on her back and her threadbare rags as she thanked him with wide eyes. Her black curls spilled out of her hood, and Isaac halted mid-step. "Wait... Mary, is it?"

"Yes," she confirmed hoarsely. Her voice sounded half frozen from the cold. "Sorry about last night." She recognised him from the tavern, hoisting her baby up securely so the child stared up at the brickwork above. "Noah hadn't eaten properly in days."

"Please don't apologise," Isaac said quickly. "I get it."

She looked him up and down, at his furs and polished boots, his clean-shaven face. "Do you?"

"I... well..." Isaac stuttered uncomfortably.

"You look pretty well off to me," she grunted. As she pocketed the handful of coins, Isaac's heart wrenched with guilt.

"Is there anything else I can do to help you?" Mary gave him a curious look as though not entirely sure she should trust this stranger. She shrugged her shoulders, and her head shook slowly from side to side. She gave him a small smile of resignation.

"I appreciate you asking, Mr...?"

For a second, Isaac couldn't remember what his name was supposed to be and panicked. "Theo. Just call me Theo."

"Alright, Theo." She eyed him through her hazel eyes. "Unless you've got something that can turn back time you can't help me."

Isaac winced. "There must be something I can do for you? I can't leave you out here on the streets…"

"Why?" Mary shot back, eyes narrowed. "Who are you? Why do you care so much?"

Isaac's fur cloak flapped wildly behind him as a cold wind rippled down the alleyway. "I'm nobody." He extended a hand to help her up off the cobblestones. "But I really do want to help you, if I can."

The swaddle of clothes gave a small cry as if in response to the sorcerer's offer. Mary huffed as she clambered to her feet awkwardly. "Come on then, although I'm not sure what you think you can do." She lived in a ramshackle old house not fifteen minutes' walk from the Sweet Siren. That would explain why the tavern was one of her regular haunts during desperate times. "It's always pretty desperate round here for me," she explained, as though reading Isaac's mind. Her house was shabby, and the furniture was in disrepair. Isaac could tell that she'd tried to keep the place clean, but there was no denying the living quarters were not fit for mother and baby.

"Do you live on your own?" Isaac asked, gently inspecting the bundle Mary had been carrying, and finding a beautiful boy who couldn't have been a year old inside. Isaac pulled a funny face at Noah, and the boy cautiously smiled back, half in confusion, half in awe at a new face. Mary nodded sadly. "I would offer you some refreshment, Theo, but I don't have anything that's worth offering. Not much of an entertainer these days…"

Isaac waved away her embarrassment with one hand. "Please, don't worry about that."

The troubled woman took a deep breath then divulged, "My husband died shortly after this little one was born." She unbundled Noah and set him down upon a blanket where he proceeded to watch the two of them contentedly and stretch out his little fingers and toes.

"I'm sorry to hear that—" Isaac began, but then Mary cut him short. It was as though she had to get all the words out at once, otherwise they weren't likely to come out at all.

"He worked in the fields that surround Blackthorn Manor, you know harvesting crops and looking after the oxen, for the baron. We used to own our own farm, churn our own butter and everything…" She nodded at Isaac, who nodded back, impressed. "But then it all went pear-shaped when the baron kept demanding more. Longer hours, less money, harsher work… It wore Stephen down in the end… and eventually he'd had enough. He tried to make the baron see sense, told him he couldn't possibly do what he was asking and live off the wage at the same time. In the meantime I was still trying to keep what was left of the farm going, but eventually we couldn't feed those poor animals."

She stopped, and took another deep breath. Isaac listened intently. "The baron murdered him. Butchered him in that very field as he worked, as though he were fresh meat to be slaughtered. He was murdered for saying no. And I was left on my own with this little one." She shook her head again, eyes glistening. "And I can't get a job. There aren't any out there! No one has money to pay wages anymore. Stephen had a small amount of money left, but that's just about gone now. Noah and I, we have to make do, and I know he misses his daddy…" Isaac's eyes stung as Mary tended to her son.

"Mary, I'm so sorry."

"It's not your fault." She dismissed his apology. Little did she know that he was apologising for so much more. When Mary was preoccupied with her son, Isaac looked into the small hallway and the kitchen beyond. Mary did not even turn around as he disappeared. All the cupboards in the kitchen were bare.

They contained traces of the fact that they had once been full – small crumbs and seeds from fruits that were drying out on the windowsill. She obviously planned to plant them in the hope that they would grow. Isaac opened the door at the end of the kitchen and found himself in another smaller room. The larder was bare. This woman and her baby had nothing to eat. Isaac closed his eyes as a small tear slid down his face. He knew this was all his doing.

He had been gone so long that he was surprised Mary had not reprimanded him for snooping around her house. But she simply sat, staring at the wall ahead, Noah in her arms. A broken woman. She turned her head slowly to look at him and peered sideways through her mane of curls. "Find anything worth stealing?" she asked good-humouredly, and then her smile vanished as she saw Isaac's face. He stood stock still, and her wide eyes met his own.

"Mary, whatever you do, you must not come looking for me."

"What? I don't understand—"

"Do not come looking for me," Isaac repeated. "No one must know I was here. I beg that of you. I wish you and your son all the best for the future." He left the house before she could even rise from the small chair she sat upon. Isaac hurried along the cobblestones in the direction of the glowing tavern windows as the small spark inside him faded.

Mary picked Noah up in her arms and stood up. She looked toward the door in confusion. The strange man did not return. "Well I never. That was a bit odd, wasn't it?" She smiled down at her son who could do no more than gabble in agreement. He did wonder where the strange man's face had gone. Mary retraced Isaac's footsteps into the kitchen. She was not sure what he had been doing in here. She hadn't really cared. She noticed that the door to her larder was slightly ajar. A strange smell pricked her nostrils, and she inhaled deeply. The scent was oddly familiar. She pushed one hand against the door, and it creaked open.

Her gasp of shock was coupled with an excited exclamation from her son. Mary gazed up in astonishment. Fresh produce packed the shelves from top to bottom. They groaned beneath the weight of fruits, vegetables, dried goods and meats galore. How was this possible? Moments ago they had been empty. She paced up and down, mouth watering, as Noah reached out his arms at the shelves. Tears of joy mixed with relief slid silently down her face. She would be able to plant the seeds from the fruits and vegetables. This would feed them for weeks, months even...

She walked out of the larder in disbelief and up the hallway. She leaned out of the front door. Theo had vanished from sight. She checked the larder three, four, five times, all the while thinking it would disappear, that it was too good to be true.

They feasted that night, and Mary carefully worked out a plan in her head to make the food last as long as possible, all the while thanking the kindness of the mysterious cloaked man. She would heed his wish, although it plagued her to know where all the food had come from. She would not go back to the tavern tonight.

Little did Isaac know, that after tonight, neither would he.

SIXTY-SEVEN

It was a quiet night in the tavern as usual. The wind blew a gale outside, and Bill had barred shut the entrance doors to prevent them from swinging on their hinges. He knew it wouldn't deter potential customers; everyone on the cobblestones had already disappeared.

Isaac and Joanna sat by the small fire. Joanna couldn't help but feel guilty as she warmed her hands in front of the flames; she knew this was probably the last of Bill's coal, and he had used it up for their benefit. He hadn't noticed Isaac's low murmuring every half an hour or so, his enchantments keeping the fire alive in the grate, something for which Joanna and the two other customers in the Sweet Siren were thankful. They sat in two musty armchairs, listening to the storm that wreaked havoc on Blackthorn outside, and put the finishing touches to their plan.

A questionable stew was served for their supper; the meat unidentifiable, the flavour odd and the vegetables a sloppy mush sat in the bottom of the small bowl. It gurgled in the depths of Joanna's stomach. She swallowed as she thought of the comforting hot meals she served to the witches before they dug their greedy talons in. As if she were missing Blackthorn House. She put an end to these foolish thoughts and focused her attention instead on the sorcerer.

He sat, gazing into the flames with a faraway look on his features, lost in a different world that nobody else was privy to. Isaac had remained unusually quiet ever since he had returned from his walk. Joanna had a sneaking suspicion that this 'walk' had been not only that; that something else had occurred during his time outside the tavern. She was not at liberty to ask what had happened; everyone was entitled to their own thoughts. Even those who were hatching a murder plot.

"Is everything alright?" she asked gently. Isaac started, as though he had been interrupted from a very deep, very poignant thought, and tore his eyes away from the disintegrating logs. He smiled wearily. His stubble was beginning to grow back.

"Yes, just…" he waved his arms about loosely, "lost in thought."

Bill bustled over to their corner. "Any more drinks?"

"Yes please, I'll take another ale." Joanna cut in before Isaac could turn him away. (He was not much of a drinker, that one.) Bill nodded and shuffled away. Joanna was going to accept all the comforts she could before they enacted the first part of their plan. It would plunge her straight into Blackthorn Manor where she was certain there would be neither ale nor a bed for her.

Bill returned moments later with an Old Pale Hen in hand. He set the bottle down in front of Joanna. She had become accustomed to that particular tipple. It was not one that the witches knew of, not… bloody enough for them, she supposed, wrinkling her nose at the thought. Bill lingered at their table after accepting the last of Joanna's coins. She paused in raising the bottle to her lips. "What's wrong? Is it not enough?"

"It's enough," Bill said, his eyes locked on the tavern door as he pocketed her payment. He proceeded to stand there, and Joanna grew more uncomfortable by the second. Isaac looked up.

"What's bothering you, mate?" Mate? Joanna winced. She had never heard Isaac address anyone by such a familiar name.

Bill shrugged, unaffected by the familiarity, perhaps even a little grateful. "I can't help but wonder if Mary's trapped outside in this storm, bangin' on that door to come in. We wouldn't hear her over this racket." He tipped his head toward the window.

"I'm sure she's just fine, Bill," Joanna began reassuringly. "I tell you what, if you're that worried about it, I'll keep an eye out for her out the window, just in case—"

"Mary's not going to come knocking tonight," Isaac said interrupting her. Joanna and Bill met his words with surprise. When he realised they were both staring at him he knew he'd have to come up with an explanation. "I-I saw her earlier," he stuttered. "Said she was going home with Noah to, er… batten down the hatches and all that, before the weather worsened. I made sure she had enough food for the night." *And for the next two months*, Isaac thought silently.

"Did you now?" Bill said slowly. "Well," he said, realising he was going to get no more out of them, "I'll leave you to it then."

Joanna shot Isaac a suspicious look. He avoided her gaze. As Bill ambled back to the bar Joanna watched him go fondly. A pang of empathy struck her. Did he once have a daughter, or a son? Perhaps there was someone that he used to share happy times with. She hoped so, she thought, as she gazed miserably out of the rain-washed window, waiting for someone who was apparently never going to come.

Isaac's eyelids drooped. It had been a long day. From discussing their plans to find Tristan that morning, to Joanna lecturing him about brewing the potion that would ultimately kill the baron, to his meeting with Mary that afternoon, he had a lot to think about. Not to mention the little spells and incantations he had performed along the way. Muffling their conversations, conjuring food out of thin air, encouraging the flames next to him to keep on burning, it all took its toll on Isaac. This was the most powerful he had felt in years. He was still not as powerful as he had been hundreds of years ago; that would take some time. But the spark had lain dormant, sleeping there all along inside him, just waiting to ignite once more. He was worried; the last time he had successfully brewed a potion it had all gone horribly wrong.

Perhaps Joanna was right. (Why was that girl always annoyingly right?) Perhaps now that he was using his magic for something useful it was more potent. He certainly would not have been capable of transforming an empty larder to one that was bursting at the seams if it had been his own. But when it had been for someone else...

He sat and pondered on these thoughts. The crackling fire, some food in his belly, the sound of the rain outside... A sleepy stupor settled over the sorcerer. His heavy lids closed.

The figure that sat slumped in the booth not far from them was almost seven foot tall. He had sat there through the exchange between Bill and the two strangers, silent, brooding. He had entered the tavern only when the landlord had his back turned, made a beeline for that particular seat and accepted only a glass of water. No one had noticed that the gloved hands were incapable of holding the glass because they hid something other than fingers. No one had thought it odd that he had kept his black hood up inside; it was cold. No one had spied the ruffled plumage of raven feathers it disguised.

Joanna absentmindedly swirled her ale round and round the bottle and did not take any notice of the black figures that swept past outside.

They descended upon the tavern.

SIXTY-EIGHT

Nothing could have prepared Joanna for the sheer brutality of the scene before her. The glass struck Bill over the head before he had time to cry out. "Bill!" Isaac roared, leaping out of his armchair. The fire in the grate disappeared immediately, and the Sweet Siren was plunged into a deathly cold. There was no time for Isaac to acknowledge the fear at seeing the foul beasts again. If he had, he may not have launched himself headfirst into the swirling pit of black cloaks, the talons and beaks tearing at his skin. Joanna held back; she had no powers to protect herself. If Isaac had not told her otherwise she would not have believed that these animals with their glowing eyes had once been human.

She tried to discern who was who through the muffled yells, ear-splitting squawks and the shattering of glass. A blind panic seized her. Joanna looked around desperately for an object big enough to wield so she could enter the fray. The poker lay in front of the fire. Isaac had been using it to prod the logs mere moments before. She picked up the iron rod. "Shit!" she yelped. It felt like being sliced by fire. But she could not afford to drop it. Clutching it tight in her grip, the end burning her skin, she advanced towards Bill, Isaac and the ravens. Her heart went wild in her chest, unsure of what she planned to do. The girl was five feet away, four, three... She narrowly dodged a flying glass...

The fighting was over as quickly as it had started. There was a great scramble, and then everybody slowed as the ravens caught their prey. There were five of them altogether. Joanna frowned.

It had seemed like more. Two of the black-clad figures held Bill in a death grip. His arms were pinned behind him, and a pair of talons rested easily against his throat.

The raven to whom they belonged had placed them there lazily, as though it were a mere precaution, not a sudden and very real threat to Bill's life. Isaac squirmed in the hold of two others. Their wings pressed him against the side of the bar. The fifth raven, the largest of them all, advanced upon Joanna. She shrank back as her heart sank. She stumbled backwards into a bar stool and dropped the poker. The skin across her right palm was red raw. "Good girl," the raven crooned. Joanna's skin crawled.

The wind howled at the doors and flung them open. Rain came pouring in sideways. A pool of water began to form. The raven who was not holding anyone hostage spoke in his strange gruff voice. Joanna took in the blood that poured down one of the other raven's beaks. The second that restrained Isaac sported badly torn feathers and winced every now and then. It seemed as though Isaac had put up a good fight. Bill, on the other hand, was terrified, and his eyes grew wider with every word that came out of the raven's beak.

"You owe the baron money." One of the smaller ravens behind Bill squeezed him nastily as the one in charge continued, "You haven't paid your taxes in two weeks, old man." Bill's eyes began to water as he pleaded with them.

"Please... you know I don't have any left... you took everything I had last time—"

"Quiet!" the raven hissed as he strode behind the bar. He began to rummage through drawers and upend jars. "I'm sure you've got something for us... Aha!" He turned an old ceramic jar upside down, and a couple of copper coins dropped into his gloved talons.

"Please!" Bill implored. "That's all I have to feed myself for the next week. I can barely keep this place running." He changed tack. "Y-you can have free beer whenever you want! All you can—" It happened within an instance. A slight inclination of the raven's plume acted as a signal to the others. Bill's head hit the bar like a sack of potatoes. They pulled him back up, and his eyes rolled in their sockets. Joanna screamed and picked the slightly cooler poker up.

"You bastards!"

The raven in charge ruffled his feathers. "Stay where you are. Unless you want to be next of course."

Joanna's heart broke as she stared at the blood trickling down the side of Bill's face. Surely the baron could not be sanctioning this? Attacking an elderly man who had no means of defending himself because he owed him a few coins? It was barbaric. Bill regained a form of semi-consciousness, but his shoulders sagged. He seemed to have given in entirely. He closed his eyes and whispered, "Take what you want." This was not good enough for the ravens.

"You lied to us," their leader snarled. "You said you had nothing. But you're hiding coins all over this… place you call a business… aren't you?" There came no reply. "If you lie to me, you are lying to the baron, and that is an act of treason, old man. Treason is punishable by death. Do you want to die?" Again, his rasping words were met with silence. "Too good to talk now, are we? I can think of one thing that will loosen your tongue. Well…" He paused and laughed nastily; Joanna winced. "It may loosen your teeth too."

The sorcerer had been oddly quiet throughout the whole exchange, and now Joanna understood why. Isaac had been recharging himself. Mustering every drop of magical power within him had taken all of his concentration. Before the raven could administer the deathly nod to his comrades, before Bill's forehead could touch the hard wood again and not bounce back up, the bar exploded.

Sparks flew from Isaac's fingertips. Glass shattered. Pumps exploded. The ravens, taken aback, loosened their grip. Bottles flew across the tavern, and everyone had to duck. They smashed against the window opposite, and the glass imploded. The wood shook in the empty frame as the boom from the explosion reverberated around the Sweet Siren. Water poured in through the empty gap where a window had been as the elements joined forces with the sorcerer. Two of the pumps sprayed foul-smelling beer that rocketed up and splintered the ceiling beams. On their way up, the jets hit the two ravens who had been torturing Bill straight in the beak. They relinquished their grip in shock as they staggered backwards through the foamy jets. One of the pumps tore free from the bar and hit one of them on the back of the head. The raven staggered against the empty shelves. Every single one of them was drenched.

Through the flying glassware, room keys and erupting beer streams, Joanna locked eyes with Isaac. He thundered one word at her: "GO!" Joanna sprinted across the room. The ravens were too shocked to understand what was happening. Her foot caught a rolling beer bottle, and it almost brought her to the floor, but she stumbled, and charged on. She took the little staircase two steps at a time leaving no moment to spare. She crashed into the musty room and fell to her knees, scattering books and papers aside, searching frantically.

There was one piece of parchment that she must find. She cursed herself for not keeping it separate. The sound of exploding glass was muffled through the floor. A heavy crunch of boots upon the stairs sounded. Joanna hesitated. She had mere seconds. She located the piece of crinkly paper and gathered all the others together so as to leave as little evidence behind as possible. She shoved them into the pockets of her coat. She was not quite sure at what point she had managed to put her coat on. She laid the single piece of paper down on the bed as the boots began to kick the door down. She swallowed her fear. She closed her eyes. She imagined the gates, the garden, the orange and lemon trees… She put a fingertip to the drawing.

The door crashed open. She did not turn around to witness the hulking beast in the doorway. He was one foot away from her when she felt herself lifting up from the ground. She gave in to the sensation, ignoring the hot breath on the back of her neck, the feathers that made contact with her skin.

Joanna departed Room One of the Sweet Siren as she passed through the pencil strokes, shades and lines that formed the gates of Blackthorn Manor. There was a brief compressing of her windpipe before it released again and she hit the ground hard, sucking in deep breaths of harsh air, the raindrops blinding her.

The raven scratched his feathers. He peered over the bed to see what the girl had been looking at, but there was nothing there.

The girl, along with the piece of paper, was gone.

SIXTY-NINE

BLACKTHORN MANOR, LETHA'S BEDCHAMBER

Her long blonde hair cast a shimmering wave down her back as she tossed it over one shoulder and continued her daydream. A sharp poker would do the trick; one straight jab right through the side of the head. Simple, clean. No, he might be too strong for that. Poison? She wouldn't know how to get hold of it. She sighed. She couldn't really kill her own father. She loved him, deep down, didn't she? Disregarding the drunkenness, general foul behaviour and complete lack of interest in his daughter, his heart was in the right place, wasn't it? Well, it had best be, she thought, if the dagger was to make its mark. She winced as a bristle caught against the side of her head. "Ouch!" she hissed, slapping the hand of the culprit away. Her maid looked at her with wide eyes, silently begging for her life. "Leave me," Letha snarled. "Both of you, go on, get out!" They exited the draughty bedroom with their long skirts billowing out behind them.

The baron's daughter sat alone at her dressing table. She stared at herself in the mirror. Her eyes glimmered, and her lips curled into a smug smile at the cruel reflection. She picked up the discarded hairbrush and moved it gently through her poker-straight hair. She cast aside these all-too-frequent thoughts of murdering her father and focused her attention on something else. She inspected her perfectly trimmed and shaped fingernails.

Rising from her seat, she took the skirts of her royal blue gown with her and surveyed her reflection in the spotless mirror.

She tossed the material this way and that, looking over her shoulder, lips pouting in a bored fashion. "I'll have to have words with Madam Faraway," she muttered darkly. Madam Faraway was Letha's seamstress. Madam Faraway was also at great risk of being on the receiving end of one of Letha's temper tantrums, for her gowns were getting boring and her needlework shoddy. At least, Letha thought as she fingered the strip of fabric running the length of her right side, she had sewn in a hiding place for her favourite weapon as requested. The riding crop could be folded in half and concealed beneath the skirts of her large gowns. She never knew when she might need it, after all.

Letha sat back down again and looked about her bedchamber. The candles in their holders flickered eerie shapes on the high ceiling. Strange shadow-like figures danced their way across the walls. Letha started at a sudden noise and then regained her composure. It was one of the maids sniggering in the corridor outside. Letha wondered what she had been snorting about, and then she heard the low voice of another, sharing some gossip about one of the boys in the stables. Letha rolled her eyes. Any other day she would have chastised them for partaking in private conversations, but she wasn't feeling particularly inspired today.

She didn't have any friends in this place. They were all too scared of her. And she was fine with that; a great leader inspires fear in others. There were those rare occasions on the loneliest of days when she convinced herself that her maids were her only friends; Lord knows she couldn't count on her father. Other times, like now, she sent them away and was reminded that they could never be true friends. They were here to serve like everyone else. Their autonomy was taken away from them a long time ago. It was only fear of the baron's daughter and the enchantment from the harp that kept them so docile.

She banged the door of her chamber shut behind her so the maids would know she had overheard them. The whispering ceased immediately. "I'm going down to the dungeons," Letha announced to an empty corridor. (The maids were hiding in the shadows.) "You may retire for the evening." Without further ado Letha strode the length of the corridor and descended the spiral staircase to the lower level of the manor. She reached a smaller corridor that broke off to the left and right; the left led to the servant's quarters at the back of the kitchen and the right led straight into the hall. She took the right and entered the cavernous room that could seat a hundred guests. The suits of armour stood still on their mounts. Half of the brackets were lit with an orange glow. No one else was about at this time of night. She manoeuvred around the long oak table at the front, thinking it would have to be moved in two weeks' time, and made a beeline for a side door at the edge of the hall. Her shoes tapped on the polished wooden floor, and the door swung inwards as she reached it. A raven must have heard her coming from the other side.

"Good evening, Miss Letha." A gruff voice came from the gloom. The raven gave a small bow as she walked past. She gave no indication that she was aware of his presence, and continued along the tunnel-like corridor, plunging downward into the depths of the dungeons. The temperature dropped. Her footsteps became an echo as she approached the dank, low-ceilinged entrance with a small smile across her face. She felt at home here. There was always someone worth less than her inside these festering walls; some desperate, lost soul begging for mercy that never came.

The dungeon guard stood to attention. She nodded at him briefly, and he inclined his head in return as the top of his helmeted feathers brushed the low ceiling. They had become acquaintances over the years. But not friends, never friends, Letha reminded herself. It always took a minute or two for her eyes to adjust to the dark. She picked up her skirts (if she had a father who cared, he would probably reprimand her for coming down here in such a beautiful gown, or at all) and began to pace the cells. The rats did not bother her. She simply shook them off her polished shoe as they scarpered across the puddles. Perhaps they lived in fear of the baron's daughter too. Even though the dungeons were underground, there was a part of the ceiling that jutted out into the open, and it was the drips from the cracks in the ceiling that formed the pools covering the dank floor. This, and a combination of whatever other bodily fluids were dispersed, but this did not bother Letha. She conjured up far worse gore in her macabre imagination.

"And who might this be?" Her cold voice echoed around the dungeon and reverberated off the bars across the cells. There was a shuffle as the prisoner tried to make an escape.

"Appeared three days ago," the prison guard grunted. "Reckon he fell through that portal thing the mad magician—" He cut off as Letha shot him a sharp stare. They were forbidden from talking about the portal. Over a hundred years ago a lunatic and his nephew had appeared in the manor. He claimed to be the creator of the realm. Of course he was laughed out of the manor and his claims dismissed as heresy, but it would have explained how people kept on landing in the dungeons, appearing from Scotch mist every now and then. They always had some cock and bull story about having been in a forest and falling beneath the earth. They would soon be either beaten into submission or hear the harp's enchantment, forget who they were, and become another of the baron's minions. Etimus had allowed his daughter to place these people about the manor as her servants – maids, cooks, pig farmers, stable hands – but they were not allowed to speak about that mad sorcerer. Admitting that the portal was real would be admitting that they were not fully in control of their lands. It would be admitting a weakness, and Etimus and Letha Villinor were anything but weak.

"Open the cell," Letha barked. "I wish to give our guest a proper greeting." The raven obeyed. With a jingle of keys and a splashing of his great boots upon the floor, the cell door was unlocked, and Letha faced the man inside. She sighed gently. She knew this was going to be boring already. She liked the ones who underestimated her. The ones that saw a little girl in a big gown and didn't fathom what she was capable of before they hit the floor. But this one knew. He saw something in the glint of her eyes that told him what a sadistic little bitch she really was. His clothes were rags, and he was beginning to show the emaciation of someone who hadn't eaten properly in a while. He was middle-aged, fairly tall, with an expression of genuine shock and desperation that Letha knew made him a good person. This may have worked in his favour had it been anybody else but Miss Villinor who stood in front of him. His wavy chestnut hair was streaked with grey, and he brushed it out of his wet eyes as the pleading began.

She thought of her father. With every thrash of the riding crop she thought of his neglect. She thought of his drunkenness. She thought of how he spent half his time feasting until he threw up and the other half pretending to pray in his private chapel, even though he was sleeping it off in there. She thought of his paunchy eyes and disgusting beer belly that had grown significantly over the years. He was no longer a trim, well-kept man who cared deeply for his family. He was a drunken fool and an awful father. She thought of the rare occasions when they spoke, only for him to tell her she was doing something wrong or to give instruction, to reinstate his authority as head of Blackthorn Manor when he thought she was beginning to forget. The prisoner's cries were drowned in the pit of her own thoughts, and her arm was only stayed by the long claws of the raven that eventually held it. "Enough, Miss Letha," he growled quietly. The raven knew that Letha would have to answer to her father if she ever killed one of his prisoners. When your choice of loyalty is split between a drunken absentee and a woman who oozed power and acknowledged your existence, Letha won that battle most times despite her many shortcomings.

She swept from the dungeon without a look back. She did not like witnessing the aftermath of her brutality. Her victims would writhe on the floor, blood streaking down their faces, incapable of the begging they had started to begin with. She had whipped that out of them. The man lay silent and shivering in the cell. His whole body shook as he thought of his beautiful wife and steadfast daughter. He looked up into the pitch black as the door to his cell was locked once more and imagined he was looking up into the stars, on a different night, in a different world.

SEVENTY

Letha emerged from the winding tunnel breathless; she had been in even more of a hurry to get away from this one, and had only now fastened the riding crop beneath the folds of her gown properly. She looked about the entrance hall as she breathed deeply, taking in its grandeur, its display of wealth and comfort. In two weeks' time, the ceremonious hall would host her coming-of-age banquet and would be decked out with no expense spared. She sighed, forgetting the lashings of her crop on the man's skin already, thinking instead about how much work she had to do to ensure the banquet went smoothly. The traditional age for a girl to have this banquet was sixteen. But age and time worked differently here and Letha understood that she was actually turning eighteen. Etimus had only just got around to realising that his daughter was indeed grown up and had begun to plan the ceremony for her. Just another reason why she hated his guts.

Thorn. She closed her eyes. Thorn was loyal, beautiful and always grateful for her attention. He was what she needed right now. She turned to her right and headed out of the main entrance to the manor. The two ravens on either side of the archway let her through and bade her a muffled "goodnight". The white light of the moon bounced off the top of her shining head like a beacon as she moved swiftly across the cobbles outside. She passed the pigsty, the cow barn and the chicken coop as she wrinkled her nose at their smell. It was rare that anybody other than the farmers and the bailiff who oversaw their work would venture into these outhouses. She spied the orange and lemon trees in the distance, the ends of their branches fit to burst with the colourful fruit, lining the pretty walkway that led to the edge of the manor and fields beyond. Her father's private chapel also lay at the back of the manor inside the walled gardens. It was a wonder that the trees blossomed with such fragrant fruit all year round; some kind of magic, they assumed. This was another thing that they didn't talk about.

The stable was the last outhouse in the row, away from the other animals, the cleanest of them all. Letha pushed open the wooden door. Thorn had been sleeping. At the hint of her presence, he eagerly scrambled to his feet, the clatter of hooves muffled by his fresh bundle of hay. His great flanks were so powerful he could outrun any of the others. His gleaming mane was brushed to perfection. Letha patted his chestnut coat that shone even in the dark as he snorted in appreciation. She entwined her fingers in his mane and closed her eyes as they had a silent conversation about her woes. They stood for a moment, beast and girl, silent and unmoving in the moonlight.

Letha's thoughts turned ever darker as they returned once more to her father and the banquet she had been left to organise. He hadn't got involved with any of the planning for it. Letha had been busy for the past few weeks instructing the cook what was to be served, barking at the maids what was to be cleaned, and sending her housekeeper on a not-yet-successful mission to acquire the finest spiced wine for the father and daughter toast. All of a sudden, Thorn whined and withdrew from her touch. Letha opened her eyes. Her hands had balled into fists and were yanking tightly on his mane. She let go with a snarl, shocked and disappointed at his withdrawal, and his wary eyes followed her. The horse backed into a corner of the stables, tripping over bales of hay in the process, not taking his eyes off his mistress.

Letha reached for the crop in her gowns, anger spiking again, and then thought better of it. The crop had not yet been cleaned and would still be stained with the blood of her last victim. She didn't want to ruin the coat of her prize horse. "Stupid beast," she muttered, leaving the stables, a tiny shard of her ice heart breaking a little inside.

As soon as the stable door closed behind Letha, Joanna let out the breath she had been holding and emerged from the shadows. So that was the baron's famous daughter. Isaac's descriptions had been correct: she was an ice queen. It wasn't safe in the stables anymore. She feared that Letha may return. Joanna tugged her coat around her, thinking how glad she was that in those final few moments she had hauled it on, for the winter night was bitter and the hay was not nearly warm enough. The coat and the piece of paper with Isaac's drawing of the gates were the only items she had about her person. She had arrived a mere hour ago, filled with worries about Isaac and hoping that he had managed to escape the ravens, and save Bill. She had consoled herself with the reminder that she had faith in him. In the past few days, a change had taken place within the sorcerer; the resolution to right his wrongs had become absolute, and his powers were growing to a height unreachable by humankind. The display of his magic would not take long to reach the rest of the land, however, and Joanna was aware that, and in her mind she used this phrase lightly: they had been rumbled.

But that did not matter now. She was inside Blackthorn Manor and Isaac would return to the hills to fulfil his side of the bargain: the brewing. For now, Joanna knew she must find a safer place in which to hide, and after waiting for a few moments to decide if anyone was passing by outside, she opened the door to the stables and left the chestnut horse alone. There was no way of telling what time it was. It had been late evening when she departed the Sweet Siren, and as far as she could tell it was fast approaching midnight. The witching hour. She shuddered and reminded herself why she was doing this in the first place. Yes, it was the right thing to do. But if Isaac could kill the Villinors, he could kill the witches too, and return one good murder for another. She hurried across the courtyard and glanced over her shoulder as she went.

In front of her lay a long pathway decorated with fruit trees. It was this path that she took. It plunged her deeper into the shadows, and she knew that she must be reaching the outside perimeter of the manor. She spied the great walls that encased the estate, a looming mass in the dark, the border between the gluttonous wealthy and the poor peasants that had been fleeced of everything. Joanna felt guilty when she arrived on the other side of the impenetrable gates and faced the starving people outside. But she had a job to do. And she wouldn't be able to do it if she got caught by one of the ravens. She had slunk away before she could be noticed, beneath the shadows of the great dragons' heads, but the peasants' wails echoed in her ears now.

Out of the corner of her eye, Joanna spotted a small building in the shadow of the ivy-draped wall and made a beeline for it. Anything had to be better than freezing out in the cold. She looked up at the triangular roof. A sigh of relief passed silently through her lips as she saw the cross that adorned the roof. A chapel had to be the safest place of them all. Surely there would be no inhabitants at this hour. She looked left and right to see if she had been followed. She had not. Joanna pushed the creaky door open before she could change her mind. Little did she know, she was entering the belly of the beast itself, for it dwelled within these unholy walls.

A faint smell of incense wafted into her nostrils. It was mixed with something else she could not discern. It must have been something the worshippers burned in a service earlier. Her footsteps echoed and bounced off the high ceiling as she walked towards the altar. She sat in a pew and took off her coat. The chapel was warm. In fact, Joanna thought as she laid her coat down beside her, it was extremely warm for this hour. She could see no sign of a fire and instead assumed it was some kind of magic that kept the temperature agreeable. Like the orange and lemon trees that seemed to be bountiful even during winter. These odd eccentricities reminded her of the sorcerer.

Abandoning her coat in the pew, Joanna began to investigate the chapel further, and ran her finger along some of the dusty prayer books. Dusty? Did that mean that the chapel was not currently in use? Or did it mean that those who worshipped here could not read? She frowned, putting one of the books back, and turned instead to the beautiful stained glass depicting scenes from the Bible. The stars twinkled through the colours and brought an ethereal light to the glass. The scenes were brought to life so vividly that Joanna was sure she would be able to enter one of them herself. They were, after all, somebody's creation; an illustration of a different world and time. Joanna took a step back and tore her eyes away from the stained glass. The last thing she needed right now was to accidentally travel through into biblical times.

She was beginning to wonder how long she would be able to hide out here when something behind her stirred. She had been so preoccupied in gazing at the architecture, she had not noticed that she wasn't alone. An embellished cloth had been draped over the table that served as an altar. At the foot of this table lay a bundle of dark clothing. The clothing shifted. Joanna panicked, looking for a place to hide, but she was standing in the middle of the aisle. She doubted herself; she hadn't seen this dark shape when she entered the chapel. Had this person been lying beneath the altar the whole time and had now rolled out?

There was no time to duck into a pew before the tangle of robes and sleeves lifted its head up and fixed her with a bewildered stare. The man blinked a couple of times, as though trying to get Joanna properly in focus, and then the stench hit her. She now identified that strange smell as alcohol. The man had been lying intoxicated beneath the altar because he had collapsed there. Joanna took a few tentative steps forward, thinking that perhaps he needed help, and then the odour hit her again and she stumbled. The pungent fumes were almost visible in the warm air, and she feared that if she were to get any closer, she too would become intoxicated.

Joanna took a seat close to him; she didn't want to leave the man, but she didn't want to advance down the aisle any further. Then she properly looked at him. At first, she thought it was Isaac, but then her breath caught in her throat as she realised who she was looking at. He was indeed the spitting image of the sorcerer, but a worse version of her friend, in every aspect. His hair was thinner and greyer. His protruding belly strained at the seams of his expensive clothes. His face looked red as though he had been out in the cold for too long. His eyes were small and watery, and he looked like he hadn't seen a sober day for a century. If he were not immortal he would have died of alcoholism long ago. Joanna straightened her back and lifted her chin. She was looking at Etimus Villinor, the Baron of Blackthorn Manor.

SEVENTY-ONE

"Who are you?" he grumbled in a croaky voice, as of one who has just emerged from a deep slumber and is not quite back in the land of the living yet. He cleared his throat and the words came forth in a more authoritative manner. "More importantly, what are you doing in my private chapel?" Fantastic, Joanna thought. She had not stumbled upon a safe place of worship as first thought but a sordid hideaway for the baron to sleep away his sins. It seemed to take an age for him to find his feet. He righted himself slowly, with difficulty, as though the ground beneath him was not level. Joanna was thankful for this delayed awakening; it bought her precious seconds to think. A half-formed idea took shape, and she leapt to her feet as it finished formulating.

"Here, let me help you." Joanna held in both her disgust and her breath as she helped the baron to his feet. "Ah... there we go." She smiled. He slumped against a bench and fixed her with a hard stare.

"What are you doing in my chapel?" he repeated and gave her a strange look. It wasn't accusatory as she had anticipated but was simply curious, as though genuinely interested in her answer, as he raised his eyebrows. Perhaps no one had ever disturbed him in here before.

"I am so sorry," Joanna began, feigning absolute confidence. "I have travelled from... from a nearby village to begin my seamstress work on the cloaks."

Etimus blinked at her. "The what?"

Joanna smiled again. She was not sure this was going to work. "The cloaks for the ravens. I haven't yet been given any sleeping quarters and to be honest," here she leaned in to him as though about to divulge secret information, "I was taking the opportunity of my spare time to explore this beautiful estate. I happened to stumble upon your lovely chapel. I didn't realise it was private, Mr Villinor." Joanna bowed her head in apology.

Etimus took a deep breath, lifted himself up and back down again in his seat, and his brows knitted together in confusion. "So you're a seamstress? But we already have a seamstress – Madam Faraway."

Joanna threw caution to the winds. She had never before had to lie so quick on her feet. "Ah, yes, but Madam Faraway makes gowns and tunics such as the marvellous one you have on here." Joanna gestured vaguely to his beer-stained midriff, and he frowned. "I am here to make cloaks, for your loyal ravens, something which Madam Faraway does not unfortunately have experience in."

Etimus chuckled at this, and Joanna looked at him in surprise. "And you have experience in making cloaks for seven-foot-tall beasts, do you?" Joanna thought back to the many hours she had spent with needle and thread, crafting embellished cloaks for the witches. She had become something of an expert in this regard. "I've encountered some beasts before, yes." The baron chuckled again, and Joanna was glad at least that he found her entertaining. This meant he probably wasn't going to kill her.

Etimus gave a great yawn. "I suppose this is my daughter's doing then?"

Joanna eyed her coat on the pew a few rows along and prayed that the drawing of the manor gates was tucked deeply in the pockets. "Yes, indeed, your daughter." Something told Joanna that this was not a conversation he would bother to have with Letha. "She sent for me to craft the cloaks, and I am to begin work tomorrow. I think she must have forgotten that I was arriving today. I know that she must be preoccupied with other important… duties—" Etimus snorted. Joanna found it easy to talk to him. She didn't know if it was because he looked so similar to Isaac or because he wasn't quite the formidable force she had been expecting. He was just a drunk. She continued before he could interrupt again. "I apologise again for interrupting your… prayer… but I am eager to get a good night's sleep so I can begin my work tomorrow." The baron rose from his seat with surprising sobriety. He looked down at Joanna with her hands in her lap.

"How old are you?" he barked, suddenly suspicious. Joanna swallowed, her throat feeling like sandpaper, and tried to assume an air of confidence once more. She often forgot that she kept the outward appearance of a pale teenager when in fact she had outlived a lifetime and more.

"I am twenty," she aimed for. "But I look young for my age." She flashed him a charming smile, a pit of disgust bubbling up in her stomach. She had never had to charm someone before and didn't like the feeling. It was necessary if she were to save her own life, however.

"Twenty," the baron repeated, and nodded, as though buying her lies. "Well, I can't say I'm surprised," he said with a small shrug and began brushing the dust off his tunic from where he had been lying on the ground. Joanna's throat loosened at his sudden matter-of-fact attitude. "My daughter is always coming up with some ridiculous plan. Here, I'll show you to your quarters, I'm done with my prayers for tonight."

Joanna's throat tightened again. Show her to her quarters? Didn't he have servants, or even ravens, to do that for him? "That's not necessary, Mr Villinor, if you give me directions I'm sure I can find the way," she gabbled. Etimus finished brushing off his tunic, gathered his robes tighter about himself, and picked up her coat. He walked over to her.

"I can't have a pretty woman like you walking about my manor on her own at this hour. Especially as you are my daughter's guest. She'd kill me," he muttered under his breath, and Joanna couldn't tell if he was joking. "Come on." He took her arm. Joanna had no choice but to fall into step with him as they walked up the aisle and toward the entrance to the chapel.

She felt uncomfortable. She wanted to get away from his stinking presence as soon as possible. They were much too close. He believed her story, however, and she knew that the only thing for her to do now was to stay silent until she could get away from him. "For a seamstress, your own clothes seem a little shabby, Miss...?" Etimus gestured to her attire.

"Woodgate," Joanna replied. It was safe to use her own name here; no one knew or cared who she really was. "Miss Woodgate. These are just my travelling clothes," she added quickly.

"Very well. I'm sure we can find you something more appropriate in your quarters."

Joanna stepped out into the night air with the baron. Their arms were still tightly linked. She could tell they would not become unlinked until it was the baron's choice to do so. It was a warning – a reminder that she was in his manor and under his control. Three ravens appeared out of the gloom. Joanna wondered if they had witnessed her entry into the chapel as well and had let her walk in. She tried not to look at their glowing eyes. "I don't require an escort tonight." Etimus waved their feathers away, and they immediately retreated into the shadows as though they had never been there at all.

Before Joanna could marvel at how quickly the baron had become sober, she was distracted by the faint melody of sweet music drifting across the grounds, growing louder. The baron's pace remained even, as though the music merely melted into the background for him. He did not say anything until the minstrel became visible in the moonlight. "Have you seen my beautiful harp?" he asked Joanna.

"N-no," she stuttered, praying that her theory about Isaac's magic was correct.

"Ah, the melody makes for a lovely... atmosphere." He smiled down at her, and it became more of a leer. Joanna stopped herself from shuddering as the minstrel passed and the music entered her ears. The harmony was so beautiful it pained her. Such melodious music seemed so out of place in this cruel setting. The minstrel passed by, and Joanna watched his curly shoes tiptoe away into the dark, his peacock-coloured tail skirts trailing behind him.

It took everything she had not to run after the minstrel and bash the harp against the stone walls of the manor. She knew that even this would not be enough to break the enchantment. But it would make her feel better. Reminding herself what company she kept, she simply smiled up at the baron, and said through gritted teeth, "Such beautiful music." He grunted in agreement as though the subject began to bore him. Joanna checked herself. She still remembered who she was and where she came from. No fog descended over her brain and clouded her judgement. She had been right: the magic of the harps did not affect her. Joanna possessed her own magic, which provided a barrier between her and Isaac's. She was also still bound by a dark curse to the witches; she could not be possessed by the baron when she belonged to another. She was immune.

She took solace in this fact while she let the baron steer her toward the manor. Knowing her own brain would certainly give her an advantage over many others in this strange place. They had reached the entrance to the grand stone building. More ravens bowed their heads as the baron passed through the archway that led into the hall, and Joanna felt more uncomfortable than ever. She looked like his plaything, hanging off his arm like that. She had planned on drawing little attention to herself, yet she was being paraded around. Thankfully, most inhabitants of the manor were safely tucked up in their warm beds and did not witness the two of them. Joanna let out a breath she didn't know she'd been holding. This was the most exquisite room she had ever been in. Blackthorn House had been beautiful, but Blackthorn Manor was breathtaking. Etimus watched Joanna as she studied the hall. He seemed pleased at her awe. "Come," he said. "If my manor is to be your home for the next few weeks, you'll have plenty of time to marvel at its delights. For now, off to bed."

He nodded sharply at a raven who stood in front of the fire. It was a wonder his feathers had not caught alight, and Joanna was sure that if she reached out a hand they would be hot to the touch. The baron unlinked his arm and let Joanna go. She had a sudden thought. "Materials." The word tumbled out of her mouth. "I'll need materials for the cloaks, Letha said... Times are hard and there are so many of them..." Joanna trailed off, fearing she had gone too far with the lie. There was a pause before the baron nodded once in silent agreement. "Thank you. Goodnight, Mr Villinor." Joanna curtseyed for added effect before following the raven out of the hall. She couldn't help but feel as though the baron had sent her off to bed like a child. And she didn't like being alone with the raven. It was huge. Its breath rattled in the quiet and a talon protruded from a rip in the bottom of the cloak. Perhaps they were in need of new cloaks after all.

Ascending a spiral staircase toward the back of the manor, the raven led Joanna onto the next level, and another long corridor faced them. He manoeuvred his body awkwardly; there was only just enough room for his hulking form to pass through. He seemed to withdraw into the wall opposite as they passed the first door on the left, and Joanna felt an icy blast emanate from the room. They passed an endless amount of closed doors until he pointed a gloved hand toward a smaller door at the end of the corridor on the right. "Guest quarters," he grunted, and disappeared back along the narrow passage into the night. Joanna watched him go, until she was confident he had descended the staircase again and resumed his post in front of the fire downstairs.

Tentatively pushing open the little door, Joanna stepped inside what was to be her living quarters for however long she managed to stay alive for. She smiled for the first time since arriving in the manor. A large four-poster bed met her eyes, and a sudden weariness overcame her as soon as she set eyes upon it. A wooden wardrobe stood to the right of the bed, next to a table, stool and large mirror. The wardrobe was full of gowns, robes and undergarments. They must have been left for whoever occupied the room. She was being treated as one of the wealthy, and this room was another display of the baron's fortune. She wandered over to the window on the left and peered out over the orange and lemon trees lit up by the stars. It seemed that her lies about the baron's daughter employing her had landed her in a guest suite.

Lying back onto the plush pillows, Joanna closed her eyes, thinking of Isaac. She must set to work tomorrow and find his nephew. For all she knew, Tristan could have been one of the ravens she had encountered already, but gut instinct told her that he hadn't been among them. Sleep began to overtake her, and as she drifted off, fully clothed atop the covers, her last thoughts were of the baron. She hoped that she would not have to spend any more time with him. Now that he believed her and she had her story set up, hopefully he would leave her alone and pass his nights in that lonely chapel.

As she fell out of consciousness she thought it probably didn't matter anyway. He had been so drunk he probably wouldn't recognise her next time they met. Hell, he probably thought there were two of her.

SEVENTY-TWO

Joanna awoke from a fitful sleep the next morning. She was still fully clothed. She did not have time to arise from the sorry state in which she had left herself the previous night before her room became a bustling hub of activity. First, the chambermaid arrived and silently went about her business before exiting the bedroom. Second, another maid dressed in a dark tunic opened her curtains and narrowed her eyes at Joanna, as though chastising her for still being on the bed. The third and final maid to arrive had been sent from the kitchens. She twisted her hands around her frilly apron after setting down a tantalising breakfast tray. "Is there anything else Miss Woodgate desires?" Joanna winced that they already knew her name.

"No thank you," she replied quickly, eyeing the plate of bacon piled high and the three different varieties of breakfast juice. "Really, all of this is not necessary," she tried to tell the kitchen maid.

The girl simply eyed her and said, "It's traditional for guests of the lord or lady of the manor to have all their needs provided for. Enjoy your day."

Joanna grimaced as she left. She had hoped that the seamstress lie would enable her to blend into the background of the manor, unquestioned, unnoticed. Guests of the lord or lady of the manor. The maid's words echoed in her ears. She was dead meat. Either the baron or his daughter was going to realise that neither of them had sent for her. They would recognise her as an intruder and string her up. "Okay, breathe," Joanna muttered. She would just have to play both of them off and buy herself as much time as possible. She could do this. But first, she had to look the part, and right now she looked like a dishevelled child in a foreign land.

Joanna thanked the Lord that she had been allowed the dignity to at least bathe and clothe herself. The room adjoining her bedchamber contained a small bath and everything she needed to wash away the memories of the midnight meeting in the chapel. The gowns were plain, but elegant, mostly dark colours with some embroidery around the neck and sleeves. She chose a dark green garment and encased herself in the velvety material. It was slightly too big for her in the sleeves, but it would have to do. She could roll them up. Joanna spent plenty of time brushing out her wavy hair, and the blonde locks trailed loosely around her shoulders. She stared at herself in the mirror. The gown did make her look older. She took a step forward and looked closer. Her nose almost touched the mirror. She peered at herself. Was she ageing? She noticed a few fine lines around her eyes and mouth that hadn't been there before. Her face no longer looked like that of a sixteen-year-old but a fully grown woman, plumper and full of colour. Was her distance from the witches loosening the bond between them? Had this strange world finally begun to whizz the hands of the clock round and round on her?

A sharp rap came upon Joanna's bedroom door. It swung inwards, and she wondered why the person had bothered to knock if they were not going to wait for a reply. Joanna tore her eyes away from the mirror. She faced a formidable woman in the doorway framed in a background of black. It was only when the newcomer took a step into the room and let the maids behind her enter that Joanna realised the mass of black was the requested material for the cloaks. The maids struggled to balance the teetering piles of it as it was carried into the room. It was hastily dumped onto the dressing table. The maids departed. "Here is the material for the cloaks." The woman speaking wore a long dark dress covered over the top with a white apron. A set of keys jangled in her pockets as she took another step forward. "I am the housekeeper here. If you need more material you are to come straight to me." Joanna eyed her warily. She had an annoying air of self-importance, and her features were extremely displeasing.

"Thank you," Joanna stuttered, wanting her out of the room. The housekeeper wrinkled her hooked nose at her.

"Where are the rest of your supplies?"

"M-my supplies?"

"Yes," she stated coldly. "The baron has informed me that you are to produce cloaks for his ravens. Your needles, your threads, the things a seamstress relies upon…" she finished sarcastically.

Joanna drew herself up to her full height, feeling confident in the new gown, and tilted her chin up to the ceiling. "The baron has entrusted me with this task. Do you doubt that I would travel here without the necessities needed?"

The woman paused, and her thin upper lip sneered. "Of course not."

"Good," Joanna continued, adamant that she was not going to let this housekeeper push her around, despite her heart hammering in her chest. Even though the housekeeper had been instructed by the baron to bring her the material, Joanna had a sneaking suspicion that this one was loyal to Letha, so decided to really drive home the impression she wanted to give. "The baron sent for me because he knew that I can do the job better than anyone else. I am assuming that you would not be disagreeing with the baron now."

The housekeeper bowed her head begrudgingly. "Not at all, Miss Woodgate, I shall leave you to your… sewing."

"There's one more thing." Joanna tried pushing her luck. "I am going to need a list."

The housekeeper bristled. "A list?"

"Yes, of the ravens. I need a list of their names. Otherwise how am I going to know which cloak is for whom? They are all made to measure. I need to take individual measurements and record them on a list. Please," Joanna added, trying to keep things friendly. The woman sighed as though she were asking a great favour of her.

"I don't know if any such list exists, and if it does, it will be within the lord's chambers which I am not granted access to." She sniffed, seeming bitter about this. "I will ask one of his stewards." She gave a haughty huff and strode out of the room in her squeaky polished boots.

Once the door had snapped shut behind her tightly pinned-up bun, Joanna slumped onto the stool at the dressing table. She was alone for the first time all morning. The breakfast tray lay untouched on the little table next to the bed. She had far more important things to think about. Fingering the silky material, she let it slide between her fingertips, and marvelled at the colour. It was black, but shimmered with a galaxy of stars, as though whirling into some deep pit in space. She had also been given a bundle of fine silk threads, some black, others silvery. They looked as though they had been gathered from beams of moonlight. How was it that all the servants of the baron were to be clad in such exquisite fabrics when the rest of the land lay to waste and starvation? The ragged cloth she had been given to fashion the witches' cloaks was far more practical. Anger boiled in Joanna's stomach. It would certainly not be enough for all of the ravens, which meant that eventually she would have to seek out the housekeeper again, a thought which furthered her bad mood. But still, to source such expensive material overnight, that could not have been an easy task. No wonder she hated her already.

But the housekeeper had been right. To produce this amount of cloaks (she still did not know exactly how many she would have to make) would be an impossible task without the instruments of her trade. It was imperative that she get hold of some sewing materials. Otherwise her whole guise would go up in flames. Joanna could not leave the manor, this much she knew. It was too risky to assume that she would be allowed back inside the gates. The baron had let slip last night that they already employed a seamstress. The mysterious Madam Faraway seemed like Joanna's only hope. She would have to become a thief as well as a liar. There was no telling when the housekeeper would return with the list, and time spent hiding away in the room was time wasted. Joanna checked her reflection once more in the mirror, confirmed that she looked the part, and tiptoed out of the room into the great expanse of the manor beyond.

SEVENTY-THREE

"Confidence is the key," she muttered to herself as she walked slowly up the corridor. She did not like the way the velvet gown trailed behind her; it would not be very practical for running away. Its long folds would, however, make for an ideal hiding place for needles, thimbles and scissors, albeit a little sharp. Maids and stewards passed her in the aisle. They were dressed to perfection, not a hairpin or ruffle out of place, and Joanna knew that these were the servants of the noble folk in the manor. Other than the baron and Letha, she had not considered who else may dwell within the stone walls, but she now realised there must have been those with enough money and land to be a part of the baron's elite when he came to power. She was among the lords and ladies of the land. Everyone she passed seemed to be half stuck in a dream. They all possessed an otherworldly air that hinted some part of them was in a faraway place. Joanna knew this was the enchantment of the harps. She had spotted it with the maids that morning. They were distant, as though constantly trying to remember something from long ago.

Joanna attempted to shrink into the shadows and avoid the hustle and bustle of the corridors and staircase. She noticed there was a flurry of excitement about the manor. People stood gossiping and exchanging looks as though a momentous event were occurring. Perhaps this was normal, Joanna pondered, as she passed two finely dressed ladies on the twisted staircase, their mouths moving rapidly in excited tones. "Sober?" one of them exclaimed, and laughed shrilly, her pearly white teeth showing. "At this hour?" They climbed up out of earshot. Joanna reached the bottom of the staircase. A steward trod on her gown, and she yelped as she almost toppled down the last few steps. The steward remained oblivious as he continued the eager conversation with a maid, who held a platter of fresh fruit as her eyes grew wider, taking in every word her friend said. "No one's seen him like this in years," the steward was divulging. "We weren't prepared – said he wanted coffee with his breakfast. Coffee!" he exclaimed, as though this were a ridiculous request.

Tugging her long skirts out from beneath the steward's foot, Joanna frowned as he ascended the staircase, still unaware of his clumsiness. She struggled to maintain her balance and had to leap off the last step in an unbecoming pirouette. She stared after the steward and maid who had taken no notice of her. Now what? Judging from the staggering amount of servants flitting about it seemed as though they had begun preparing lunch already. They seemed to be emerging from the left of the staircase and then scattering out over the manor. Thinking that Madam Faraway may reside in the servants' quarters, Joanna took a left, and fought against the oncoming tide of people coming out of the kitchens, scullery and cellars. She dodged great platters of food and narrowly avoided being tripped up again by a rolling barrel that had broken free of the cellar. A servant boy gave chase closely behind it. On his way past, he shot Joanna a suspicious glance, and she realised she must look out of place in these quarters.

There was a brief pause in the hubbub, and Joanna found herself standing alone in the corridor. She gave a great sigh, realising she had made a mistake, and turned her back on the kitchens. Madam Faraway was not going to reside down here. If she really was the baron and Letha's appointed seamstress, her accommodation would be far better than the kitchen maids'. Back at the bottom of the twisted staircase Joanna had three options: go right along the opposite corridor, walk straight ahead and into the grand entrance hall she had seen last night, or turn around and go out of the back exit and into the gardens. She made the decision in a split second. Trying her very best to not be put off by the two ravens standing guard, she entered the entrance hall, and immediately became distracted.

A great variety of dinner plates, drinking vessels and decanters had been laid across the trestle tables, as though on display. "No, not those ones," a voice snapped. "Take those back to the kitchens, they're far too ugly." The voice belonged to the hook-nosed woman who Joanna now knew to be the housekeeper. One of the maids standing to attention immediately removed the offending items and scurried back past Joanna in the direction of the kitchens. Joanna retreated along the right side of the wall behind a suit of armour; she didn't fancy another encounter with the housekeeper just yet. "That one, there," she was now barking to a sullen-looking girl. "No, not that one, that one." She pointed ferociously to a large glass decanter. "That one is perfect for the toast." The maid under her authority picked up a large vessel with all the fear that it may smash at any given moment. Joanna assumed that they were preparing for some kind of banquet. She looked for an exit, anywhere that might lead to other accommodation, but stopped short. A door had opened a mere few feet in front of her, hidden by the wood panelling, and there was someone emerging through it.

Joanna cursed and backed behind a nearby suit of armour. There was an almighty crash as she misjudged the space and caused the suit to topple on its plinth. A pair of hands caught the heavy plates before they hit the floor, and everyone in the hall turned to scowl at Joanna. They quickly turned away back to their chores as they saw who she was standing next to. The baron eyed her. "Are you going to make a habit of destroying all my artefacts, Miss Woodgate? A great man wore that one." He inclined his head toward the now upright knight. The baron's voice was devoid of emotion, but his look was dangerously playful.

"I-I-" Joanna stuttered as she tried to come up with a feasible excuse as to why she was skulking about the hall. The baron sighed and gave a small smile.

"I never really liked him anyway. Come, walk with me."

SEVENTY-FOUR

Joanna could not ignore his brisk command. She fell into step with him as he led her out of the hall, past the spiral staircase, and through the exit into the courtyard. Maids and stewards scattered when they saw him coming, which left the two of them in silence. Instinct told Joanna to keep quiet. She glanced sideways at the baron. There was something different about him today. As they walked side by side across the cobbled pathway and approached the animal pens, it clicked in Joanna's mind.

The baron was sober. This simple fact was headline news in the manor. His face was clean-shaven. His chestnut eyes, when Joanna looked into them briefly, sparkled with the morning sun and held none of the watery confusion of the night before. His clothes were clean, without a trace of the beer stains Joanna had spied in the chapel, and his skin, although still flushed, was of a brighter complexion. He looked, with the exception of the bushy beard, much more like the Isaac with whom she had become friends and allies.

The pair reached the long pathway lined by fruit trees without exchanging a word. Joanna could not help but breathe in the fresh scent of the citrus as they walked the length of the gravel. They had taken a few steps when the baron paused and gestured for Joanna to take a seat on a nearby bench. Joanna did so, and her velvet gown puffed up around her. She was grateful of having chosen one with long sleeves, for the air was cold. The baron perched beside her and stared ahead. She swallowed. She could feel the power emanating off him.

This manor, this world, belonged to him. She glanced over her shoulder at the ravens who had subtly followed them out into the gardens. "Oh, don't worry about them," Etimus said slowly, noticing Joanna's unease. "They're just keeping watch on things." Joanna tore her eyes away from the glowing ones and found the baron looking intently at her.

"I'm sorry – about the armour, Mr Villinor." She didn't know how she was supposed to address the baron, but Mr Villinor seemed to do, and he raised his eyebrows.

"Are you going to begin all of our meetings with an apology?" Etimus asked her. Joanna frowned. She did not like the way he addressed her; it was always with a question as though teasing her, playing with her. She also did not like the assumption that there would be more of these meetings to come.

"No," she replied firmly. He looked taken aback and brushed an invisible fleck of dirt off his emerald tunic.

"I must apologise for the smell. I have just come from the dungeons."

Joanna's stomach bubbled unpleasantly. "Is that so?"

"Yes." Etimus turned his face away from her and up to the sky. "A dirty beggar was caught at the gates. The old man was trying to harass my guards. As though he stood a chance," Etimus snickered. Joanna felt sick. This was not the Isaac she was friends and allies with. "I felt it was my duty to pay him a personal visit in his cell – to show him what his disloyalty truly means."

"Disloyalty?" Joanna repeated.

"Yes." The baron looked at her quickly. "That man could have offered to work here and earn his keep. He could have had a place among my servants and off the streets. Instead he steals from my land and bothers my ravens."

"Perhaps he was just hungry," Joanna stated before she could stop herself.

"Perhaps he was," the baron murmured. "But that's not my problem. He made his choice to beg and starve rather than serve me." *Rather than be your slave*, Joanna thought bitterly. She readjusted the sleeves of her gown.

A sudden breeze disturbed the orange and lemon trees. It caught a lock of Joanna's hair, and Etimus's gaze travelled to her once more as it deposited the lock on her shoulder and almost touched his fine fabrics. He stood up brusquely. "Shouldn't you be hard at work by now?" His tone had changed, as though he suddenly remembered he had important business to attend to. Joanna rose from the bench. She didn't like the way he towered above her, blocking out what little of the morning sun there was, and formed a lie out of the truth.

"I'm looking for Madam Faraway."

The baron's brows knit together and then slowly relaxed. "And what do you want with her?"

"Merely to meet her," Joanna countered. "Two seamstresses working in such… close quarters… it seems rude not to introduce myself. That way we can ensure our work does not overlap and we won't get in each other's way." It wasn't a very strong lie, but Joanna suspected the baron had little interest in the goings-on of his seamstresses.

"Very well." Etimus reached for her arm. Joanna reluctantly obeyed. "I shall take you to her. I could do with checking my tunic for the banquet." So there was an upcoming event, Joanna thought. She felt it best not to probe further and let herself be steered back toward the manor. She hated this. Hated playing a game, hated where the game had taken her, and hated the proximity the foul baron had assumed. She tried not to breathe in his musk tinged with something metallic. She could only picture what he had done to the poor beggar man. Not soon enough they walked back into the hall. It was empty. The housekeeper had disappeared, and the maids were left scrubbing the floor and tables. They scrubbed so ferociously Joanna was sure they had been threatened with something awful unless they could see their own dejected reflections in the polished surface.

The pair passed, arm in arm, and received a few bowed heads mixed with some disgruntled looks. Joanna felt as though she'd be more at home scrubbing the floors than hanging off Etimus Villinor's arm. She could not fathom why the baron had taken such a liking to her. If it aided the plan to finally destroy him, the baron's intentions were to be ignored, for now. They turned left and walked along the corridor that Joanna had decided against earlier. It led to another staircase, this one less ostentatious than the main spiral one, and Joanna noticed the paintings on the walls as they ascended.

She would have an escape if she really needed one. Being of magical origin, the baron did not have any descendants' portraits with which to adorn his manor, and his immortality meant that there was no family tree. The paintings were of stark landscapes instead. A pack of wolves stood among moonlit trees, a solitary tower rose atop a dark mountain, and a great expanse of moorland stretched with no sign of life... Joanna shuddered. Perhaps these paintings were better off unexplored.

"Come," the baron instructed, and Joanna quickened her pace, realising she had been lagging behind on the staircase. This part of the manor was colder than Joanna's room, and the harsh air shocked her lungs for a few seconds. The baron led her past room after room, giving no indication that he had noticed the change in temperature, and did not look at her as she followed behind. These bedchambers were for those who were employed by the baron, not of high enough rank to dwell among the lords and ladies, but not of low enough status to be put in the servants' quarters below. Those like Madam Faraway.

"Here we are." The baron stopped abruptly, and Joanna crashed into him. She winced at the physical contact. They faced a small door halfway along the wide corridor. Another door shut near to them, and Joanna jumped. People really did hide away from the baron. The single window at the far end of the corridor didn't provide enough light for her to see how many other rooms there were. He knocked thrice upon the door before them. Joanna panicked. She hadn't actually determined what she was going to say to Madam Faraway. In her original plan she had never intended on meeting the woman. A whisper of relief passed through her as no one answered. The baron banged on the door impatiently, as though never having to ask for anything twice before. There was still no response.

"It seems she is off advising someone else about their gowns." Etimus broke the silence. "You'll have to try again later, Miss Woodgate."

"I will, thank you." Joanna twisted the folds of her gown awkwardly, wishing he would leave. He turned to face her, and all of a sudden the corridor seemed much too small.

"That colour rather becomes you." He gestured to the velvety material. Joanna paused. He examined every inch of her. The gown became itchy, and she scratched at the neckline. Before she could try and pass off the compliment and hint that she did not want any more, the baron turned his back on her and strode away down the corridor. "I trust you can find your own way back to your quarters." Joanna felt too uncomfortable to give a reply, but he clearly didn't expect one as the tails of his tunic disappeared from sight.

Joanna tucked her hair behind her ear and pressed it to Madam Faraway's door. It was possible that the seamstress was inside, had heard the baron's voice, and decided not to answer. Joanna wouldn't blame her. She didn't know what their history was. She was met only with silence. She needed those materials. Glancing behind her, Joanna pushed on the door, and held her breath.

Madam Faraway had left her room unlocked.

SEVENTY-FIVE

Adjoining Madam Faraway's room was a parlour stuffed to the brim with sewing materials. She really should think twice about her security, Joanna thought, as she winced at every other step. The twisted staircase proved difficult to manoeuvre. Joanna had to tuck the needles and thimbles in the waistband of her gown, which was unnaturally tight for her liking, and beneath her neckline. One wrong movement and she could be impaled. She wondered if Isaac was going to such great lengths to carry out their murder plot on the other side of the gates. If he had escaped from the ravens, of course. Joanna pushed this thought aside, convinced that her attempts would pay off, and stepped robotically up the stairs to avoid being speared by her own spoils.

Thanking the Lord that she had not been waylaid, she stepped foot into her own room on the other side of the manor, and took a few deep breaths. A rustling over by the window caught her attention. A small black shape hopped over the ledge. Joanna ran over to it, but the raven was already gone. She closed the window firmly shut. One of them had been in her room. She looked about. She had left no visible sign of foul play. A horrible thought struck her. Had the baron engaged her in conversation so as to give his raven time to search her room? Or had it been a mere coincidence that the two had occurred at the same time? Joanna fiddled with the catch on the window again, checking it was locked, and peered into the gardens below. No sign of any ravens. They were good at disappearing when they needed to.

She checked the dressing table, bathroom and even in the bath itself. She couldn't afford any more malicious spies.

Finally satisfied that whoever had been in her room was long gone, Joanna let the gown fall to her feet, and all of the stolen materials came tumbling out. She laid them on the table next to the materials and pulled the gown back on. They looked like they had always been there. Trying not to dwell on the fact that her room had been searched, Joanna began to think about how she was going to fashion the cloaks, and how long it was going to take. She really did need to get close to the ravens; she had no idea of the extent of these beasts or how to dress them. Recording their measurements individually and making each cloak to suit seemed like the best idea. This lengthy process would also buy her and Isaac time. She hoped that his cauldron, or whatever he used, was already brewing away with the deadly draught.

Joanna sat down on the bed. Tiredness overcame her bones. She sat up straight. She could not afford to sleep – could not afford another unwanted visitor in her room. With this thought she got up and locked her door from the inside. Joanna's reason for needing the list of all the ravens was twofold. She could begin work on the cloaks, and the baron and Letha would see that she was not lying about being a seamstress. She was also looking for a name. Tristan Brewer should be on that list. She needed to find Tristan, but first needed to check that he was among them, and this list would give her faith that he resided in the manor. All these thoughts brimmed around Joanna's mind as she began to pace, and pace, and pace…

The sky outside had grown a navy-blue shade of night before the list was delivered to Joanna's door. Her stomach had begun to grumble, and she was grateful of the supper that had been served in her room moments before. The housekeeper's wan face drifted in her doorway as she handed the papers over. "The ravens will assemble for you in the morning so you can measure up for the cloaks." She strode away in a huff grumbling at the amount of work she had to do. Joanna looked down at what she had been given. It wasn't a list, but a book. An old, leather-bound book.

She dropped onto the bed at once and began poring over its contents. The pages were yellowing, and she feared that as soon as her fingertips touched the delicate surface it would disintegrate before her very eyes. The names had been scrawled in faded black ink, and time's wicked hands had meant that some were indecipherable. The names went on and on. Joseph Hemlock, Ivan Roberts, Alexander James, John Rivers, William Sharp, Adam Thomas... Joanna paused. She stopped rifling through the pages and looked about the dark room. Nausea washed over her. There were thousands of names in the book. Isaac had been forced to perform the monstrous transformation on every one. No wonder it had broken him. Joanna thought of the endless amount of families that had been ripped apart by this magic. Husbands, brothers, sons... They were all gone, all no longer human.

It took her a few minutes to look at the small book again. She forced herself to continue studying it, to find some kind of pattern, to make sense of it. There were various annotations in a different hand next to the names. Some had been crossed through with a single black line. Some were marked with a 'T', some with a 'D' and some with an 'R'. Joanna worked out that the ones marked with an 'R' often had the same surname. This annotation meant that they were related. It hadn't been enough to take just one member of a family away. Most of the names marked with a 'T' had been crossed out, and it was only when Joanna came across the odd word scribbled in the margins of the page, like 'rebel', 'deserter' and 'treason', that she understood the meanings. 'T' stood for traitor and 'D' stood for deceased. Whether accidental death or murder she could not tell.

The list was not alphabetical, and there were no dates marked on the papers. She had been flipping through aimlessly, trying to interpret names at random, when something clicked. It was simply a list from the first raven to the last. When someone had been transformed, they had been forced to give their name, and it was written down here. It was in order of who had been transformed first. Joanna returned to the very first page in the book as her heart skipped a beat.

There it was, Tristan Brewer, the very first raven.

But it had been crossed through with a single heartbreaking line.

Tristan Brewer T. D.

SEVENTY-SIX

The sun had not yet risen before Joanna made up her mind. She had to leave this place. Isaac's nephew was dead and she could not do this alone. For all she knew, Tristan Brewer could have passed out of this world a hundred years ago, and the sorcerer had merely been mourning his memory. It had been another sleepless night during which Joanna had exhausted all the possible scenarios in which this would end. Most involved her death by some grotesque means. She hadn't even entertained the possibility that Tristan could be dead. Perhaps Isaac's naive belief had rubbed off on her more than she had realised. No, it was time for reality to kick in; she was too late, and there was no hope.

The lamentations of the poverty-stricken families had echoed in her ears ever since arriving in the manor. She silenced their cries in her mind. The plan could not possibly be carried out without the help of an insider. After hours of pacing her room, tearing out her own hair in anguish and holding her head in her hands, Joanna Woodgate did something that she never usually did. She gave up.

Joanna grabbed her coat and the drawing of the shepherd's hut. The sketch was awful, only just lifelike enough to picture the real hut in her mind, but it was the only place she could think of that Isaac would go. She wouldn't go back to the witches yet. She had to deliver the solemn news first. She would have to break the news of his nephew's death before she confessed to him that she could no longer help. That he would have to live out his endless life in the hillside pining after the ghost of someone he never got to say goodbye to. Just like everyone else in his life.

Joanna stopped pacing. She collapsed onto the bed and gazed desperately at the ceiling. "I can't do that to him," she muttered softly. The room was silent in reply. Joanna sat up. Her elbow brushed against a small object, and she looked down. The little book of names lay innocently next to her pillow. A sudden rage bellowed forth from her, and she threw the book across the room. It was Isaac's fault in the first place! His bitterness had torn families apart. His hatred for his own brother had lost him his nephew. His arrogance had led him to complete and utter loneliness. She had simply been trying to escape from the witches and now look where it had got her! In that moment she felt nothing but anger for the sorcerer and all that he had done.

A single piece of paper fluttered to the floor as the book hit the wall opposite. She propped herself up on the bed as the sun began to rise. The weak morning light illuminated the paper slightly. Joanna narrowed her eyes. She had not spotted it before. It must have been hidden within the folds of the old pages. The bed creaked as she lifted herself off it to go and investigate. She bent down, head still whirling with bitter thoughts about Isaac, and blew the dust gently off the piece of parchment. It was old and yellowed, barely intact, with inky scribble across the single page that was only just legible. Across the top had been underlined:

KNOWN FOLLOWERS OF THE FIRST

Joanna's anger ebbed away. Her brows knitted as she took the book and the slip of paper over to the window, to further inspect. "Followers of the First," she repeated in a whisper, still not understanding the title. There followed a list of names. She recognised some of the names from the original book of ravens. The odd name had been crossed through, and Joanna knew that meant they had died. The list was double-sided and some of the names had been inked over twice, three times, as though someone had tried to highlight their importance. At the bottom of the list was a squished column with a handful of ravens entitled:

WATCH LIST

Joanna looked up, suddenly fearful that she was being watched. The baron had not intended for her to see this; he had probably forgotten that he had tucked it into the folds of the old book many years ago. Questions raced through Joanna's mind. Why would Etimus have a separate list of his ravens that he was keeping a close eye on? Who were the Followers of the First? Were they dangerous? Perhaps some kind of threat? Did these names mean anything now? Or were they irrelevant to her plans? Anyone who was a threat to the baron was a friend to her, raven or not.

The courtyard was a teeming mass of talons and feathers. Joanna found herself amidst the mayhem ten minutes later. She shuddered at the sudden thought that struck her: how on earth was she going to get close enough to these beasts to measure them? She was a seamstress, she reminded herself firmly, setting down her bag of measuring equipment on the bench. She didn't have a clue how to use half of the things she had obtained. Madam Faraway's boudoir was a treasure trove of strange-looking items that she could not identify yet had deemed worthy of stealing. Anything she could stuff down her dress had been taken. The witches had not afforded her such luxuries when designing their cloaks. She was used to a pair of blunt scissors and a faded measuring tape conjured from mid-air.

The ravens took little notice of her as she perched awkwardly on the bench. Every so often two of the bulky birds would get too close to each other, not knowing the span of their own wings, and a cloak would tear and a shriek sound. Joanna now understood why no one had batted an eyelid when she claimed the ravens needed new cloaks. They looked clumsy, somehow. Their inability to function in an enclosed space was a potential weakness that she hadn't considered before. She eyed them warily.

She did not fancy her chances at shouting over the top of all that noise. A couple of minutes passed in an uncomfortable fashion. Joanna began to fidget and was about to fill up her lungs to shout something out when a distraction arrived. Joanna started up from the bench, trying hard to ignore her panicked throat, which had now filled up with cotton wool. Seeing the baron's daughter in the moonlit stables was different to being close up. Joanna managed a small curtsey, and her knees wobbled. Letha's ivory skin was even paler than usual as the cool winter air danced against the sides of the glacier. She sported no rosy cheeks or signs of life. She inhaled a deep breath of bitter air and smiled cruelly as though it didn't sting her insides.

"What, may I ask," she began expectantly, "is going on here?"

"I-I-" Joanna hated herself for stumbling, but the ravens had stood to attention, and the silence was deafening. The ice queen raised her perfectly plucked eyebrows and shook her head in disgust.

"Are you going to do me the dishonour of ignoring my question?" The question was a threat, and Joanna knew it. She willed her fluttering heart to calm down and mustered what composure she could find.

"M-my apologies, Miss Letha." She curtseyed again. "I thought that you knew. Your father asked me to design new cloaks for the ravens." Letha's eyes narrowed into inhuman slits.

"Why?" The word pinged across the courtyard and ruffled the ravens' feathers. Joanna threw caution to the wind.

"I suspect it is for the... upcoming event... so that everyone can look their best." Something flickered across Letha's face.

"My father," she repeated the words, "has sent for you to design new cloaks? Why not ask Madam Faraway?" Joanna again hedged her bets and lifted her chin slightly.

"Perhaps he thinks her needlework is getting shoddy?" The comment seemed to surprise the baron's daughter, and her next sentence was thawed out a little.

"And you have experience with this sort of thing, do you?" Joanna was relieved that her next reply was the truth.

"Yes, this is not my first time fashioning cloaks." Letha nodded slowly and swished the skirts of her satin gown around her. The pale blue material suited the icy atmosphere. Joanna held her breath.

"Very well." Letha turned to the ravens. "You heard the girl. She's fashioning you new cloaks. Now form an orderly queue and stop all this squawking. You're giving me a headache." She strode from the courtyard, and Joanna was dismissed.

SEVENTY-SEVEN

Joanna wondered if she had unknowingly hit a nerve. Blackthorn Manor had spared no expense when it came to preparations for the upcoming event. She still didn't know what was planned. Perhaps it was something to do with Letha after all. Had the flicker of emotion across her face been disbelief; that her father was capable of doing something nice? Joanna could only pray that both would ignore the other on the matter of who had asked for the cloaks.

She turned to face the hulking figure in front of her. The raven first in line looked at her expectantly, not quite sure what to do, or how to arrange his limbs. Joanna grabbed the stolen tape measure out of her bag, praying that no one would recognise it, and set to work immediately. She took each raven's name down in the notebook she had been given. Next she wrote down their measurements in the chart she had prepared which would tell her their wing span, arm length, height and collar size. She had initially given the quill to the ravens to hold, but they were unable to grip it for long enough to write anything down.

Measuring the collar size also proved problematic. Joanna had to lift away the thick layer of feathers around their necks, and that was the most intimate she ever hoped to get with these creatures. Thankfully they didn't seem to mind her poking and prodding. Their feathered bodies emitted warmth for Joanna in the cold courtyard. She bristled every now and then as she recognised some of the names from the list.

There was no easy way of instigating a conversation with a raven. Once they had got past the name, the beasts would grow silent, grunting at her feeble remarks about the weather and the new cloaks. Joanna knew that she was going to have to probe further if she wanted new information. She decided upon a direct approach. "So, do you have ranks to organise you? You know, like the First, Second etc... Ow!" Joanna withdrew her hand. The raven had snapped back his wing protectively, and his red eyes were now upon her. He skulked away without letting her finish his measurements, eyeing her from the other side of the courtyard, before shrinking into his smaller form and flying away across the manor grounds.

"Friendly," Joanna mumbled as she turned the page of her list, trying to remain calm. The second raven she attempted to engage in conversation was slightly more interested but still wary of speaking to her at all.

"Yes," he grunted, standing stock still as she took his height. "We have ranks. The baron rewards the more... trustworthy of us." Joanna noted that his height exceeded many of the others' and thought that he may very well be among the higher ranks.

"And, er... what would they call someone who holds such an important position? A leader, a... a First as such, or something else?" Joanna knew she'd made a mistake as soon as the words were out.

The raven moved stealthlike, and a talon rested against her throat. Joanna thought she might pass out. She chanced a look over his wing as he bent down, but there were no onlookers. She doubted that anyone would come to her aid even if they did spot that she was being threatened. The raven's hot breath rattled in her ears, and she could feel the sharp end of its hooked beak pressed into her cheek. "I don't know who you are or what you're up to," it squawked hoarsely, "but if you ever mention the First again, you'll be hung, drawn and quartered by the baron quicker than I can fly across this courtyard. Understood?"

Joanna nodded breathlessly, and the raven withdrew his talon. He strode away from her, and she dropped onto the bench, massaging her throat.

Joanna thought suddenly of Bill and understood how he had felt pinned back behind the bar. She didn't know if it was the thought of the landlord or her recent encounter but tears pricked at her eyes. That was enough for one day. Once the ravens noticed that she was packing up her supplies they lost interest and began to flutter off into smaller groups. Joanna cleared her throat and shouted as loud as she could, "Same time tomorrow, please!" Some grunted in response, others merely ignored her, but she had already left the courtyard before most of them realised what was going on.

*

Joanna flopped down dejectedly on the edge of her four-poster. Her ridiculous skirts puffed up around her, and she pushed the frills away irritably. She was no farther along in her plan than when she had left the bedroom that morning. Gleaning information from the ravens was tricky when they were so loyal to the baron.

"Joannaaaa..."

Joanna spun around on the bed and cricked her neck. "Ow... shit..." She stood up and tripped over the skirts of her gown. She crashed to the floor. Massaging her behind, she picked herself up from the wooden floorboards and rushed over to the windowsill, but there was no one there. She strode the length of the room in three large steps and pressed her ear to the door. Nothing. Unlocking the door to her quarters, Joanna poked her head up and down the corridor. It was deserted. She swallowed hard and shut the door. Someone had definitely said her name. It was faint, as though they were pressed up against glass, or trying to shout through fabric. She even checked under the bed and in the adjoining bathroom. She was very much alone.

After lunch Joanna squeezed in some sleep to make up for her disturbed night. She was soon awoken by a faint tapping sound. As she opened her bleary eyes, a dark shape came into focus at the window. All traces of sleep left her immediately once she recognised what it was. A raven sat on her window ledge pecking to be let inside. Joanna panicked and looked away, as though she hadn't seen it. Was it here to harm her? The tapping sounded, faster and more insistent, and she turned her head back. The bird fixed her with its beady eyes and tapped on the glass again. It hovered in mid-air before alighting on the ledge and cocked its head to the side as if to say, 'I'm not going anywhere.' Joanna rose from the bed, and a sharp pain on her backside reminded her of her fall earlier. As she undid the latch on the window, wincing, she convinced herself that if the bird had come to harm her it probably wouldn't have bothered to knock.

SEVENTY-EIGHT

The raven hopped delicately inside. Its small feet left behind three-pronged dust prints on the sill. The black feathers atop its head inclined toward the open window. It took Joanna a minute to work out that he was asking her to close it. She leaned awkwardly over him, praying that he wasn't about to change form, and pulled the window to. She backed off a few steps, knowing what was about to happen next, and hoping the ceiling was tall enough to accommodate it. The change happened in the blink of an eye. One moment, he was a small raven on a window ledge, the next he was a hulking form brushing his top feathers against the beam of her ceiling. There was no slow, grotesque transformation; no gruesome half-formed features to plague her nightmares.

"Hello," the raven said quietly. "I'm Conrad."

"Uh, hello," Joanna said tentatively. The raven slowly extended a gloved talon in greeting and Joanna realised that he wanted her to shake it. What in the birds' nest was going on here? She obliged, after determining that it wasn't going to rip her to shreds, and grabbed hold of a single talon.

Conrad nodded, and then, "I realise you may be wondering what the hell I'm doing in your bedroom."

"That was one of the questions that came to mind," Joanna replied a little breathlessly.

"I'm sorry for disturbing you like this. But it's the only way of sharing a private conversation." His red eyes blinked at her slowly.

"And why would you desire to share a private conversation with me?" Joanna was not going to let her guard down that easily. This could be a test: a raven sent from the baron to do some snooping on her.

Conrad shifted uneasily on his heavy boots and glanced out of the window before continuing. "Because I heard you asking about the First earlier in the courtyard, and I wanted to talk to you. To warn you before you go blabbing to the wrong people and get your tongue cut out of that pretty face." Joanna took a step back and scrabbled around for anything that could be used as a weapon. The sewing needles had been discarded on the other side of the room. "I'm not here to hurt you," the raven said in a hoarse whisper as he noticed her looking around for something. "I'm here to help you."

Joanna fixed him with a defiant stare. "I'm sorry, but I don't know what you're talking about. I suggest you vacate my bedroom and get back to your duties before the baron finds out you're here." Conrad scanned her bedroom lazily.

"Is the list in here?"

"Wha-what list?"

"Stop acting dumb, Miss Woodgate. I know you don't have shit for brains. Why else would you be asking around about the First? You know the baron keeps a list of us."

Joanna raised her eyebrows, taken aback by his directness. "A list of you? So you're a follower... of the First?" Conrad sighed and strode across the room. He pulled out the little stool from beneath her dressing table, perched awkwardly atop it, and tucked his wings neatly behind him. He gestured for her to take a seat on the bed. She did not want to obey his instruction but was still afraid of what might happen if she didn't. She sat slowly across from him. He looked over her shoulder out the window again. Seeming satisfied that they were not being watched, he began to speak.

"I don't know who you are or why you've come to Blackthorn Manor. But the fact that you've showed up out of nowhere and are asking questions that could get you killed hints to me that we may be on the same side." He didn't bother to wait for a reply. "You're obviously not loyal to that bastard. In fact," he looked her up and down, "I'm certain that you're not who you say you are."

"You don't know anything about me," Joanna countered.

"No, I don't," the raven admitted. "And I'm taking a huge risk just by being here. But there is something about you. Like you are from a different world, a different... time?" Joanna avoided his gaze. "So that means that you must be here for a reason and you are after information, but if you carry on the way you did today, you won't be alive for much longer."

Joanna forgot herself for a moment and said sarcastically, "Well, that's only the second threat I've received today."

Conrad looked at her and leaned in. Joanna could have sworn that the redness in his eyes dimmed a little. "Like I said, I'm not here to hurt you. Why would I want to see you get killed if you're on our side?"

"You talk about sides as if I know what you mean. What side am I supposed to be on? What side are you on? How do I know I can trust you?" Footsteps on gravel sounded from below the window, and Conrad's feathers ruffled. He arose from the tiny stool, which Joanna noted was still intact.

"You don't. But if you want more information you can meet me beneath the willow tree at midnight tonight."

"Are you kidding—"

"I have to go, someone may be watching." The raven crossed her bedroom and peered out of the window. He scanned the empty walkway below and turned back to her. "Bring the list." Joanna watched him unlatch the window and fly into the sky. Conrad became a black speck in the distance.

SEVENTY-NINE

A thin layer of frost sparkled on the cobblestones as Joanna hurried across them. She picked up her skirts and tugged the long sleeves of her gown further down. Glancing over her shoulder, she fumbled in both pockets of the navy-blue dress, double-checking that her contingency plan was still hidden there. She had tied up her wavy blonde hair and tucked it into the back of the gown thinking it would make her less conspicuous. In her left pocket lay the baron's little book containing the list of the followers, and in her right was a crumpled piece of paper on which was her sketch of Isaac's shepherd's hut. If everything went horribly wrong her drawing would ensure that she had somewhere to travel through to.

"If you're not already dead, I'm going to kill you for all this, Isaac," Joanna muttered bitterly. She made a beeline for the willow tree that stood proudly at the other edge of the manor. Thankfully she had spotted it on her first night when she had stumbled upon Etimus in his private chapel and he had escorted her back through the grounds. She prayed to a god of her own that he would not be out and about tonight, drunkenly stumbling through the orange trees and across the courtyard beyond. She had heard rumours lately among the servants that his taste for alcohol had been dulled, however.

Joanna checked behind her for what seemed like the hundredth time that she wasn't being followed. She even peered up into the skies in case any ravens circled overhead. The grounds and the sky were empty. The minstrel with the hideous harp would soon be prancing about if she didn't get under the cover of the willow tree soon.

Similar to how the citrus fruit grew all year round, the branches of the willow remained bedecked in feathery tendrils, despite the winter night. If Joanna wasn't preoccupied with contemplating possible death she would have marvelled at another extraordinary piece of magic in Blackthorn. She took a deep breath and ducked beneath the arms of the willow. She struggled for a few moments; there was a thick layer of leaves to get through before she reached the middle. They hid a small, shadowy meeting place, and Joanna emerged on the other side, breathless, trying to get her bearings. She stopped in her tracks.

Approximately fifteen ravens stood in a small circle around the hollow of the tree. They were silent as they watched her arrive. They no longer sported the uncomfortable armour of the day and simply wore a long black cloak over their feathers. Their helmets concealing everything but the red eyes had disappeared, and for the first time Joanna was able to look upon a raven's face. The nose and mouth of a human had been replaced with a small beak. Although their features were otherworldly it was still possible to see the hint of a human man or boy behind the mask. Joanna tried not to stare. Feathers protruded out of their heads, and as she scanned down their forms she noticed that they still wore gloves. Perhaps this was more out of practicality than anything else. Their faces were not as awful as what she had been picturing. She thought that the witches' hooked noses and warts were far uglier than these man-birds.

A raven advanced towards her, and Joanna took an instinctive step back. She felt the dropping branches of the willow press into her back. "Joanna, it's me, Conrad."

Joanna loosed a breath. The ravens were indistinguishable from each other, and she had not recognised the male who had been in her bedroom hours earlier.

"I'm glad you decided to come." Joanna remained silent and once again checked her pockets. "If I tell you who we are, will you tell us what you're really doing in this godforsaken place?" Conrad left a few paces between them. Joanna surveyed his companions. They remained rooted to the spot, blinking at her curiously. She nodded once. Conrad turned to the raven behind him. "Still clear at the sentries' stations?" The other raven nodded in the affirmative; they too were keeping watch.

Conrad's beak clicked in fast motion as he gave Joanna the explanation she had been seeking. "Let me tell you our story. We haven't felt what it is to be human in 140 years. All of us had normal lives out in the country, peaceful even. Most of us had families – people we loved, and people who loved us." Joanna had never seen an expression so melancholy as the one that hung over his face. She let him continue as her heart wrenched. "Until the sorcerer arrived in Blackthorn." A dark thundercloud replaced his sorrow, and a ripple of anger vibrated through the ravens.

"The baron's loyalists dragged us into the manor, and the sorcerer transformed us into these beasts."

"We're a lot less handsome," one of the ravens commented as a half-smile formed across his beak. Joanna didn't smile back and waited for Conrad to continue.

"As you can imagine, we were outraged at the baron for tearing us away from our families. Not only that, but he expected us to be at his beck and call, torturing his victims and enabling his greedy ways. There was a rebellion, an uprising, if you will." Conrad narrowed his eyes and shook his head as though remembering something he wished he could erase from his memory.

"The bastard left us to rot in the dungeons. Most of us died of starvation. The others were killed by the baron's guards; kept in cages until they were too weak to fight back. There were those that were already loyal to the baron, you see." Joanna winced as fury bubbled inside her. "Our leader of the rebellion died that day." Conrad bowed his head, and the ravens simultaneously lowered their beaks to the mossy floor. "We called him the First because he was the first raven to be transformed," Conrad explained. "Tristan Brewer was one of a kind. Led us right till the very end, he did. He wanted to get home so badly, back to his Luna, he kept on saying." Conrad paused again, and the night air became thick. "Tristan was murdered by the baron himself."

Tears burned Joanna's eyes. Isaac's nephew was dead, and he had no idea. "What happened after that?" Joanna asked hoarsely. The ravens looked toward Conrad.

"A lot of us gave up after that. They saw how barbaric the baron could be and reckoned their lives would be easier if they just gave in. But there were some of us that didn't switch our loyalties. There was, and still is, a band of us loyal to the First and everything that he stood for. Our numbers have dwindled over the years, but we seek to overthrow the baron and return to our human forms." Conrad's wings ruffled as he finished sombrely, "Of course, we can't go back to our families now, they'll be long gone, but we could at least live out a normal life where we get to make our own decisions."

A few moments' silence passed before Joanna's voice returned. "It seems we have more in common than I thought." Conrad locked eyes with her, his full of expectance, a steadfast swirling pool of rubies and fire. She knew it was time to explain who she really was.

"My name really is Joanna Woodgate," she began. "I'm not a seamstress, I'm just a girl, well, a very old girl. I'm trapped, the same as you..." She trailed off miserably as she struggled to find the words to denote the heartbreak and loneliness she had felt in Blackthorn House.

"How do you mean, you're trapped?" Conrad asked as Joanna realised she hadn't spoken for a minute. She didn't want to divulge the details; her past before meeting Isaac was irrelevant.

"Let's just say I know what it's like to be held against your will. To be forced to do someone's bidding. To know that your family is ageing, and you will still exist years after they are gone. Centuries after." Tears pooled in Joanna's eyes. The ravens both on the ground and in the branches were silent as they shared a heartbreak that few could ever understand.

"I... temporarily escaped from my captors." Joanna skipped over the part where she could travel through paintings; she had to keep some things close to her chest. "I found myself on a windswept hillside in your world. A hillside where a very old man lived." There was a rustle to her left, and Joanna's head snapped to the side as a feathery arm of the willow lifted. Her heartbeat slowed as she watched a raven check the boundaries. He bowed his head at her in apology, inviting her to continue, and Joanna took a deep breath. "The sorcerer and I formed an unlikely friendship. We both realised we had nothing to lose. I've been travelling with him, with Isaac, for the past few weeks, you see, and—"

"Sorry," a croak to her right interjected. "Begging your pardon, Joanna, if I may call you as such, and my name's Daniel by the way, but are you saying that the sorcerer who did this to us is... still alive? After all this time?" Joanna knew that her reaction would crush the ravens. But they deserved the truth. She bowed her head once in answer.

The uproar was instantaneous. Joanna looked up. Beaks squawked, feathers ruffled, and branches creaked and snapped as hundreds of black shapes flitted to and fro irritably in the arms of the willow. She fumbled quickly for the piece of paper in her long pockets. It seemed the Followers of the First were far more extensive than she had realised. "Quiet!" a voice thundered. Conrad's eyes burned as he spread his wings and issued a command. The noise died down. "Do you want to get us all killed?" he hissed at the branches above.

The ravens begrudgingly remained silent. Conrad held up a hand to Joanna as the boundaries of their meeting place were checked for intruders. Once he had determined that the alarm had not been raised, he turned back toward the girl. He narrowed his eyes. He took in the long gown that did not fit her, the sleeves that draped over her hands, the hair tucked into the back of the navy-blue material to hide her appearance. He understood that she was an ancient soul akin to him; the shell outside hid her identity, and she had an important tale to tell.

"I'm sorry," he whispered. "This is not easy to find out that—"

"Please don't apologise," Joanna interrupted. She dropped the piece of paper back into her pocket. "I get it." She could feel the burn of each eye upon her. "To find out that the person who did this to you is still out there. Has let you carry on like this while he hid away." Daniel nodded in earnest. "But there is something else that you must know. The sorcerer's full name is Isaac Brewer. Tristan was his nephew. And Isaac has no idea that his nephew is dead. Isaac tried, for years and years, to get into the baron's stronghold, to find Tristan and undo what he'd done. He's lived with an indescribable guilt. All he wants is to find redemption for his actions. He wants to undo all of this, to destroy all the magic. He wants to help—" The ruffle of feathers above threatened to break out into a full-on protestation again, but Joanna's heart beat faster, and her voice grew louder.

"I'm not here to apologise for the sorcerer. That's up to him to do. And whether you deem him worthy of forgiveness is up to you. I am not his messenger. I am here to free the lives of people who have been trapped in this nightmare. People who never asked for this. People who deserved so much more." Joanna swallowed as she thought she'd never related more to anyone in her life. "I know you're angry with Isaac, and you have every right to be," more squawks from above sounded, "but he is out there right now brewing a poison for the baron and his daughter. He is out there right now with a plan, with our plan, to finally destroy what he created. He, the Sorcerer, is your only hope right now. So, you can either accept that and we can work together to free all of you, or you can sit here in misery and bitterness for the next 140 years."

There were no clicks of beaks or snapping of twigs from above. Joanna's speech had stunned them into silence. Conrad and Daniel held a silent conversation as their eyes met. The air was punctuated only with the faraway sound of the minstrel's harp as the memory magic settled over the manor again. The cruel melody affirmed something for them as they bowed their heads in unison. Conrad tucked his wings neatly behind his back and opened his beak. "I think I speak for everyone here when I say that no matter how much hatred we feel toward the sorcerer, our loyalty to Tristan will always be more important than anything else." Daniel nodded in agreement, and the ravens overhead were so quiet you could hear a feather drop. "We will work with you, Joanna Woodgate, and together we can wake from this nightmare." Joanna's shoulders relaxed. Conrad raised his voice and spoke now to the branches above. "All those in agreement, please fly down here now, and those who are left above will be welcome to have their say."

Joanna dared not move as the weight lifted from the willow tree and the branches creaked upward toward the sky. A mass of feathers descended. They covered the mossy floor and turned it from green to black. Joanna watched in amazement. She looked up at the bare branches. Not a single bird remained above. Daniel's beak clicked as he spoke for the people. "What do we need to do?" Joanna tore her eyes away from the feathery floor and began to think logically about the next step of the plan. "I left Isaac a few days ago in a tavern. I couldn't tell you which town it was in, as I don't know the area. But it was called the Sweet Siren, and the owner was a man named Bill."

"I know it!" a raven called out. "That's my hometown – Armsville. When I left, the owner must have been Bill's…" his eyes narrowed as he tried to work it out, "great-grandfather. Does it have a bar on the right-hand side and a crest above it with a siren of the sea on?"

"That's it!" Joanna exclaimed. "That's the one! We were ambushed by a group of ravens loyal to the baron. I managed to escape here, but Isaac was left behind. He was supposed to return to the hut on the hillside to brew the poison, but I don't know if he... got out of there alive."

The raven who had recognised the name of the tavern walked a few steps toward her. He nimbly avoided treading on any of his companions in their smaller forms. He looked at Joanna with a burning resolution in his eyes. "We will find the sorcerer, and the poison, and bring them both back here."

Conrad nodded in agreement. "We can leave the manor every now and then, for short periods, and we'll go in alternate groups to avoid suspicion." Conrad raised a glove toward Joanna. "Do we have an agreement?" She did not hesitate as she took the outstretched talon into her grip.

Their eyes met, ancient soul to ancient soul, and they sealed the bond between them.

EIGHTY

Joanna walked the manor in a high state of anxiety. It had been five days since her meeting with the Followers of the First. Five days and no indication of how the search for Isaac was going. It was a frosty Friday morning and Joanna was measuring the last group of ravens for the cloaks. She had worked her fingers to the bone over the past five days, wanting to maintain her disguise as experienced seamstress, and had almost finished all the cloaks. The burn across her hand from the poker had only just healed properly. It would have been nice in all that time to have spoken to somebody, but Joanna could not tell if she was among friends or foe. Knowing that a lot of the followers had departed the manor to search for Isaac, she determined that mostly she was among foe, and therefore it was sensible to keep her mouth shut. She felt as though she had been silent for so long that she was in danger of losing her voice.

"Ow!" a raven grunted and looked at her in derision. Joanna quickly removed the stuck pin from where it shouldn't have gone.

"Sorry," she mumbled. "I-I think I'm done here now." The last raven flapped irritably away, the pin falling to the ground as he took flight, and Joanna cursed herself silently. She had to stop with these daydreams. Had to stop wondering what was going on outside of the manor and focus instead on inside the gates. As she packed up her materials, prising some of them off the frozen bench, she considered herself lucky that all the occupants of the manor were so preoccupied with the upcoming banquet that no one had really taken much notice of her.

Joanna made it her mission to stay out of Letha Villinor's way. The baron's daughter patrolled the manor in a constant foul mood. She swept her long skirts down the corridors as she supervised her maids with disdain. She bellowed in the kitchens until her face was blue and the cooks were shaking. She strode across the polished floors of the grand hall and commanded the servants to clean the impeccable surface again. She told her maids to collect all the silverware and polish each individual piece, until their cloths were ragged, and sent anyone to the dungeons overnight who dared complain that their hands were stiff. Letha's obsession with the banquet, which Joanna had learned from gossip in the corridors was to take place on Sunday, had allowed for her to melt into the background of the manor as she awaited word from the followers.

The illusion was shattered when an aggressive rap came at her bedroom door late that afternoon. The door swung open on itself before she could reply, and Joanna knew who it was before they entered. The housekeeper looked down her hooked nose and arranged her sallow features into a displeasing grimace. "Miss Letha has requested your presence in her bedchamber." Joanna swallowed and tried to remain calm. *Don't give up the game now*, a little voice inside her head whispered, *you are seamstress Woodgate, remember.*

"Of course," Joanna replied briskly, as though she had been expecting this invitation all day. The housekeeper narrowed her eyes and sniffed disdainfully as her prying eyes travelled around the bedroom. Joanna wondered if she was trying to find something incriminating.

"Bring some of the cloaks. She wants to inspect your handiwork. I wouldn't keep her waiting." The housekeeper wiped her hands on her frilly apron as though getting rid of something

Joanna had given her and turned on her polished heel. The door clicked shut behind her.

"Shit shit shit," Joanna cursed as soon as she was alone. She was not ready for this. Yes, the cloaks were ready, but she herself was not. Taking a few deep breaths, Joanna wandered over to the bathroom mirror, and attempted to compose herself. She patted down her gown until the skirts sat neatly. She gave her hair a quick brush until it fell in golden locks around her face. Lastly, she pinched her cheeks to give some colour. As an afterthought she checked that her fingernails were clean (she'd heard rumour this was a particular annoyance of Letha's) and peered at her reflection in the mirror.

She paused for a few seconds. There were lines on her face that hadn't been there before – around her mouth and across her forehead. She certainly did not look like the sixteen-year-old girl that had snuck into the manor two weeks ago. Joanna swallowed hard. She was ageing. Not overly so, but enough for her to notice, and this thought both worried and intrigued her. Had the bond between her and the witches loosened? Had the distance between her and Blackthorn House weakened their magic?

There was no time to dwell. Joanna had been allowed to store the finished cloaks in a room on the same floor as her chambers. It was plush, with velvet stools and plump cushions, as though previously used as a fitting room for gowns or tunics. She unlocked the door and faced the heap of cloaks. They hung neatly, with name tags on each, and Joanna knew that Letha had access to this room herself. Which meant that she didn't really want to see the cloaks; she wanted to see Joanna. As she stood on a nearby stool and picked out the best of her handiwork, she mentally prepared herself for a kicking. Letha had imposed her power upon the manor lately, and it seemed that Joanna was to be the next victim. She had no choice but to obey; a direct refusal would surely land her in the dungeons.

Letha's quarters were closer toward the main spiral staircase whereas Joanna's were right at the end of the manor in a darker part of the winding corridor. The rooms that branched off into the dark recesses were reserved for those that could not be demoted to the servants' quarters but were not important enough to dwell on the level above. Joanna had never found out who lived in the rooms on the third level. Her best guess had been some of the higher-ranking ravens and lords and ladies of the land who had fallen in kindly with Etimus. *Privileged bastards*, she thought darkly; they were probably as drunk and greedy as the baron himself.

Knowing that it was going to take her five minutes to navigate the winding corridor towards the staircase, Joanna set off at a brisk walk, awkwardly dropping the key to the fitting room in her pocket. She draped three of the cloaks across her arms to prevent them from dragging along the floor. Not that the floor was dusty anymore thanks to Letha's tantrum two days ago. Even three of the cloaks were proving difficult to carry. The material was so heavy and the cloaks so large that Joanna wouldn't have been able to carry any more.

Those dressed in finery shot her suspicious glances as she manoeuvred past them. Joanna ignored them, increasingly aware that it had been almost ten minutes since the housekeeper's request. She approached the hulking figure that always stood guard at Letha's chamber. Joanna studied the raven for a few seconds. It was impossible to tell if they had been one of the hundreds she had met with five days ago. If they did know her, they were doing a very good job of hiding it. They knocked with a fisted glove upon Letha's door.

The doorknob turned from the inside, and the raven took a step back. Joanna hurriedly followed suit and stumbled on a cloak. She righted herself quickly and bowed her head as the baron's daughter emerged from her ice chamber. "You're late," she announced to the corridor. "I wasn't aware you had more important things to do, Miss Woodgate." Joanna assumed an expression of deepest humility and began to murmur her apologies. "Spare me." Letha sighed. "I don't have all afternoon."

She disappeared behind the door, and the raven indicated for Joanna to enter. Her mouth had gone extremely dry. Joanna shivered as the door shut behind her and they were left alone in the cavernous room. The icicles that ran down the walls and snaked across the bed posts found their home in Letha's heart. She turned to Joanna and fixed her with cold blue eyes. Her white hair sparkled ever so slightly as though encrusted with snowflakes.

EIGHTY-ONE

"Is that all you brought with you?"

"Begging your pardon, Miss Letha, but the cloaks are heavy, and it was all I could manage." Letha sniffed and tucked her blonde waves behind one ear. She gestured wordlessly over to the bed and Joanna quickly laid down the cloaks. The inspection was silent and thorough. Letha walked around the bed three times as she peered at the material and attempted to unpick the needlework. She picked up the hem of a cloak and let its folds run down her arm as she took it over to the window for the last of the afternoon light. Joanna waited with bated breath. Letha set down the shimmering material. The silvery threads danced off her eyes as she tore them away. Although Joanna's pulse threatened to give her away, she was confident that Letha would struggle to find fault with her handiwork. The cloaks were beautiful; fit for a king, let alone a slave.

Letha remained unsmiling, clearly dissatisfied that she was unable to find fault. Her gown rustled softly across the floor in the silence. "They will do," she stated. Joanna's heart lifted a little, thinking that this encounter would soon be over, and she nodded her head humbly in reply. "I take it they are all finished?" Letha barked, stepping uncomfortably close to Joanna's face.

"I took the measurements for the final few today, and everything will be finished tomorrow."

"When you are done you must bring them to my housekeeper. She will distribute them before the banquet."

"Yes of course." Joanna was struck with a sudden thought. "How will I move all the cloaks, Miss Letha? There are hundreds, and they are all very heavy." She regretted the words the moment they were out. Letha's face was far too close, and her eyes shone with malice.

"Are you an idiot, girl? You'll carry them. All of them. Down to the hall. I'm sure you can make more than one trip." Joanna dared not reply. They both knew that this would take her hours. "Is there a problem?" Letha asked, a cruel smile playing about her pink lips.

"Not at all." Joanna bit her tongue. Letha's disappointment at Joanna's reserve was written all over her face.

"Are you sure there's not something... wrong... Miss Woodgate?" Letha played with her, teased her, wanting her to erupt and validate punishment. Joanna watched her sickeningly twirl a lock of hair about her finger.

"There's nothing wrong, nothing at all."

Letha's malevolence burst forth. She extended her arm towards Joanna's face and pinched her right cheek. Joanna bore the violence without flinching. "How old are you?" Letha's fingers remained in a tight grip, and Joanna knew the quicker she answered the quicker they would be removed.

"Twenty, Miss Letha," she forced out through gritted teeth. The grip lessened but did not cease.

"You don't look twenty. You look older." Before Joanna could try and explain that she was in fact centuries old, Letha removed her hand and turned toward the window.

Joanna massaged her stinging cheek. She whizzed her hand back down to her side before Letha could see that she had hurt her. "Follow me." Letha swept her skirts out of the bedchamber. She had almost reached the top of the steps before a bewildered Joanna hurried after her. She had never walked up the deathly staircase before and tripped on her own gown in her haste to follow. Maids and stewards cleared the way as soon as they got wind that Letha was about. Those under her authority scattered. Joanna's mind raced as she considered the possibilities. She could be going to the baron. Her stomach turned, but then she rationalised. How often were the baron and his daughter spotted together? Their hatred for each other was common knowledge, and Joanna could think of no reason for his being involved at present. Perhaps it was a trick and Letha was going to lock her away in a room at the top of the manor so she would get in trouble for not finishing the ravens' attire. But this banquet seemed important to Letha; she would not risk anything going awry.

A long time ago the baron had widened the corridor on the top level of Blackthorn Manor. It had been necessary to accommodate the protruding bellies and bosoms of the lords and ladies who supped there. They passed a few of these despicable creatures on the way to the unknown location. Joanna hid her disgust at their paunchy, powdered faces; the way they sauntered back and forth as though they deserved every little bit of this luxury they had gifted themselves with. They stepped down from their self-allocated pedestals, however, to bow their heads at Letha Villinor as she passed. They had to keep in good company if they wanted to continue their sickening lifestyles. Coins clanged in large purses hung from drawstrings on their arms as they eyed Joanna curiously. Coins that they would never need. Blood money from those who had died of poverty whilst labouring for them. "Keep up," Letha hissed. Joanna tore her accusatory eyes away.

Letha stopped abruptly and rummaged in her gown. She unearthed a long bronze key. Unlocking the door in front of them, she gestured for Joanna to follow her into the room. Gowns of every shape, form and colour bedecked the right side of the wall. Some fluttered like glittering jewels in the breeze from the corridor, while others maintained their structure as the heavy velvet stood staunchly on the floor. Rich burgundies, dusty roses and deep violets were among the hues. They were all pristine; perfectly cared for by an attentive someone lest any speck of dust fell upon the luxurious fabrics. The left side of the room was adorned with floor-length mirrors to ensure that the gown in question could be viewed from every angle. Joanna had never owned anything quite as spectacular. Quickly, she hid her awe, remembering who she was supposed to be. A seamstress who was surprised at fine fabrics? Now that wouldn't do.

Letha unlocked a second door hidden behind the racks of gowns and they delved deeper, into her personal fitting room. This room was small but featured a large window. "What do you think of this?" Letha stepped aside impatiently, gesturing to something on the back wall. Joanna could not believe what was happening. Letha was asking for her opinion on a dress.

The dress in question was a deep aubergine colour with a plunging neckline and three-quarter-length sleeves. The silky material flowed down to the ground from where it hung on high. "It's... it's beautiful," Joanna stammered in earnest. Letha looked at her and narrowed her eyes. She walked over to it and fingered the material with her head cocked on one side.

"What do you really think of it?" Joanna hesitated for a moment. She decided to throw caution to the wind.

"It's a lovely gown, really, Miss Letha. The material is exquisite, however, if I was to suggest anything that could be improved, I would say it's a little... plain?"

Letha looked her over, not displeased this time, but curious, expectant. Joanna took the cue and hurried over to the back wall. "Say you were to add some white lace embroidery, here, and here," she gestured to the neckline and down the back of the dress, "and perhaps along where the sleeves end, it would really contrast with the colour and bring out your hair and eyes."

Letha clapped her hands together in what Joanna supposed could only be glee. "Yes, that's it! That's what you'll do. And I'll show that useless spinster when you're done to prove that not all her dresses need be so boring." Letha continued talking, her mouth opening and closing in quick succession, before Joanna could get a word in. This was the closest to happy Joanna had ever seen her. "It's for my banquet on Sunday, so ideally needs to be embroidered tonight, so I can check it tomorrow. I trust you have enough white lace to finish the task this evening?"

"Y-Yes," Joanna said with a heavy heart, thinking that another raid of Madam Faraway's store was in order. She was beginning to panic about finishing both the remaining cloaks and Letha's dress before tomorrow. But she couldn't let the baron's daughter down. Not when she was in her favour now and drew attention away from the ravens that flew continually in and out of the boundaries.

Letha handed something over to Joanna who accepted the heavy bronze object and held it tightly in her palm. It was the key to her fitting room. Letha raised her eyebrows and smiled slightly. Joanna looked at her. Did this girl trust her? Was that a smile? They held each other's gaze for a few seconds: the girl that secretly craved friendship and the girl whose only companion had been loneliness for the past century. Joanna wondered at this other side to Letha. The side that was friendly and trusting enough to place her faith in a fellow companion. But then Joanna felt an ache on her cheek and remembered who Letha truly was.

She was Isaac's creation, born out of bitterness. She was a manifestation of his darkest thoughts. She was beyond even the sorcerer's control; simply a figment of his imagination, existing in an alternate world, filled with malice and greed. The smile faded from Letha's face, and the illusion was shattered as she filled the silence. The glacier iced over once more. "Have you gone mute? Or are you just stupid?"

After a quick eye roll and swish of her skirts Letha departed the fitting room. Joanna slumped down on a nearby stool and sighed. Her shoulders sagged with the thought of how much work she had to do. The remaining cloaks would have to wait for now; Letha's gown was her priority. Her stomach churned at the thought of raiding Madam Faraway's stores again. She was risking too much, and she knew it. If she were found out now the whole plan would go up in flames. Joanna arose from the low stool with a small groan minutes later. What's life without a little risk, after all?

EIGHTY-TWO

Joanna's stomach grumbled as she sat in the hidden room and worked furiously to embellish Letha's gown. For her banquet, she had said. Her obsession with perfection now made sense – even down to the lace on her gown. Groaning plates of sumptuous banquet food slid into Joanna's mind; her mouth watered over sizzling joints of meat, heaps of buttery potatoes and decadent desserts. A great groan sounded from her stomach again. She would have to sneak down into the kitchens later and find some supper. If she were to bring one morsel into the fitting room Letha would sniff it out like a bloodhound and dole out a horrific punishment.

The last of the light faded, and the window outside showed only blackness. Joanna sat in the candlelight and listened to the wind blow as she worked. Her thoughts trailed again to the ravens who were searching for Isaac. Would they be able to find shelter in such horrible conditions? Two hours passed, and Joanna's eyes grew bleary. The needle punctuated her fingertips more times than the fabric, and she had to be careful not to get smears of blood on the gown. She attached the final piece of lace to the back of the dress and yawned. Standing up to survey her handiwork, she blinked a few times, and the dress came into focus in the gloom.

She had woven delicate trails of white lace up and down the dress. These in turn were interwoven with silver threads that glimmered in the moonlight on top of the rich material. The gown was breathtaking. It looked as though cobwebs and icicles had attached themselves to it. Letha had instructed her to leave the masterpiece in there, lock up the fitting room, and return the key to the housekeeper the next day with the cloaks.

Joanna returned to her bedroom on the floor below. She soaked in the bath for a while, not yet having the energy to finish the last of the cloaks, thinking she would do them first thing in the morning. Her hands were growing sore with the effort of it all, and she stretched them out before her. The water droplets ran off her tired skin. They did not look like the hands of a sixteen-year-old. The skin was stretched, and a few age spots had appeared on the knuckles. They looked weathered, as though reflecting the weariness within. "Strange," Joanna muttered, and her voice echoed in the bathroom. "Time seems to work differently here."

The service bell had remained in the same place for the duration of Joanna's stay. She picked up the little bell off her bedside table, and a maid arrived in her room moments later, a little flustered, and adjusting the white cap atop her head as though just having awoken. "What can I do for you, miss?" she asked, a little breathless.

"I apologise for the late hour," Joanna said guiltily, "but is there any chance of a little supper? I had other engagements and wasn't around for my evening meal." The maid bowed her dazed head, and the hat flopped to one side.

"Of course," she said with a smile, "I'll bring it right up."

Joanna sat in her nightdress and ate her supper in bed. Once her belly was full, she set down the empty wooden plate and blew out the candle beside her. It wasn't long before sleep came and took her. At three o'clock in the morning she grew fitful. She tossed and turned in the bed sheets, sweat rolling down her back, entangled in a maze with no exit. She dreamt that she had woken up to find an ancient woman staring back at her in the cracked mirror. Saggy skin, drooping jowls and white hair that all withered away before her very eyes as she watched herself turn into a pile of dust. She could not scream because she had no mouth; no arms nor legs, not limbs of any kind.

It was only the insistent tapping at her bedroom window that dragged her away from the horror. She took in a massive breath of air and felt a sharp pain in her chest. She clutched at the corset fitted into her gown and managed to loosen it a little. Cursing herself for having fallen asleep in such restrictive clothing, she massaged her chest, and looked toward the window. The night sky outside gave little away. But then the tapping sounded again, and Joanna's heart lifted at the sound. Hurrying across the room, she patted down the gown to ensure she was decent and undid the latch. A howling wind begged for entry along with the raven. Joanna shut the window quickly and shivered in the sudden cold. She backed away from the ledge a few steps, allowing the raven to transform, and Conrad materialised before her eyes.

Joanna was so overjoyed to see a friendly face that she could have hugged him. Refraining from doing so, she said breathlessly, "Boy am I glad to see you."

Conrad opened his beak, and Joanna could have sworn that a smile formed as he replied, "Joanna, it's good to see you too." He rubbed his gloved hands together, thankful to be out of the cold. "I'm sorry it's so late."

"Don't worry." Joanna gestured to him to sit atop the stool by her dressing table. "I'd rather hear your news—"

"Well." Conrad took a deep breath and looked at her as though preparing himself. "We found him."

"You found Isaac?" Joanna repeated, eyes wide.

"Yes, about four hours ago. He was a bit surprised when we turned up." Conrad chuckled. "But once he realised we weren't there to reveal his whereabouts to the baron he was eager to hear news of you. We've hidden him in one of the outhouses for now. Daniel's snuck into the kitchens and got him some supplies for a few days. Figured it was too risky to try and bring him into the manor." Joanna listened to Conrad with mouth agape. She couldn't quite believe what he was telling her. They had found Isaac. Her friend was alive. "We traced him all the way to his little hut on that…" here Conrad shivered and shook the feathers atop his head, "that awful hillside. The wind was so severe that we could barely fly in a straight line. Almost gave up at one point. The tavern, the Sweet Siren, it was abandoned, you see…" Conrad trailed off. He looked awkwardly over Joanna's shoulder.

"What is it?" Joanna watched the raven as he stood up from the stool without warning and crossed the room. He stood in front of the bedroom door and shifted awkwardly from foot to foot. Joanna waited, thinking perhaps that he had heard someone in the corridor outside, but Conrad wasn't concerned about that. He kept stepping from one great heavy boot to the other. He was evidently keeping something from her. She stood up and faced him, eyes ablaze. "What happened in the tavern, Conrad?" Her voice was flat, and her stomach churned.

He swallowed audibly. "Joanna, I—"

"Just tell me, please." Joanna's voice had reduced to a whisper.

"The sorcerer said there was some big fight, between you lot and some of the other ravens…" Joanna thought back to the scene that she had left. Isaac had blasted apart the bar, and shards of glass flew everywhere. The pumps had exploded, the jet streams having torn through the ceiling and windows, but she hadn't stayed to see what had happened to Isaac and Bill.

"The old man's dead." Conrad's words sliced through her heart like a shard of ice. Joanna put a hand on her chest, experiencing a sudden sharp pain, but it wasn't from her corset this time.

"A-are you sure?" she asked, stupidly hoping there had been some mistake. Conrad approached her and sat back down on the little stool. He bowed his head, and the blow caved in upon Joanna's heart. She found the edge of her bed and was glad when her legs collided with the solid furniture.

Silence filled the room for a couple of minutes until Conrad whispered, "I'm sorry, Joanna. I wish I had better news for you."

The dull aching in Joanna's chest morphed into something else. A bubbling pit of fury rose within her. Bill's kindness in this bitter world had meant so much to them. His little spark had gifted them with warmth when they had needed it most. And now he was gone; he was another victim of a violent murder. His blood was on the baron's hands. Joanna looked up at Conrad with fire burning in her eyes. Something in Conrad shifted when she spoke, as though he had seen something unexpected, as though he were suddenly afraid.

"Where is the sorcerer?"

EIGHTY-THREE

The stars that twinkled down from a clear sky and lit up Blackthorn Manor were the only observers as Joanna and Conrad hurried across the courtyard below. Joanna wrapped the heavy cloak tighter about her as the wind threatened to freeze off her ears. She had taken advantage of the excess material and fashioned a cloak for herself. Conrad led her to the most dishevelled-looking outhouse. Before they hurried inside Conrad turned to her. "Joanna… I must get back to my post. I'll have to leave you here… I'll be in contact." Joanna nodded up at him, and he swept his feathers away into the darkness. Before he fully shrank into the night, he turned his red eyes upon her. "Oh, and Joanna…" she turned back around from the pigsty, "be careful, the servants will be up soon. You don't have much time."

"Thank you," Joanna whispered, not entirely sure if she was thanking him for his concern or for finding her friend. Conrad transformed into a raven and took flight into the night.

Joanna picked up her feet as she entered the little shack. She was met with bales of hay and animal droppings. Wrinkling her nose at the odour, she blinked a few times into the gloom, and was at least thankful for the warmth. The pigs snorted out of her way, disgruntled at having been woken again, and rolled back in the hay. Joanna hesitated, suddenly fearful that something was wrong, but then a figure emerged out of the shadows, and her heart lifted.

His mop of brown and grey curls had grown back, along with the beginnings of a bushy beard. But his familiar grey eyes blinked back at her as they swelled with emotion. Joanna smiled. "Look what happens when I leave you alone for a few weeks. You go back to looking like the wild man of the woods." She laughed out loud as the sorcerer wrapped her in a gigantic hug. An emotion that Joanna hadn't felt for a long time overcame her. A relief that eased the tension in her shoulders. A warmth that gave her hope and comfort. Something that made her feel, somehow, more at home. Something akin to family.

"Joanna," Isaac said softly, still hugging her tightly. The sorcerer released her and held her at arm's length. His eyes narrowed. "You look—"

"Yes, I know," Joanna returned as he struggled to find the correct words to describe the way in which she had aged in the time they had been apart. "But let's not focus on that now, please, I just can't believe you're here, in the manor."

"Tell me about it." Isaac's hands dropped down from Joanna's shoulders and swept his heavy furs across the hay. He looked through a crack in the building at the darkness outside. He turned to Joanna and smiled. His ancient features were lit only by the candles the ravens had stolen from the kitchens, and Joanna spied the pile of food and water supplies in the cleanest corner of the outhouse. "I'm so glad to see you," he said in earnest. "You became my only friend over the past month and not knowing if you were okay has been awful. I know you wanted to help with the plan we made," here Isaac peered toward the entrance of the outhouse, "but I didn't want you to become another victim. You don't deserve that."

Tears pricked in Joanna's eyes. "Don't be silly," she said with a small smile. "I've been alone and alive for long enough now to know that the freedom of a whole other world is more important than any misgivings I may have had about all this." Isaac nodded gratefully and sat down on a large bale of hay undisturbed by the pigs. He knew there was nothing else he could say to express his gratitude for her. He gestured for Joanna to take the bale opposite.

She arranged her cloak around her to keep from draping it into the animal droppings and fixed her friend with a woeful look. "Tell me how Bill died." Isaac closed his eyes, and his shoulders sagged forward. His voice was thick when he looked up again.

"The ravens got to him first. After the bar exploded and you disappeared, I tried to get to Bill. But it was all so confusing. It was raining inside the tavern. I couldn't see anything at first in the chaos but once I'd flung the broken chairs aside that were blocking my path, I-I saw Bill, and I saw that it was too late. I was too slow." Isaac's words were filled with guilt. "He was already dead." His voice cracked.

"What did they do to him?" Joanna asked as the pit of fury bubbled again.

"Broken bottle," Isaac said hoarsely. "Straight to the neck." Through Joanna's heartbreak she was glad that he had told her bluntly. She didn't need things flowering up for her. She wanted to know every gory detail.

"Bastards," she stated fiercely. Isaac nodded his agreement as his face set. They silently expressed their condolences for Bill in the minutes that followed until Joanna said, "What happened after that?"

"Well… I'm not entirely sure," Isaac said slowly.

"What do you mean?"

"I sort of… lost it," Isaac explained. "It was like all the magic that I'd been keeping at bay for so many years just burst forth from me like a broken dam. I knew that I wanted revenge on the ravens. I knew they couldn't live." Joanna nodded, hoping against hope that somehow, those ravens had paid the price for the death of an innocent soul.

"I managed to control the elements," Isaac continued. "The storm that was raging outside – I brought it inside. Inside the tavern," he clarified as Joanna's confused expression met his. "I imagined the tavern as a vessel, like a ship going under at sea. The water filled the room all the way up to the ceiling, and I shielded myself in a bubble." Joanna's eyes grew wider as she tried to imagine the scene. "I watched as they drowned." Isaac's voice was flat. "I drowned them in the salty water to pay for their sins. Then just like that, after they had all perished, the room was empty. Wet through, but empty, and the storm calmed again. I got out of there quick after that and travelled back to the hillside. I needed somewhere to brew the poison. And I knew I could do it this time, Joanna. I knew it was going to work. All my magic is back... I feel... powerful again."

Joanna looked at the sorcerer and swallowed. She had never quite understood the true extent of his power. And she was glad that she was not on the enemy's side; if he could control the elements to murder for him, he was more formidable than she had ever thought. He had just needed something inside him to break to release his magic. As Joanna came to terms with who her friend really was, Isaac rummaged eagerly in the deep pockets of his furs and unearthed a little bottle.

"This is it." The tiny vial was encased in twisted glass. The curved diamond shape ended in a pointed stopper at the top. The liquid inside was so clear it was possible to see through it. "Odourless, colourless, in short, the perfect poison," Isaac whispered. The sight of the glass bottle gave Joanna chills, and suddenly their plan felt very real.

"You're sure it's going to work?" she questioned, wanting every loophole in their plan accounted for.

"Yes," Isaac confirmed without hesitation. "It will work." Joanna nodded, trusting him, and shifted awkwardly atop the pile of hay.

"There is a banquet," she divulged, "in a couple of days' time. I don't know much about it, but it seems like it's going to be a pretty big deal. Letha's been heavily involved. It will be the perfect time to administer the poison. I'm sure there will be separate food reserved just for the baron. If only we could sneak into the kitchens and make sure it's in there."

"I'll see if the ravens can get me in," Isaac said. "I'll speak to them tomorrow. I couldn't believe when I heard that you'd managed to get some on side."

A blinding realisation hit Joanna in the face. They had addressed the death of one who they held dear but not another. She took a deep breath and steeled herself. "Isaac. Did Conrad tell you about your nephew?" Isaac looked at the ground grimly. Joanna averted her eyes respectfully for a few moments as he wiped away tears. His voice was heavy with years of regret.

"I think I knew a long time ago that he was dead. I just didn't want to admit it to myself. I'm so proud of him though, for standing up to the baron, for leading them in horrific times. And the fact that some are still loyal now, well..." Isaac sniffed. "He must have made quite the impression."

"It sounds like he was a great leader."

"All the things I wanted to say to him, to say sorry, for everything, for all of it..." Isaac's voice cracked. Joanna leaned forward and took Isaac's shaking hand in hers.

"I know. So, let's do this for him. Let's end this once and for all."

Isaac stood up and startled a few pigs. His face was resolute. "Tell me what you've been doing. Have you met the baron? What's he like? How did you learn about the followers?" Joanna thought back to the uncomfortable meetings between herself and Etimus Villinor. The drunken stumble back from the chapel, arm in arm, the stench of his sin sickening her. The uncomfortable closeness in the corridor when they had gone to find Madam Faraway. The way his eyes had lingered over her for a little too long, and she had spied the malice and intent behind them.

"He's nothing like you," she summarised, and Isaac smiled. "Let's just say I've had to come up with my own disguise." Joanna filled him in on everything that had occurred the past few weeks: her position as seamstress, measuring up and fashioning the ravens' cloaks, her encounters with Letha and the housekeeper, and her meetings with Conrad and the followers.

Shortly after their exchange, Isaac and Joanna bade each other goodnight, Conrad's warning echoing in Joanna's ears. They had agreed that Isaac was to keep the poison with him in case Joanna's room was searched. They would meet again the next night on the eve of the murder to finalise things. Joanna left him in the pigsty, turning around at the door before scurrying back to her chamber, and watched as the bottle glinted in the dim light before it disappeared safely into Isaac's pockets.

EIGHTY-FOUR

"For goodness' sake, girl, what on earth do you think you're doing?" Joanna looked at the housekeeper in exasperation. This was the tenth time she had been up and down the spiral staircase, laden with heavy cloaks, depositing them in the entrance hall. Crafting intricate needlework in the early hours of the morning had not been an easy feat. She hadn't been able to sleep after seeing Isaac and had taken advantage by finishing the few remaining cloaks by candlelight.

The morning before the banquet Joanna had done as Letha had instructed: to bring the cloaks to the housekeeper in the hall so they could be distributed. "I repeat, Miss Woodgate, what are you doing?" The housekeeper's long dark dress was dusted with streaks of flour. Tendrils of greying hair escaped from her usually perfect bun. She had been up at an ungodly hour overseeing preparations for the next day, and her already lacking patience was running thin.

"I'm bringing the cloaks down to the hall like Miss Letha said to." Joanna panted, wiping a bead of sweat from her forehead.

"What, one by one?" the housekeeper exclaimed, throwing her arms up in the air. "I don't have time for this. I need to get rid of them this morning, not wait till dusk when you're finished." A maid scurried past them in the corridor, and she scolded her as she passed. "Why aren't you polishing the silverware, Lily?" The housekeeper turned back to Joanna and sighed with irritation. She lifted the cloaks out of Joanna's arms and hurried to the staircase, groaning as she went. It took

Joanna a few moments to understand that the surly woman was helping her.

After enlisting the help of three maids and one steward who looked thoroughly displeased at being disturbed from his post it took another hour to shift all the cloaks. The six of them stood breathlessly around the large table, looking at the mass of silken material, all neatly tagged with names. As soon as the housekeeper had obtained the use of her lungs she barked, "Right, as you were!" The maids and stewards hurried off into different corners of the manor.

Joanna dithered on the spot, unsure if she was dismissed. Technically she had finished her job. The housekeeper leaned over the table, cheeks flushed, under the pretence of inspecting the name tags on the cloaks but just taking another minute to recover. She straightened and half-heartedly attempted to tuck back in her loose strands of hair that had gone awry. It seemed she had forgotten Joanna was there for a moment as she muttered, "At least they will be dressed appropriately for the coming-of-age banquet."

"Thank you," Joanna said cheerfully. The housekeeper looked at her and sighed as though disappointed she had said something nice. "The… coming-of-age banquet?" Joanna probed. She was desperate to find out anything she could about tomorrow night. Anything that might help them administer the poison.

The sallow features regarded her as though she were idiotic. "Yes," she replied curtly. "The coming-of-age banquet is tomorrow evening. Surely you know that by now, Miss Woodgate? The banquet that I have been putting my blood, sweat and tears into for the past few weeks? It's very important to Miss Letha, you know." She spat the words out and lifted her head high on her shoulders. Joanna nodded quickly.

"Yes of course, I just wondered if… if there was anything I could do… to help?"

The housekeeper's shoulders drooped, and she looked at Joanna as if no one else had ever asked her that question. She was utterly perplexed. "Well, there's…" She looked about the bustling hall distractedly, wringing her hands together. The housekeeper sucked in a deep breath and launched into a flowing rant. It sounded as though all the air was slowly being sucked out of a giant balloon.

"I keep instructing the maids to polish the silverware, but they simply don't do it well enough. If you can't see your reflection staring back at you in the spoons, it's not up to scratch and that's that. The floors in here have been waxed from top to bottom, but with all the hustle and bustle they're scuffed again, so I'll have to ask them to do it again tomorrow morning before all the guests arrive in the evening at six o'clock." She sucked in another breath and continued.

"The stewards are supposed to be attending to the suits of armour and the paintings to make them presentable, but they're more interested in raiding the kitchens and annoying the maids. Cook's bouncing off the walls saying she hasn't got this or that, and especially all the herbs for the pheasant – that's been an absolute nightmare. The wine merchant's disappeared and no one can find him, probably drunk in one of his own barrels again, but we're desperate to get…" here the housekeeper swished about invisible large skirts, "the finest spiced wine in all the land. That's for the toast, you see—"

"The toast?"

"Yes, the toast, girl! There's a special toast at the end. Letha toasts her father as a thank you for, well… bringing her up, and the baron toasts his daughter to acknowledge her going out into society. It's all very formal and what have you. This banquet should have happened years ago, but the baron's been a little preoccupied by all accounts. The spiced wine is reserved for the toast, but we haven't even got it because we can't find the sodding wine merchant!"

Several heads turned. The housekeeper's voice had slowly crept up in pitch, and she had practically squealed the last few words. Joanna's mind was racing. The housekeeper stood in silence for a few moments as though a little relieved she had just offloaded this information to someone. Joanna struggled to find a reply but was saved from doing so by the sudden appearance of a steward. He was dressed in a neat tunic, and his cheeks were flushed as he came to an abrupt halt. "We've found him," he blurted out proudly, as though this statement would earn him a crest of honour. "The wine merchant. He was out yonder in the vineyard, drunk as a skunk, but we've sobered him up for the time being." Clapping her hands together with newly found vigour, the housekeeper followed the steward out of the hall immediately, without another word to Joanna.

EIGHTY-FIVE

Joanna sought out Isaac without a moment's hesitation. However, she had to swerve in her path on approach to the outhouses under the pretence of taking a walk through the orange and lemon trees. Two ravens stood either side of the pigsty entrance. They looked disgruntled at having to guard the pigs, and their glowing eyes followed Joanna as she walked away.

"Shit," Joanna muttered. She felt a vice-like grip on her shoulder and panicked.

"It seems you are lost, Miss Woodgate. You're looking for the chapel, I suppose, for your morning prayers?" The raven looked down at her with a strange expression. The two guards watched from their post. "It's me, Daniel," the raven hissed. "Just play along."

"Y-Yes," Joanna stammered loudly, projecting her voice in the direction of the guards. "Gosh, this manor is so large it's a wonder anyone can find anything in it!" she shouted in a high-pitched voice. Joanna could have sworn that Daniel rolled his eyes before escorting her away. "What's going on?" Joanna muttered, but Daniel simply shook his feathers.

"Are you sure the baron's not in here?" Joanna asked as the heavy oak doors swung shut behind them.

"He's not," Daniel said quickly, but looked through the stained glass suspiciously. "The baron's stopped coming in here... ever since he sobered up... The place is practically abandoned now."

"But why are we here?"

"Thank God I found you when I did." Daniel ignored her question and continued reproachfully, "You looked right suspicious dawdling by the outhouses—"

"I wasn't dawdling," Joanna retorted. "I was—"

"Looking for Isaac." Daniel finished her sentence through gritted teeth. "Yes, I know. He only just escaped from that pigsty last night. A raven heard noises at dawn and raised the alarm. Thankfully Isaac managed to slink away before they found him, but they did notice his food and water supplies. They know there's an intruder about. We've had to move him into a room at the back of this chapel. I've been waiting around in case you turned up, just keeping an eye on things." Daniel had a habit of continually surveying his surroundings. It was ingrained into him after all these years of being a follower.

"Thank you," Joanna said softly. Daniel inclined his head down the aisle toward the back of the chapel.

"He's in there. But you don't have long. Conrad's got followers posted all around the manor grounds, but the other ravens are starting to get suspicious. Especially after the discovery last night. We need to put this plan into action as soon as possible. Isaac's told me about the banquet tomorrow."

Joanna nodded. "Yes, and I have more information about that, something that could be a potential opportunity—"

The raven interrupted her. "Sorry, Joanna, but you should speak to the sorcerer. I'm wary of being in here too long. Isaac can fill the rest of us in tonight when it's dark. If I'm not here when you come out it's because I'm keeping watch." Joanna took heed of his words and hurried up the aisle.

The little room was empty when Joanna stepped inside. She looked at the velvet curtains, the stacks of prayer books long forgotten and the warm blankets that were draped over the furniture for a makeshift bed. "Isaac," she hissed. "It's Joanna." A long curtain was disturbed, and Isaac stepped out from behind the plush material.

390

"Sorry," he said sheepishly. "Can never be too careful. Things are getting a little risky around here."

"Daniel told me they found your things." Joanna's voice was full of concern. Isaac strode over to her.

"Yes, but it will all be over tomorrow. They have no idea that the intruder was me, and I still have the poison with me. I carry it about my person in case I must make another quick getaway."

"Good thinking," Joanna agreed. "I need to tell you something about the banquet tomorrow."

"Go on." Isaac's eyes were wide, his bushy eyebrows narrowed.

"There's going to be a toast at the end. It takes place between Etimus and Letha. The housekeeper is reserving the best spiced wine just for them. It will be the perfect opportunity to slip the poison in. It will probably be in a large crystal decanter or something. I don't know exactly, but—"

Isaac clapped his hands together and then looked regretful at the noise it made. He looked to the window. "Joanna, that's perfect," he whispered. "The poison mixes better with liquid, and if it's reserved only for them no one else will dare touch it."

"Okay." Joanna nodded and tucked her hair behind her ear to think better. "So that's how we'll administer the poison, but how do we get into the kitchens to do it?"

"Don't you worry about that," Isaac said quickly. "I'll take care of that part. You've done quite enough, my dear girl."

A spark of hope alighted in Joanna at Isaac's words. She knew that she could trust him to play his part, not to mention the help of all the followers they had enlisted, and their plan was bound to work. Yet there was something in the back of her mind that had been nagging her ever since she had seen the little bottle of poison in Isaac's hands.

"What's wrong?" He peered at her worriedly.

"What's going to happen if we succeed?"

"If?" Isaac repeated her word incredulously. He looked at her. "Joanna, I promise you, this is going to work."

"Okay, when." Joanna reluctantly changed her wording, and Isaac looked momentarily satisfied. "When we succeed – when the baron is dead – what's going to happen then?"

"Well..." Isaac pondered for a moment. "The baron is the source of all the magic in Blackthorn. Killing him will therefore remove that magic. Which means that the ravens will return to human form, the harps will no longer harbour any magic, and all the inhabitants here will remember who they are."

"But," Joanna couldn't stop herself from interrupting, "aren't you the source of all the magic here?"

"My dear girl, no, it doesn't quite work like that," the sorcerer explained kindly. "I am from another world completely, much like you in that regard, and am simply trapped here inside this portal. Yes, I created the baron, but no, we are not the same person, and he is capable of his own thoughts and feelings, which unfortunately in this case have been malicious and tyrannical. His creation was a mistake. He should never have existed. His undoing is the key to all of this."

Joanna sighed and removed some prayer books from a little chair so she could sit down. Her silence troubled Isaac. "Why, you're not suggesting that I kill myself, are you? Because I've been down that path, Joanna. It cannot be done. I am but a vessel. An ancient reminder of the man I used to be. I am cursed to walk this place until I undo what I have done. It's just taken me... a rather long time to get here."

"I'd never say that," Joanna said quickly. "That's not what I'm suggesting, but..." She paused. She tried to make sense of a world that she didn't belong in; a world in which no one had truly belonged. "I just want to make sure that you know the consequences of murdering the baron. Everyone is going to have a lot of questions about who they are and why they are here. They've been living an illusion for as long as they can remember."

Isaac sat down next to her and fixed Joanna with a hard stare. "Portals and alternate worlds are a part of dark magic that should never be tampered with. They destroy people's lives. I know that now. The baron isn't real. Letha isn't real. They're not human. They're born out of dark magic. My magic. I have lived with that guilt for hundreds of years, Joanna, and if I have to sit down each and every inhabitant of this world and explain to them over and over again my mistakes, then that is what I will do. I will explain until they understand that they are finally free. I will experience all the heartache, all the loss, all the anger with them. I will stand by them and give them their long overdue freedom. What you're saying is, that when the baron is dead, I've got my work cut out for me?"

Joanna gave him a half-smile. Isaac let out a deep sigh of resolve. "But, after all this time, my dear girl, isn't that the least that I owe them?"

The door to their hideaway burst open and their exchange was cut short.

EIGHTY-SIX

"You need to leave now, Joanna." Daniel's huge frame filled up the whole doorway.

"Wha—"

"Don't ask questions, just listen to me very carefully." His features were sombre. "Walk out of the chapel. A raven will approach you in approximately one minute." Joanna gathered up her cloak as she listened. "He is one of them. There is a summons for you from the baron. Tell the raven that the baron has given you permission to use the chapel as it suits you. Keep walking, guide him away from this place. Go, now!" Joanna took one last look at Isaac and closed the door behind her with a grimace. She walked up the aisle being careful not to hurry in case anyone was watching.

Once she had exited the chapel, Joanna made straight for the citrus trees, as though she were returning to her chamber, and pretended not to notice the black figure that approached. He blocked her path with his wings. She stopped abruptly as though startled. "Miss Woodgate?"

"Yes," Joanna confirmed confidently. "Can I help you?" She ignored her beating heart as the raven looked over her head and bristled at where she had come from. "What were you doing in the baron's private chapel?"

"I was praying of course." Joanna managed a sincere smile. "I do hope that's not a problem. The baron has kindly told me I am welcome to use the chapel as I wish." Joanna repeated Daniel's lie.

"Very well." The raven bowed his head. "The baron has summoned you to his private quarters. I will show you the way." Joanna fell into step behind the raven and allowed herself to be guided into the manor. She wondered why he had believed her lie so quickly.

A breeze ruffled the hem of Joanna's long skirts and snaked all the way up her back. The shivers began at the thought of being near Etimus again. She tried to calm herself as she struggled to keep pace with the raven and breathed in the sweet citrus scents that wafted on the air. They walked through the entrance hall and approached the twisted staircase. The raven motioned for her to follow. The great beast stretched out his wings across the width of the stairs and toppled people over in his wake.

Joanna looked back in horror at those he had felled. Many of them massaged their limbs and scowled up. Some had tumbled six or seven steps and cried out in pain. "Keep up," he grunted. She took the next steps two at a time. Joanna thought the manor had only two floors, but she was wrong. The staircase narrowed as they approached the next level, and the raven had to be careful not to stumble on the smaller steps. Joanna thought he would wholeheartedly deserve it if he slipped up and injured a wing. The steps had clearly been designed to admit only one person. The general clatter of the manor died away when they reached the upper level, and the raven came to a halt.

Joanna begrudgingly listened to his instructions as she spat out a mouthful of feathers after colliding with his back. "The baron's private quarters are to the right. Knock once upon the door before you enter. Do not delay." He inclined his helmet down the small corridor and abruptly departed. Joanna's mouth went dry as she watched him disappear. She peered back down the perilous staircase. She could turn around and pretend she was never there. But that would draw attention and the guards would search for her. She couldn't afford any more searches being conducted in the manor grounds. She must face the beast herself.

Joanna's hand shook as she knocked upon the only door she could see. A brief clearing of the throat sounded before a deep voice boomed, "Enter." Joanna struggled with the heavy door for a moment before stepping inside. She let her eyes adjust to the gloom; the room was windowless and lit only by candlelight despite it being the middle of the day. Her eyes flitted from the candles in their holders to the giant bookshelves lining the walls. They harboured books with glossy volumes, some of which were in a different language, their spines glittering with handwritten embellishments.

A grand wooden desk took centre stage in the large room. Stacks of papers teetered over the edge as they threatened to touch the open flames. As the candlelight flickered over their contents, Joanna realised they were land deeds, all signed by the baron's hand, above the unintelligible scrawling of peasants who had probably been forced to put ink to paper. Quills were positioned in a neat line across the top of the desk. The feathers had been plucked from rare birds and handmade for the baron's use. They stood to attention as their tips quivered slightly in the smoky air.

Coins lay scattered across the desk, some arranged in obvious piles, others discarded along with empty bags, as though he had just been counting them. Joanna couldn't help but notice that some of their edges were stained with blood. In short, the room was exquisite. It was just a shame about the person sitting in it.

"Your talents speak volumes, Miss Woodgate." The baron's lips curved upwards into a smirk as he gestured for her to take the seat opposite. She did so, gingerly, fearing something would come out of it and spike her. Joanna fixed him with an unassuming expression. It was still strange to look upon the face of one she knew so well – someone that was friend, yet foe.

"Do they indeed?" she mused, trying to match his playful air. Joanna thought back to the last time she had spoken to him. It had been outside Madam Faraway's room, which she had raided shortly after, in the corridor that had seemed much too small and the dress which had felt far too itchy. That familiar itching feeling took hold of her again as he fixed her with his chestnut eyes.

"I have heard great things." Joanna's own eyes narrowed. She was trying to determine if he was taking the piss out of her or if he was being sincere. It seemed it was the latter. "Both my housekeeper and my daughter have expressed... how shall I put this..." the baron ran his hands through his curls which seemed glossier and browner than the last time she had seen him, "... something like joy at your handiwork."

Joanna's eyebrows raised in genuine surprise. "Miss Letha has seen the embroidery I added to her gown?"

"Yes." The baron leaned back in his chair. "She was very excited to see if you were up to the task, and it seems you were..." He raised his eyebrows at the woman who was plotting his murder. Joanna bowed her head in appreciation. She did not want to accept his praise, keen to ensure this conversation was as short and sour as possible. The baron seemed slightly disappointed at her silence and gave a small huff as he reached below his chair and began to rummage for something. His eyes never left hers as he did so.

Just as Joanna was thinking he was about to produce some kind of weapon he flung a large coarse bag over the desk toward her. It skidded to a halt as it reached the other edge but didn't fully stop and cascaded straight into Joanna's lap. "Oh!" she exclaimed. She noted the unmistakable clang of coins as it hit her knees.

"Payment," the baron declared with a smug smile. That would explain the piles of coins about his desk. Joanna wondered how many of them were stained with the blood of their former owners. One thing was certain: it was more money than Joanna had ever had in her life, and it was entirely useless to her. The thought of accepting the sum made her feel sick.

"Th-thank you," Joanna stammered. She realised they had never actually agreed a sum of money before the work had taken place; she had been too eager to establish a way into the manor. The baron had decided the sum of her worth for her.

"Consider it payment for the cloaks and Letha's gown but also..." he paused and leaned one arm on the side of his chair as though about to make her an offer, "payment up front for future commissions."

"Sorry, I-I don't understand."

The baron took immense pleasure at Joanna's confusion. A wide smile stretched across his smooth features. Suddenly, he unearthed a decanter half full of pale yellow liquid from beneath his papers and placed it between them. "Join me for a drink, Miss Woodgate." Joanna began to stammer her apologies for not drinking in the daytime, but he cut her off. "'Tis merely a concoction cook has fashioned from the apple trees in my courtyard. It contains nothing that will... dull the senses, shall we say." Joanna did not like the way he played with her, how he teased her with his power games, and how she had to play along for fear of arousing suspicion. She was beginning to wonder if she had played her part a little too well.

She accepted the cool glass of liquid and mirrored him as she tasted its sweet flavour. It was extraordinary; like no apple juice she had the pleasure of sampling before. She knew the fruits must contain Isaac's magic for it to taste that way. She set down her glass slowly and gave the baron a small smile of thanks. "A toast," he declared. Joanna's thoughts strayed jarringly to the colourless bottle of poison as he put the glass to his lips and smacked them together in a way that made her shrink in her chair. "I propose a toast to the new permanent seamstress at Blackthorn Manor." It took a few seconds for his words to sink in.

"Thank you, Mr Villinor—"

"Etimus, please." He cut across her. She wondered how many of the others he employed were on first name terms with him.

"Thank you, Etimus." Joanna continued her feigned gratitude. "I didn't expect this at all. In fact, Madam Faraway, will she be—"

Etimus Villinor had an annoying habit of cutting across people's words as he butted in: "Let's just say that the people I no longer have need of tend to… disappear. Madam Faraway won't be a problem. She won't be in your way."

"Oh, that wasn't what I was—"

"Nonsense," he declared with a small burp that was the result of having downed the last of his drink. "I know how these things work. You won't want anyone stepping on your toes. Her work has become so shoddy lately it will be a breath of fresh air to have you as a new member of the household."

Joanna didn't have the heart to correct him. The thought that she may be responsible for the exile, and perhaps even worse fate, of the woman she had never met horrified her. "Now." Etimus clapped his hands together and placed both elbows on the desk. He perched his chin atop his hands and blinked at her a couple of times. One of the candles flickered and extinguished itself. "Let's get down to business." His upper lip curled in an alarming manner as he continued to fix his gaze on Joanna, who now felt wholly uncomfortable in her own skin. A few moments' silence passed where he surveyed her. Joanna felt as though he were taking in every fine line that had appeared since her first night here, every curl that had withered ever so slightly, and the pools of time that hid behind her blue eyes. He eventually seemed satisfied with his scrutiny of her. "Now that you are a permanent member of the household you are obligated to attend the banquet tomorrow night."

Panic seized Joanna. "That's not necessary, Etimus, I will be perfectly fine dining in my quarters. Please don't make extra allowances for me." Etimus withdrew his elbows off the table. He brushed down his elegant tunic with irritation.

"Is there a reason you don't want to attend my banquet, Joanna?" His use of her first name sent another jolt of panic through her. It was a closeness; an intimacy that she thought she had kept well-guarded from him.

"Not at all," Joanna said quickly, knowing that her refusal had been a mistake. "I just know how hard everyone has been working towards tomorrow night, and I wouldn't like to add another place last minute."

"It is of no consequence adding another place to the table. Besides," Etimus said as he cocked his head on one side, "did I say you had a choice?" He remained unsmiling as she writhed in her seat. He inspected his fingernails as though growing bored with the conversation and ignored her obvious discomfort.

Joanna's mind raced as she tried to come up with an excuse that would let her be far away from the scene of the crime. She drew a blank. It wasn't even as though she could use the petty excuse of having nothing to wear. She hadn't planned on witnessing the baron's demise, but it seemed she was going to have a front row seat to the tragedy. Besides, declining the baron's invitation would hint that there was something wrong. She could not jeopardise the plan now. She changed tack. "I would be delighted to attend." She drained her glass and set it down firmly on the desk. Hoping this conversation was coming to an end, she shifted the bag of money on her lap, indicating she was ready to get up. The smoke from the candle wicks was beginning to irritate her eyes, and she was eager to get out of the gloom. She pretended to admire his books to avoid eye contact with him.

"Have you ever considered marrying, Miss Woodgate?"

Joanna could only stare at him in disbelief. He raised his eyebrows in enquiry. "M-marrying?" she repeated as though the word were alien to her.

"Yes," the baron said amusedly. "Taking and obeying a husband. At your age and... well, manners... I am surprised that you are not already."

"I have no time for marriage," Joanna blurted out in anger. "My work comes first."

"Some might say that marriage is work," the baron rebutted instantly. Then he chuckled quietly as though having had first-hand experience of this.

Joanna dared not ask about Mrs Villinor. No one knew who Letha's mother was, but perhaps the first Mrs Villinor had been another of those useless things to him that had simply disappeared. "No, it's not something I had considered," she concluded flatly.

"Very well." The baron bowed his head. "I can see I have shocked you. Things are changing in the manor, Joanna. Perhaps something to consider." Etimus arose from his seat as Joanna was still trying to understand what she was supposed to be considering. He gestured behind her, and Joanna stood up, needing no further indication to get out of there, grabbing the bag of money and departing the study.

"I shall look for you at the banquet tomorrow." She turned around and gave a brief nod in reply as her heart hammered against her chest. His eyes narrowed as he fixed her with them, and they glinted in the reflection of the flames. "It's going to be a night to remember."

EIGHTY-SEVEN

The hog rotated slowly on a spit as its fatty juices dripped into the hearth below. The animal's glassy eyes reflected the great hall around it. A red apple had been shoved crudely into its mouth. Joanna swallowed as the bile rose to her throat. She was no vegetarian, but there was just something grotesque about the scene before her. She fiddled with the goblet in her hand, raising it to her lips every now and then, but never letting the liquid touch her mouth. She would not taste a drop. There had been no word from Isaac or the ravens to confirm that their plotting was going to plan. Joanna had thought it too risky to seek Isaac out. There was no telling where the poison was hiding. It could have been slipped into the spiced wine as planned, or it could have gone wayward and ended up elsewhere on the table she now sat at.

Guards had been posted about the manor, more of them than usual, as though they were expecting something to happen. Joanna put the goblet down and fidgeted with the lace constricting her neck. The material had created a red rash already. The pale blue gown had been delivered to her door two hours earlier. The maid had announced it was a "gift from the baron" and that's when the sickness in Joanna's stomach had begun. She had slipped on the silken material, knowing she had no choice but to accept the strange gift, and the long sleeves and high neck instantly restrained her. It was both demure yet revealing; the way the thin material clung to her made her feel as though her body was on show.

Letha Villinor was resplendent in her aubergine gown. The silver threads that Joanna had woven into the lace caught the candlelight, and many a guest at the banquet admired her. Her blonde hair lay in wavy tresses down her back, and silver clips were pinning back the locks at various intervals giving the impression that she wore a braided crown. Her head was held high as she smiled smugly at the musicians, jesters and entertainers that surrounded her, knowing the display was all for her benefit.

The floors were so polished that a jester had slipped on the dangerous surface. The suits of armour were so shiny it was difficult to look directly at them. The long table groaned beneath the weight of all the lavish food. The fire blazed in the grate so aggressively that the heat was becoming uncomfortable in the winter evening. A few women fanned their paunchy faces, red lips puckering up like frogs, as they indulged in the interminable supply of alcohol and delicacies before them. The noble folk were content to sit and soak up the plentiful luxuries the baron had afforded them whilst those less fortunate struggled to pay their taxes and afford a loaf of bread. The whole thing disgusted Joanna. She had not sampled a drop of liquid nor touched a morsel of food. She was trying to prevent herself from throwing up at the long table that she shared with forty other guests.

Joanna had been horror struck when she was shown to her seat on the left-hand side of Etimus Villinor. She had been sat near the head of the table, which unfortunately meant that she also had the displeasure of looking diagonally across from his daughter. Why she had been seated there was a mystery to her; the only explanation was that her last-minute seat had been placed at the end of the table. As far as she was concerned, she would have been happy dining in the cellar with the rats.

There was a sudden break in the music where the musicians changed their instruments over. Joanna couldn't help but notice Isaac's harp in the corner, away from the other entertainment, the horrible minstrel continually plucking at the sweet strings. Only the simple melody of the harp remained. There was a brief pause where the guests ceased their eating and drinking as the memory magic washed over them. Joanna watched as they became disorientated and their eyes glazed over. The baron continued piling a plate of roasted meat into his mouth. Letha dismissed a servant who had asked if she required more and inspected her fingernails. Something strange began to happen to Joanna.

She too became dazed, as though also affected by the harp's magic. But this was a different kind of magic. It was pulling her up, up and away from the very seat that she sat on. So much so that she clutched at the edges to clamp herself down. The magic was drawing her away from the banquet and wanted her to be somewhere else.

"Joaannnaaaaaaaaa..." She shook her head a few times to dislodge the rasping voice within her mind. "Come back to usssss..." The bottom of her gown lifted about her ankles in a phantom breeze. No one else seemed to notice. She blinked continually, trying to bring her plate of untouched food back into focus, trying to ground herself within the world she was in. A vision blazed like fire in her mind: a twisted staircase, a house hidden in ivy, black cloaks flapping about her like hands snatching out. She slapped the hands away in her mind and rocked back in her chair, having been thrown back down unceremoniously from the couple of millimetres she had been hovering above it. Letha eyed her suspiciously but was mercifully distracted by the musicians beginning a jolly tune after the lull.

Joanna tried not to let the smell of roasting pig flesh upset her stomach and fought against what was pulling her back. She knew it was the witches. She knew that her time in this world was coming to an end; the witches were reaching out with long talons and clawing her back through their bond. She was still bound to them and to Blackthorn House. She knew that she would have to return eventually; no magic can reverse a curse as binding as theirs. She just thought that she had more time.

Cursing the witches' impeccably bad timing, she realised that a voice had started up to her right, and tuned into what the baron was saying. Etimus had relaxed his alcohol ban that evening. His words grew gradually slurred and his face blotched red as he downed the strong spirit before him. Letha had also clocked onto the beginnings of his intoxication and turned her head away in disgust. She pretended not to listen to their exchange and watched an acrobat swirl expertly in the air to the musician's tune. Her eyes narrowly followed the ribbons as they slashed through the smoky air.

"You are pleased with your gown then, Miss Woodgate?" the baron asked Joanna, and shifted slightly in his seat to peer at her. Joanna wanted to say no. She wanted to tell him that it was the most uncomfortable piece of clothing she had ever had the displeasure of scratching her body with, that it was entirely inappropriate and demeaning that he had forced her to wear it, and that she could think of no greater pleasure right now than ripping it off herself and throwing it into the fire beneath the roasting hog.

Instead, she took her satisfaction in the hope that this man had mere hours to live, and simpered, "It's beautiful, Mr Villinor."

He smiled smugly. "For such a special occasion I thought it was only fitting for you to wear something that shows off your true beauty." Joanna paused. Letha tilted her head toward their conversation but kept her gaze trained on the acrobat. The glacier may have been impenetrable, but it was certainly not deaf. Joanna wondered what all of this had to do with her; this was the father and daughter banquet, was it not? "I-I appreciate that, however I'm sure no one can look as resplendent as your daughter tonight."

Etimus waved his hand airily. "Yes, yes of course. Tonight is all about my daughter..." His lip curled as he spoke.

Pretending to pick at her food, Joanna moved the morsels around her plate to try and make it look like she had touched it, busying herself. She felt a clamminess attach itself to her arm through the thin material. The baron had laid a hand upon her. "I'm just glad I've got someone to share this special occasion with, for now, and for many years to come." Joanna resisted the urge to snatch her arm away. She turned to face the baron. His eyes glittered with intent like the night before as she had left his study.

Letha's head slowly turned toward the table, and her eyes darted back and forth between Joanna and her father. She noticed the physical contact between them, the luxurious yet simple gown Joanna had been adorned with, and how her maids had fixed her hair into an elegant style. Joanna's eyes met the cool blue of Letha Villinor's. They held each other's gaze for a few moments as the realisation hit them like a thunderclap. Letha's nostrils flared, and she looked daggers at her father. Joanna's eyes widened as she was snared in the trap she had willingly walked into.

The baron had prepared her like a pig for slaughter.

Tonight, he planned to make her his bride.

EIGHTY-EIGHT

The weight lifted from her arm, and Joanna looked down at it, not quite registering if it was hers, still reeling from what was expected of her that evening. She turned toward the baron, not even sure what protestation she was going to come up with, but he had already grown bored with the conversation and shovelled heaps of potatoes into his mouth as the butter dribbled down his chin. Letha eyed her for a few seconds more before pursing her lips and setting her stony face in a bitter expression. As she turned her withering gaze away, Joanna swallowed hard and thought that perhaps she was the most likely victim of murder that night after all. Just as Joanna was about to excuse herself from the banquet table, a horn blasted, and the doors to the entrance hall burst open. She was too late. She had run out of time.

Three ravens bore a great big silver platter atop their shoulders as they walked ceremoniously into the hall. Their newly fashioned cloaks fanned out behind them and Joanna, amongst all the other emotions she was battling with, felt a surge of pride at her handiwork. The cloaks truly did make them look regal.

As they deposited the platter in front of the blazing fire, a plethora of ravens joined the suits of armour standing guard, until the edge of the hall became a wall of obsidian. Maids scurried about at the sides and arranged goblets for the other guests to eventually share in the spiced wine. The chatter of the noble folk died down. Both Etimus and Letha positioned themselves upright in their chairs. Joanna shrank in hers.

All the musicians departed the hall apart from one. She plucked at the lyre strings, and a quiet melody filled the background. The jesters and acrobats made themselves scarce. Joanna looked past the baron to the front of the hall where the toast was to take place. She could easily see the sparkling silver decanter from where she sat, and the spiced wine sloshed slightly as the stewards set it down. The dark red liquid stuck thickly to the sides. If the poison was in there, it was impossible to tell.

The stewards delicately picked up three goblets from the platter. They walked over to the seated guests who watched expectantly. One was placed in front of Etimus, one in front of his daughter, and Joanna's heart sank as the final goblet was set before her. This only confirmed her suspicions that she would eventually be part of the ceremony. Whispers echoed down the table, and Joanna could feel multiple sets of eyes upon her. Some even strained in their seats to try and get a better look at the seamstress who had somehow captured the baron's attention. She considered feigning a sudden illness, but the two figures to her right rose abruptly from their seats. The stewards lined the hall on the opposite side. Etimus and Letha stood on either side of the fire as they faced their guests, goblets in hand.

Joanna's heart beat uncomfortably in her chest. She grew cold and wished she could make herself disappear. As Letha began her speech, the awful whisper in Joanna's mind started up again, and she struggled to concentrate. "Joaannnaaaaaa... we call you back to us. You cannot hiiiiiiiide..."

Adamant that she was to remain in this world for the next few minutes at least, she gritted her teeth and shook her head, not caring that the other guests thought this odd. The whispers in her head ceased, and she was able to turn her cloudy head toward the front of the hall again. Letha was saying something about how thankful she was for her father's guidance. Joanna couldn't help but notice that her teeth were gritted.

"...and now I am of age I shall take his wisdom and courage into the world with me. I pay tribute to my father and thank him that he is always by my side..." This continued for five minutes or so, and some of the guests slumped in their seats, intoxicated from the food and wine, as the pleasant music continued in the background.

"I toast my father." Joanna watched with apprehension as she lifted the goblet higher. "In recognition of all that he has done for me." Letha lifted the goblet to her pink lips and took a long drink of the spiced wine. Joanna waited with bated breath. Etimus began to clear his throat in anticipation of his speech. Joanna bit her lip and sat up straighter in her chair. She stared at Letha.

Her heart sank. There was no sudden closing of the throat, no spluttering or discolouration of her face. The poison was not in the spiced wine. Or if it was, it had not worked. The baron began his speech as Joanna quickly realised that she needed an escape plan. She would not marry him. The thought disgusted her. He had not even given her the opportunity to say no. She must flee. Flee this place and this world. She had tried to help the sorcerer to save Blackthorn, and she had failed. She intended to slip out when the baron drank from his cup, distracted, and head straight for the paintings lining the staircase. She would disappear through one of those and buy herself some time.

Readying herself toward the end of his speech, Joanna gathered up the skirts of her long gown and bunched them in her fists, to ensure nothing could hinder her escape. The doors to the hall were still open from when the ravens had arrived; if she was quick, she would be able to walk straight through without anyone stopping her. Once out of the hall she could travel through one of the canvases within minutes. She carved out her path with her eyes and prepared to bolt at any second.

"…and so I present you with a gift, my daughter," the baron announced and ushered over one of the stewards who carried a leather pouch. The steward handed the pouch over to Etimus with a bow and then a nod toward Letha. He withdrew to the side of the hall. Etimus held out the long pouch to his daughter and invited her to open it. "Take this into the world with you, as a symbol of my protection, and a reminder of my love for you." Letha eyed the pouch suspiciously as one might eye a poisonous snake. She took it from him. Everyone strained to see what it hid.

Letha reached a delicate hand inside. Her eyes glinted as she held the object out of sight for a few seconds. The blood red of the rubies encrusted into the hilt made several people gasp as Letha smiled and held it high for all to see. Etimus beamed as his daughter showed off the gift. The steelwork glinted and shone all the way down to the sharp point at the end of the dagger. "Now, before I toast my daughter," Etimus continued, "I must propose another toast tonight." He locked eyes with Joanna as she bunched her fists tighter around her gown. "And all are welcome to attend the ceremony which will be conducted in a couple of hours." He finished by addressing his guests. Excited chatter broke out from the noble folk, and Etimus had to raise his voice to be heard before they quietened again. "I drink to both my daughter and to my new br—"

Before Etimus could finish his last word, he spluttered, and a bright red stream bubbled out of his mouth. He dropped the goblet, and it rolled away. It left a trail of the blood red wine that mixed with his own as it splattered across the polished floor. His eyes widened in shock as he looked down at his chest to see the ruby-encrusted dagger sticking out of it. Letha had stabbed him straight through the heart.

Joanna stood up as the hall erupted. Screams began as the guests realised what had happened, and scattered. They ran for the exits, some too drunk to align their limbs, and tumbled over each other as they jostled to get out. Some slipped on the long trail of the baron's blood that snaked down the hall. Etimus had tried and failed to pull the dagger free and had made the wound worse. The blood exploded forth from him and sprayed the bottom of Letha's gown as he dropped to his knees. Clutching at his chest, he looked over at the woman who would never be his bride, as the life left him, and his limp form collapsed at the feet of his daughter.

EIGHTY-NINE

Joanna locked eyes with Letha. Her lips were drawn back in a snarl, and her eyes had narrowed into malevolent slits. She looked inhuman. Bending down, she yanked out the dagger her father had gifted her, and held it poised in her hand. Etimus's chest had been carved in two. His blood dripped down Letha's wrist as she formed a word and spat it across the room. "You."

Joanna bolted. She tripped over the baron's empty chair and scaled the table. She had to go over it to avoid running toward Letha who stood mere metres away. A pot of scalding hot gravy tipped over onto Joanna's arm, and the thin material she wore was not enough to shield her from the pain. She slid across plates of hot food and cursed as they too burnt her. Dropping down on the other side, shaking out her sleeve, dress torn and stained, Joanna saw Letha move towards her, and knew she was next.

There was not enough time; she would not reach the exit before Letha reached her. Joanna knew that if she kept running, Letha would stab her from behind, and she could almost feel the cool dagger in her back already. Letha was three feet away, and Joanna turned to face her with a grimace. Instinctively, she grabbed the silver platter on the table before them with both hands, and the remainder of the spiced wine flew straight into the fire, causing the flames to leap out of the grate and distract Letha for a second. She turned back to Joanna and saw what she was holding. She laughed icily. "You think that's going to save you?" Joanna would not beg this woman for her life. She had lived far too long for that and was far too wise to think that this girl had a drop of mercy in her blue veins.

Joanna felt the tight sleeves of her gown rip as she raised the silver platter up high to shield from the dagger that had been stabbed down toward her neck. "Bitch!" Letha cried, as the dagger went straight through and missed Joanna's neck by two inches. Letha removed the weapon quickly, and Joanna slammed the now sharp edge of the platter into her face before she could stab again.

Blood dripped down Letha's cheek, and she wiped it away furiously, turning to the side as she did so, spitting bitterly on the floor. Joanna took her opportunity and sprang toward the exit. She was halfway across the hall and saw figures emerging out of the exit door. A teeming mass of black and a man cloaked in grey furs moved toward the fight. The ravens and Isaac had come to Joanna's aid. But they had underestimated how quickly the baron's daughter could move.

Joanna felt the slash of the dagger before she realised that Letha was behind her. She stopped and clutched her right arm as the blood dripped along the thin red line. It was only a flesh wound. But Letha was not done. She advanced on Joanna like a wild animal, and the dagger glinted in the air as she took aim. Joanna braced herself, knowing she had no weapon and not enough time, and closed her eyes for the final moment.

When it did not come, Joanna opened one eye in confusion, and wondered if it had been so quick, she had not even felt it. She looked up at the girl trying to kill her. Letha had stopped mid-stab, clutched at her throat, and blinked at Joanna dumbfounded. Her eyes streamed as she lost the ability to breathe. The pupils darted back and forth between Joanna and the ravens as she struggled to put two and two together. She dropped to the floor and began to convulse as the foam bubbled at her lips. The dagger collided with the polished floor, and Joanna kicked it away in case of a last-ditch attempt from Letha.

She was dead within seconds. She lay on her back in the hall, the whites of her eyes face up to the ceiling, blonde tresses all a-tangle from the fray as her crown became unwoven.

Joanna's body failed her as she stumbled away from the corpses. She was violently sick. As she tumbled backwards into the feathery arms of her comrades, all she could see was Blackthorn House, the violent visions punctuating her mind, before fading to black.

NINETY

Isaac watched over Joanna as she slept. He would not leave her side for fear that he was going to lose the girl. He owed her too much for that. She awoke a few hours later, stiff and uncomfortable from lying on the floor, and stretched out with a yawn before remembering where she was. She sat up, still in the same soiled gown from the banquet, and a heavy blanket fell off her. She gave a weak smile at the sight of Isaac's face.

"Joanna," he said with relief. "You had me worried there." Joanna cleared her throat and accepted a glass of water from someone who stood over her.

"You could have told me that the poison takes a few minutes to work," she said with a wry smile. Isaac laughed and shook his head. His smile faded.

"I can't believe she killed him."

"I can," Joanna said flatly. She sat up straight, her back propped up against the edge of the hall, and had to blink a few times before it came into focus. The bodies had been removed, and the blood had been wiped away. "How long have I been out?"

"Only a couple of hours," a voice said from above. "We took care of some things while you were... recovering."

The man smiled down at her. He was tall, sporting a full head of black curls, and as he bent he took both of her hands gently in his. "I can't begin to tell you how grateful we all are for what you've done. After all these years, I can take control of my own destiny again." It took Joanna a few moments, only after meeting his kind eyes, to recognise who knelt before her.

"What's wrong?" Conrad joked. "Didn't recognise me without a beak, eh?" Joanna smiled and grasped his hands in return.

"So it worked? The baron's death has removed all the magic from Blackthorn? All the ravens, they're...?"

"Gone!" Daniel exclaimed as he too joined them on the floor. "We're all human again, thanks to you." Joanna's heart rejoiced as the Followers of the First gathered around her, proclaiming their thanks, hugging and greeting each other like very old friends.

"And what about the others?" Joanna turned to Isaac. "Everyone's memories, are they...?"

Isaac gestured around the hall. Groups of people had gathered, some looking confused, others looking angry, but all scratching their heads and furrowing their brows as though recollecting something from long ago. "They've been like this for hours," Isaac explained. "Their memories are slowly returning. They'll soon remember everything. Where they came from, who they are, their families..." Isaac trailed off. He swallowed back tears and nodded gravely. "I'm going to have a lot of explaining to do, to help them come to terms—"

"And grovelling, by the looks of it," Daniel interjected and nodded his head over to a large group by the fire. They appeared to be rallying each other, looking for someone to blame for their situation, and kept eyeing the sorcerer. "Looks like you might have an angry mob coming, Isaac, once they figure out who you are."

Isaac nodded gravely but then fixed them all with a determined look. "I'm going to rebuild this society. These people deserve that. I need to get a group together to go out into the towns and spread the message. I want everyone to come to the manor so I can explain. I want to make this world a civilised place again. No baron, no poverty," he paused and looked at

Joanna, "no magic." Joanna nodded. She felt so weak. She was glad it was not her faced with this difficult task. The ravens began to trail away and formulate their plans. Joanna's head was so very cloudy. She pulled Isaac toward her.

"Isaac," she croaked.

He looked fearful at how feeble she sounded. "Joanna, are you okay—"

"Please," she whispered, sliding back down beneath the blanket. "Just listen. I don't have much time left." Isaac's eyes widened but he remained quiet. He watched Joanna close hers. "The witches are pulling me back. I can feel it. We still share a bond. I knew it would happen eventually, but I feel so weak, and I don't think I can fight it anymore." Isaac took her hand in his.

"Joanna," he said as his voice cracked. "I wish you could stay here with me and see everything you've achieved. But we are both ancient souls, and I understand that you belong in a different world."

Joanna nodded, eyes still closed. She blocked out the witches' voices in her mind as the pain in her head began. There were so many things she wanted to say to the sorcerer. She wanted to tell him how happy she was that she had helped him right his wrongs. She wanted to explain how he had blocked out the miserable loneliness she had been cursed with for so many years, how she had found a spirit akin to hers, and would be forever grateful for his companionship. She wanted to thank him for giving her the adventure of a lifetime. The pain in her head was becoming unbearable as the witches clawed at her mind and body. She only managed one line that she hoped conveyed everything she felt.

"I'm glad I met you."

She felt the splash of Isaac's tears upon her closed lids. She heard him scrabbling for something and felt something cold press into the palm of her hand. He closed her fingers around it.

"Take this with you into the next world," he whispered thickly. "You are the most extraordinary person I have ever met."

A small smile tugged at her lips as she heard his words. She clutched onto the object the sorcerer had given her with all her strength as she departed this world for another.

NINETY-ONE

Lifting the lids from the many pots atop the stove, Joanna peered into their contents, and watched them bubble away. The smells were phenomenal. Freshly snared rabbit, potatoes dug up from the ground with her very hands that morning, and root vegetables bursting with flavour. Joanna had been back in Blackthorn House with the witches for three days. She had managed to avoid most of their beatings upon her return. They had thrown little spells at her here and there, burning her skin, creating red welts upon her arms. They mingled with the dagger wound from Letha where the skin was still healing over the pink line.

The second day was spent removing the filth that the witches had wallowed in during her absence. The pantry was bare, and the paintings were dusty. Joanna had restocked the shelves with the help of the witches' magic and harvesting the ground around the borders of the house. She had left the paintings alone. If there was one thing she had learned from Isaac Brewer, it was that magic was dangerous and it was high time she eliminated it from her life.

This of course she meant, except for one last piece of sorcery, and she upended the contents of the little bottle into her 'apology' meal for the witches. Joanna was sure that Isaac intended the poison for the witches. He too wanted her to be free, and had finally given her the answer for which she had been searching for the past century. She delivered the plates to their table with a sickeningly sweet smile and watched in disgust as their blackened talons instantly reached out and snatched at the food.

"You can leave," Krista barked at her as she filled her warty mouth with her undoing. The other witches took no notice of her. Joanna would not have stayed to witness what was about to take place. She could only hope that it would sever the bond that had chained her to this miserable place.

Having had previous experience with Isaac's poison, Joanna knew that it would not work instantly, and retreated to the upper levels of Blackthorn House into the library to save her waiting anxiously in the corridors. She took the window seat and gazed up at the stacks of books she had lovingly restored over the years. They all told great stories of adventure and magic, but none, she thought, could ever compare to her own.

She turned her attention to the world outside. Her little world, which had only ever existed of this house, these paintings, and this clearing, had now changed forever. There was so much more out there than she had ever thought. She thought fondly of the people she had met along the way. Ten minutes passed. As Joanna watched a raven hopping from branch to branch out of the window, she felt an immense weight lift off her body, and her shoulders sat up straighter for it. The red welts on her arm disappeared, her mind was clear and open, and her body felt so weightless she was surprised she had not floated toward the ceiling.

The trees out in the clearing suddenly looked greener, she opened the window and the air smelt fresher, the flowers bloomed with colour despite the season, and Joanna knew that the bond was destroyed. The witches were dead, and she was free. The joy washed over her. She watched the beautiful forest outside with tears in her ancient eyes. She revelled in this moment, finding an inner peace she had never known, and gave a nod of thanks to Isaac.

Joanna's limbs ached. Her bones grew weary. Her heartbeat slowed. Her body was giving up on her. She was, after all, over a hundred years old. It wasn't natural. Joanna knew that the only thing keeping her alive in this world had been the witches' magic. She had come to terms with the fact that her time in all the worlds was fast coming to an end. She raised herself up from the window seat with a small smile, content with her lot, and left the library.

There was one task she wanted to accomplish before she died. She had sought out the blank canvas three days ago, dusting it off so it was ready for the final painting, the last depiction of magic in Blackthorn.

Joanna's gift had always been a gift. She'd just never had the opportunity to look at it this way before. It was only now, as she walked peacefully through Blackthorn Forest with the canvas in hand, both aching yet so powerful, that she truly appreciated her own uniqueness. If she could bring paintings to life, she knew that she could also trap objects inside them. It was time to finally eliminate all the magic from this little village.

Magic brought chaos and hubris. It was now time to pave the way for peace and humility.

She sought out the portal deep within the trees that Isaac had painstakingly described to her. Its reverberations called out to her, as though wanting to be found, as though it grew tired of sucking up unassuming victims. Joanna approached the white beams of light. They grew smaller and larger, pulsing with a hidden world, emitting a strange ethereal sound as they disturbed the forest floor.

Forcing the last few steps, Joanna cried out in pain, and dropped to the earth. She gritted her teeth and crawled to the portal's edge. Outstretching her shaking hand, she offered up the canvas to the portal. The edge of it touched the beam of light, and Joanna felt a great power judder through her. Her world slowed as the last bit of magic in Blackthorn absorbed into the canvas and was trapped forevermore.

Joanna unclenched her teeth and rolled onto her back as she peacefully drifted into an unconsciousness and then nothingness. The most extraordinary woman that Isaac Brewer had ever met passed from this world. The canvas at the tips of her fingers depicted only a shining white circle; an entire world hidden in a few simple brushstrokes. Only a circular patch of burnt grass remained where it had been.

The last of the winter sun dropped down beneath the trees.

Blackthorn Forest was still, and the grass began to grow.

EPILOGUE

It was the height of summer and the sun beat down upon the village. "Mummy, Mummy, when can we go inside?" The little girl tugged at her mother's hand as her father ruffled her locks with a chuckle. He replaced her sun hat and looked at his wife.

"What do you think, love? Worth the queue?"

"Pleeeeease," the little girl implored, her bright eyes shining up at them.

"It is supposed to be very interesting," the mother said slowly with a smile. "If we're going to live in the village we may as well find out a bit about its heritage – even if we don't really believe in all these things." The little girl's father winked at her and hoisted her up onto his shoulders.

"Apparently it used to be a big house, but now they've turned it into a museum. Come on then, chicken, let's go and find out about magic!" The mother rolled her eyes but followed behind with a grin.

"Come on then, folks, let's get a move on," a booming voice said from atop the twisted staircase. "Use the lifts please or the steps to my right for accessibility." The queues snaked their way around the house and into the lifts, obeying the voice of the guide, who ushered groups of varying sizes inside toward the front desk.

"Queues for the Blackthorn Museum of Folklore are here at the main entrance! If you're looking for this month's exhibition, The Massacre of the Witches, queues are at the back of the house! Please note the exhibitions are always age-restricted and photo IDs will be required!" He tutted and shook his head at a sniggering group of teenage boys meandering their way across the freshly cut grass to the back of the house.

The little girl looked up in awe at the sparkling windows thrown open onto the green lawn. Her innocent eyes widened at the gargoyles adorning the front entrance which, they had been told, were exact replicas of those which had stood hundreds of years ago.

"It's beautiful," she whispered, excited for what magical marvels lay within.